A NEW INTRODUCTION TO OLD NORSE

PART I: GRAMMAR

A NEW INTRODUCTION TO OLD NORSE

PART I

GRAMMAR

THIRD EDITION

BY

MICHAEL BARNES

VIKING SOCIETY FOR NORTHERN RESEARCH
UNIVERSITY COLLEGE LONDON
2008

© M. P. Barnes 1999/2004/2008

ISBN: 978-0-903521-74-1

First published 1999
Reprinted with corrections and additions 2001
Second edition 2004
Third edition 2008
Reprinted 2016
Reprinted 2018

Printed by Short Run Press Limited, Exeter

Preface

This *Grammar* is intended for university students with no previous knowledge of Old Norse. It covers considerably more than the essentials, however, and is suitable for study up to first degree level. Full account is taken of the fact that grammatical concepts may be unfamiliar to many using the work, and all but the most basic are explained. Comparison is made with English where helpful, and a glossary of grammatical terms included at the end. Although it is possible to study the *Grammar* on one's own, the guidance of a tutor is strongly recommended.

The bulk of the *Grammar* was available in draft by the time of the 1998–99 session, and was tried out by several teachers at British universities. Content and presentation have benefited greatly from the comments and suggestions of both teachers and students. I would like in particular to thank Alison Finlay, Judith Jesch and Svanhildur Óskarsdóttir, who offered many valuable insights, Peter Foote, who read the whole work and improved it in countless ways, and finally Anthony Faulkes, who not only commented on numerous points of detail but designed the layout and saw the production of the book through from start to finish. Needless to say, such faults as remain are my responsibility.

Michael P. Barnes
University College London
July 1999

Preface to second edition

The necessity for a further reprint has made it possible to introduce a number of corrections and changes, and to add a new section on points of syntax (3.9.9).

Users will also be pleased to know that there is now a CD that can be obtained from the Viking Society containing extracts I, II, IV, VIIB, VIII (b) and (e), IX and X from *NION* II read with Modern Icelandic pronunciation by Icelanders: *Selected Readings from A New Introduction to Old Norse*, published by The Chaucer Studio, 2003.

April 2004

Preface to third edition

The book has been corrected and revised throughout, and a postscript added (pp. 262–3).

May 2007

Contents

Abbreviations and Symbols xii

1. Introduction
   1.1 The aim of the *Grammar* 1
   1.2 What is Old Norse? 1
   1.3 Old Norse and modern English 2
   1.4 Pronunciation 3
   1.5 Orthography 4
   1.6 General advice to the student 5

2. Pronunciation and Orthography
   2.1 Old Norse 8
       2.1.1   Pure vowels 8
       2.1.1   *Exercise* 9
       2.1.2   Diphthongs 9
       2.1.2   *Exercise* 10
       2.1.3   Consonants 10
       2.1.3   *Exercise* 12
       2.1.4   Syllables 13
       2.1.4   *Exercise* 13

   2.2 Modern Icelandic 14
       2.2.1   Vowels 14
       2.2.1   *Exercise* 16
       2.2.2   Consonants 16
       2.2.2   *Exercise* 20
       2.2.3   Syllables 20
       2.2.4   The epenthetic vowel 20
       2.2.3/2.2.4 *Exercise* 21

3. Morphology and Syntax
   3.1 Noun inflexions and their function 22
       3.1.1   Number 22
       3.1.2   Case 22
       3.1.3   Gender 27
       3.1.1/3.1.2/3.1.3 *Exercise* 28
       3.1.4   Basic noun inflexions 28
       3.1.4   *Exercise* 31

3.1.5	Examples of noun usage		31
3.1.5	*Exercise*		37
3.1.6	Difficulties in recognising noun inflexions and ways of overcoming them		37
3.1.6	*Exercise*		39
3.1.7	Important variations in noun inflexion		39
	3.1.7.1	Labial mutation	39
	3.1.7.1	*Exercise*	41
	3.1.7.2	Front mutation	41
	3.1.7.2	*Exercise*	44
	3.1.7.3	Breaking	44
	3.1.7.4	Deviations from the basic endings	45
	3.1.7.5	Minor irregularities	45
	3.1.7.3/3.1.7.4/3.1.7.5 *Exercise*		46
3.1.8	Examples of noun inflexion		47
3.1.8	*Exercise*		53
3.1.9	The suffixed definite article		56
3.1.9	*Exercise*		58
3.2 Pronoun inflexions and their function			60
3.2.1	Personal pronouns: form		61
3.2.2	Demonstrative pronouns: form		63
3.2.3	Indefinite pronouns: form		65
3.2.4	Negative pronouns: form		66
3.2.5	Interrogative and distributive pronouns: form		67
3.2.1/3.2.2/3.2.3/3.2.4/3.2.5 *Exercise*			68
3.2.6	Examples of pronoun usage		68
3.2.6	*Exercise*		76
3.3 Adjective inflexions and their function			77
3.3.1	Number, case and gender		77
3.3.2	Definiteness		78
3.3.3	Degree (comparison)		79
3.3.1/3.3.2/3.3.3 *Exercise*			79
3.3.4	Basic adjective inflexions		80
3.3.4	*Exercise*		84
3.3.5	The free-standing definite article		84
3.3.5	*Exercise*		86
3.3.6	Examples of adjective usage		87
3.3.6	*Exercise*		95

3.3.7	Difficulties in recognising adjective inflexions and ways of overcoming them	96
3.3.7	*Exercise*	97
3.3.8	Important variations in adjective inflexion	98
3.3.8.1	Labial mutation	98
3.3.8.1	*Exercise*	99
3.3.8.2	Front mutation	99
3.3.8.3	Suppletive forms	100
3.3.8.4	Deviations from the basic endings	101
3.3.8.5	Minor irregularities	102
3.3.8.2/3.3.8.3/3.3.8.4/3.3.8.5 *Exercise*		103
3.3.9	Examples of adjective inflexion	104
3.3.9	*Exercise*	111
3.4 Numerals		115
3.4.1	The numerals and their inflexions	115
3.4.1	*Exercise*	119
3.4.2	Examples of numeral usage	120
3.4.2	*Exercise*	123
3.5 Adverbs		124
3.5.1	Adverb formation	124
3.5.2	Inflexion for degree	125
3.5.3	Examples of adverb usage	127
3.5.1/3.5.2/3.5.3 *Exercise*		129
3.5.4	Adverbs and adverbials	130
3.6 Verb inflexions and their function		131
3.6.1	Person and number	131
3.6.2	Tense	132
3.6.3	Mood	134
3.6.4	Voice	135
3.6.1/3.6.2/3.6.3/3.6.4 *Exercise*		136
3.6.5	Basic verb inflexions	137
3.6.5.1	Endings	137
3.6.5.1	*Exercise*	139
3.6.5.2	Vowel alternations	140
3.6.5.2	*Exercise*	143
3.6.5.3	The *-sk* form	144
3.6.5.3	*Exercise*	146

3.6.6	Finite and non-finite forms; principal parts	146
3.6.6	*Exercise*	152
3.6.7	Preterite presents and other irregular verbs	152
3.6.7	*Exercise*	155
3.6.8	Examples of verb usage	155
3.6.8	*Exercise*	164
3.6.9	Important variations in verb inflexion	164
	3.6.9.1 Phonological variation	165
	3.6.9.2 Morphological variation	168
	3.6.9.3 Idiosyncratic variation	169
	3.6.9.1/3.6.9.2/3.6.9.3 *Exercise*	171
3.6.10	Examples of verb inflexion	171
3.6.10	*Exercise*	177

3.7 Prepositions 181

    3.7.1   Prepositions triggering the accusative 182
    3.7.2   Prepositions triggering the genitive 184
    3.7.3   Prepositions triggering the dative 185
    3.7.4   Prepositions triggering the accusative
             and dative 189
    3.7.5   Prepositions triggering the accusative and
             genitive 196
    3.7.6   Preposition triggering the accusative,
             genitive and dative 197
    3.7.7   Residual remarks 197

3.7 *Exercise* 199

3.8 Conjunctions 200

    3.8.1   Coordinating conjunctions 202
    3.8.2   Subordinating conjunctions 204
            3.8.2.1   The particle *er* 204
            3.8.2.2   The particle *at* 212
            3.8.2.3   Interrogative pronouns and adverbs 215
            3.8.2.4   Other adverbial sentence introducers 218

3.8 *Exercise* 221

3.9 Residual points of syntax 223

    3.9.1   Sentence word-order 223
    3.9.1   *Exercise* 228

3.9.2	Word-order in noun phrases	228
3.9.2	*Exercise*	230
3.9.3	Impersonal constructions	230
3.9.3	*Exercise*	236
3.9.4	Accusative and infinitive	236
3.9.4	*Exercise*	240
3.9.5	Omissions	240
	3.9.5.1 Objects	241
	3.9.5.2 *vera*	241
	3.9.5.3 Verbs of motion	243
3.9.5	*Exercise*	243
3.9.6	Points of nominal syntax	244
	3.9.6.1 Idiomatic uses of personal pronouns and possessive adjectives	244
	3.9.6.2 The genitive and dative of respect	246
3.9.6	*Exercise*	248
3.9.7	Points of verbal syntax	248
	3.9.7.1 The perfect and past perfect	248
	3.9.7.2 The passive	251
	3.9.7.3 The 'dative absolute'	253
	3.9.7.4 Present participles expressing potentiality or obligation	254
3.9.7	*Exercise*	255
3.9.8	Points of syntax affecting more than one type of phrase	256
	3.9.8.1 Adjectival and adverbial complements	256
	3.9.8.2 Agreement between subject, verb and subject complement	257
	3.9.8.3 *-sk* verb forms and 'preposition adverbs'	259
3.9.8	*Exercise*	260
3.9.9	Adverbial *ok*	261

A postscript on 'impersonal constructions' ... 262

References to linguistic terms explained in the *Grammar* ... 264

Select glossary of linguistic terms not explained in the *Grammar* ... 266

Bibliography ... 270

Abbreviations and Symbols

acc.	accusative
act.	active
adj.	adjective
art.	article
aux.	auxiliary
comp.	comparative
COMP	complementiser
dat.	dative
def.	definite
f.	feminine
gen.	genitive
imp.	imperative
indic.	indicative
inf.	infinitive
interrog.	interrogative
m.	masculine
n.	neuter
NION I–III	*A New Introduction to Old Norse* I: *Grammar*; II: *Reader*; III: *Glossary and Index of Names*
nom.	nominative
NP	noun phrase
ON	Old Norse
pass.	passive
pl.	plural
pos.	positive
pp.	past participle
pres.	present
refl.	reflexive
REFL. POSS.	reflexive possessive
sg.	singular
subj.	subject; subjunctive
sup.	superlative
vb.	verb
*	reconstructed form; ungrammatical sentence
>	develops to
<	develops from
~	zero ending

1 Introduction

1.1 The aim of the Grammar

From the point of view of the student, many existing grammars of Old Norse suffer from two major defects. First, they are largely constructed on historical principles and thus contain detail about earlier stages of the language and linguistic development, little of which is of direct use to someone seeking to acquire a reading knowledge of Old Norse. Second, they assume a level of linguistic sophistication which the school system no longer cultivates, and so leave unexplained many things which to the modern student are opaque.

The present *Grammar* has been written with one aim only: to facilitate the learning of Old Norse for as wide a range of students as possible. It therefore eschews historical digressions except where they throw essential light on the workings of the language, and an attempt is made to explain all but the most basic ideas, concepts and terms on their first appearance or, failing that, in the Select Glossary (pp. 264–6). The emphasis throughout is pedagogical, and the work thus represents not so much a re-think of Old Norse grammar as a re-think of the ways in which the basics of Old Norse may be best presented to the learner.

1.2 What is Old Norse?

The term 'Old Norse' has been used in various ways. For some it is a broad concept covering the language of Denmark, Norway and Sweden, as well as Iceland and the other Scandinavian colonies, throughout the Viking Age (*c*. 750–1050) and the early and high Middle Ages (*c*. 1050–1350). At the other extreme it has been taken to mean only the Old Norwegian of the early and high Middle Ages. In the present context it is used principally to signify the language of Norway in the period *c*. 750–1350 (after which Norwegian changes considerably) and of Iceland from the settlement (*c*. 870) to the Reformation (*c*. 1550 — a date that sets a cultural rather than a linguistic boundary). Known in modern Icelandic as *norræna*, in Norwegian as *norrønt* and in English sometimes as Old West Norse, this type of speech is a western variety of Scandinavian. Scandinavian itself represents the northern branch of the Germanic group of languages, whose western branch includes Dutch, English and German.

As a result of Viking-Age expansion, Old Norse (in the sense just defined), which had its origins in Norway, came to be spoken in such widely different places as Faroe, Greenland and Ireland, but it was only in Iceland and Norway — especially the former — that a significant scribal culture developed, and it is upon manuscripts in Icelandic and Norwegian written with the roman alphabet that our knowledge of Old Norse is chiefly based. The earliest Icelandic and Norwegian vernacular manuscripts that have survived are dated to *c.* 1150, but the bulk are from the thirteenth and fourteenth centuries, and many Icelandic manuscripts are later still. For insights into Old Norse prior to 1150 we are dependent on runic inscriptions, bits and pieces preserved in foreign language sources, and verse composed in the Viking Age but recorded in medieval manuscripts.

Although Icelandic *c.* 870–1550 and Norwegian *c.* 750–1350 are here given the designation 'Old Norse', it would of course be wrong to think of this language as entirely uniform, without variation in time or space. The form of Scandinavian spoken in Norway around 750 differed in a number of important respects from that spoken around 1350, and by the latter date the Norwegian carried to Iceland by the original settlers had begun to diverge from the mother tongue. Nevertheless, in the period *c.* 1150–1350, when the great medieval literature of Iceland and Norway was created, there existed an essential unity of language in the western Scandinavian world, and it is on that unity that the present *Grammar* is based.

1.3 Old Norse and modern English

A major difference between Old Norse and modern English is that Old Norse is a much more highly inflected language. Modern English still has certain inflexions, by which is meant that words change their form according to their function in a sentence (e.g. ***she*** *came*, *I saw* ***her***; sg. *cat*, pl. *cats;* pres. *r***u***n*, past *r***a***n*), but Old Norse has a far greater number. In English the function of a word can often be deduced from its position in relation to other words. We understand:

Olav saw the old woman

to mean that Olav was the one who saw and the old woman the one who was seen because *Olav* precedes *saw*. Reverse the order and the opposite applies. In a corresponding Old Norse sentence it would be perfectly possible for the order to be reversed without a change in meaning. Everything would depend on the inflexions. Thus:

Óláfr sá konu þá ina gǫmlu

and

Konu þá ina gǫmlu sá Óláfr

both mean 'Óláfr saw the old woman', because the forms *Óláfr* and *konu þá ina gǫmlu* are unchanged. If we wish the sentence to mean 'the old woman saw Óláfr', we must alter the forms of the words so that *Óláfr* becomes *Óláf* and *konu þá ina gǫmlu* becomes *kona sú in gamla*.

It is obvious, therefore, that from the very start the student will have to pay the closest attention to inflexions. Failure to do so will result in the regular misunderstanding of Old Norse texts.

1.4 Pronunciation

Even in the case of dead languages, pronunciation is of some importance. If students cannot translate letters on the page into sounds, it becomes well-nigh impossible for them to discuss the language they are trying to learn. Furthermore, for those without an exclusively visual memory, the association of image and sound is a valuable aid to learning.

The pronunciation of Old Norse, like that of Latin, varies from country to country and sometimes from teacher to teacher. In the English-speaking world a widespread practice is to adopt modern Icelandic pronunciation. Although it is often claimed there is little difference between modern Icelandic and Old Norse (and this is true enough as regards the inflexional system and the basic vocabulary), the pronunciation has changed a great deal since the first centuries of the settlement of Iceland. The adoption of modern pronunciation, while putting the learner at some distance from the speech of those who wrote the literature s/he is reading, nevertheless has the great advantage that one can in effect listen to native speakers reproducing the language, and thus learn to read aloud not only with fluency but with natural intonation (patterns of voice pitch). For those whose chief interest is Old Norse literature, modern Icelandic pronunciation has much to recommend it. The pure language student, on the other hand, will find the modern pronunciation frustrating: not only does it obscure the relationship between several common sounds — and thus also between large numbers of words or word-forms — it can render meaningless rules involving syllable length (especially important in poetry). In the present work, therefore, an outline is given of the pronunciation both of Old Norse and of modern Icelandic. For the former we can rely to a considerable extent on a twelfth-century work, the so-called *First Grammatical Treatise* (ed. Haugen 1972; Hreinn Benediktsson 1972), which discusses in some detail the vowel and consonant sounds of the Icelandic of that age. This, together with what we can deduce from spelling, historical comparisons and modern pronunciation (Icelandic and different varieties of Norwegian) means that guidance on the essentials of Old Norse pronunciation during the golden years of literary production can be offered with reasonable confidence.

1.5 Orthography

The scribes who wrote Old Norse did not conform to standardised rules of spelling, any more than their counterparts in medieval England and elsewhere. They wrote words more or less as they had been trained to do at the scriptorium where they studied, although they might also be influenced by forms in an exemplar from which they were copying — and occasionally by their own pronunciation. The result is that most Old Norse words appear in manuscripts in a variety of spellings. In order to facilitate the making of grammars, dictionaries and text books, therefore, and to help the learner, modern scholars have adopted a normalised orthography for Old Norse. Some editions of Old Norse writings, designed more for the philologist and linguist than the literary reader, follow closely the spelling of the manuscript or manuscripts on which they are based, while in others the normalised orthography may be adapted to bring it into greater harmony with that of the manuscript source. This last practice means that normalisation of Old Norse does not conform to an immutable standard. Even between grammars, text books and dictionaries a degree of variation can be found. The present *Grammar*, for example, does not always acknowledge the lengthening of *a*, *o*, *ǫ*, *u* which took place in twelfth–thirteenth century Icelandic before various consonant clusters beginning with *l* (e.g. *hjalpa* > *hjálpa*, *folk* > *fólk*, *hjalmr* > *hjálmr*), although such lengthening is generally indicated in Parts II and III (*Reader* and *Glossary and Index of Names*) of *A New Introduction to Old Norse*. The conventions adopted here are in the main those found in E. V. Gordon, *An Introduction to Old Norse* (1957), which deviates little from usage in many of the major editions and dictionaries. It should be noted, however, that the two dictionaries most used by English-speaking students, Richard Cleasby and Gudbrand Vigfusson, *An Icelandic-English Dictionary* (1957) and Geir Zoëga, *A Concise Dictionary of Old Icelandic* (1910), make a few concessions to modern Icelandic orthography (for which see, for example, Stefán Einarsson 1945, 1–31).

1.6 General advice to the student

The present *Grammar* is intended primarily for university students, and how it is used will be determined largely by individual tutors. Nevertheless, it may be helpful to both students and staff, and to anyone studying on their own, to offer outline guidance on the learning process — not least because it is the author's understanding of how Old Norse can most effectively be learnt that has determined the structure of the *Grammar*. With the emphasis on learning, the following remarks are addressed direct to the student.

Decide at the outset which pronunciation to adopt, and stick to it. Vacillating between rival pronunciations is confusing. Having decided, read through the relevant part of section 2. Do not attempt to learn all the rules of pronunciation at once. Read words, then phrases, then whole sentences aloud, referring to the rules as and when necessary. If you adopt modern Icelandic pronunciation, try to obtain recordings of native speech.

Your learning of morphology and syntax should initially be concentrated on the basics of nouns, pronouns, adjectives and verbs. These are the most highly inflected word classes in Old Norse, and the most central to the understanding of what you are reading.

Begin with the nouns. If you are uncertain about concepts like 'number', 'case' and 'gender', read sub-sections 3.1.1, 3.1.2 and 3.1.3 and do the accompanying exercise. Now learn the endings given in 3.1.4, noting the patterns. If you find this material too abstract, you can compare the endings with those of the actual nouns listed in 3.1.8. There is much greater variety of inflexion there, though, and that may confuse rather than help you in the early stages. The noun paradigms of 3.1.8 are meant primarily for reference as the learning proceeds. When you are satisfied you have mastered everything in 3.1.4, do the exercise. Next, study in detail the examples of noun usage given in 3.1.5, paying particular attention to the accompanying notes. This is your introduction to the basics of Old Norse syntax, and you should be prepared to spend a fair amount of time on it. When you have assimilated all the information in 3.1.5, do the exercise. Then read through 3.1.6 and answer the questions at the end of it. Now try the exercise in 3.1.8, using a dictionary or the Glossary in *NION* III and the noun paradigms listed in this sub-section. Do not worry if you do not get all the answers right straight away; this exercise is part of the learning process as well as a test of knowledge. Sub-section 3.1.7 on the most important variations in noun inflexion is not intended to be read at one go and learnt, but is there to be consulted as and when problems arise. You should, however, familiarise yourself with the fundamentals of labial mutation as soon as possible.

Following the nouns, section 3.1.9 on the suffixed definite article should be studied and the accompanying exercise completed.

Now go on to section 3.2. Learn the pronoun paradigms set out here, noting the correspondences between them, and follow this by doing the exercise covering 3.2.1–3.2.5. Next, study in detail the examples of pronoun usage given in 3.2.6, paying due attention to the accompanying notes. When you have assimilated all the information in 3.2.6, do the exercise.

Section 3.3 on adjectives follows largely the pattern of 3.1 on nouns, and the various items should be tackled in the same order and manner (with 3.3.8 for consultation as necessary, and the paradigms in 3.3.9

for reference). Note, however, that the free-standing definite article is treated immediately after basic adjective inflexions; it should be studied before you go on to the examples of adjective usage, where this form of the article occurs quite widely.

From adjectives proceed to section 3.6 on verbs. Work through subsections 3.6.1 to 3.6.8 in the order they appear (3.6.1 to 3.6.4 may be omitted if you are familiar with the concepts discussed). 3.6.9 is for consultation as necessary. The paradigms in 3.6.10 are for reference; the exercise at the end of this section is, however, an essential task.

Having assimilated the basic forms and functions of Old Norse nouns, pronouns, adjectives and verbs, you should go on to tackle numerals (3.4) and adverbs (3.5). When studying the numerals, note in particular similarities with other inflexional types and the various idiomatic usages detailed in both 3.4.1 and 3.4.2. Regarding the adverbs, pay particular attention to adverb formation and inflexion for degree (3.5.1, 3.5.2).

As soon as practicable, you should begin to read an Old Norse text. It is recommended you start with the extract from *Hrólfs saga kraka* in Part II of *A New Introduction to Old Norse*, which has word-for-word linguistic commentary on the first 40 lines. While reading this (or another) text you will meet prepositions, conjunctions, and various syntactic structures not dealt with in sections 3.1 to 3.6 of the *Grammar*. That is where sections 3.7, 3.8 and 3.9 come in. As you read, you should consult them regularly for such information as you may require on the areas they cover. The exercises in these sections should be attempted when you feel you have reached an appropriate level of expertise.

It is of course possible to work through 3.7, 3.8 and 3.9 in the same methodical way as the earlier parts of the *Grammar*. This should not, however, be done before starting on your first text. The importance of reading a continuous piece of Old Norse at the earliest possible opportunity cannot be emphasised too strongly.

Finally, an important piece of practical information: where nothing other is stated, Old Norse words are given in their dictionary form, i.e. nominative singular for nouns, nominative for personal pronouns, nominative masculine singular for other pronouns, strong nominative masculine singular positive for adjectives, nominative masculine singular or plural (as appropriate) for numerals, positive for adverbs, and infinitive for verbs.

2 Pronunciation and Orthography

2.1 Old Norse

Stress was in principle always on the first syllable. About intonation nothing is known for sure, but it probably varied somewhat from area to area.

Regarding the speech sounds themselves, we have a good idea of the system as a whole, but are less certain about precise shades of sound. The equivalents in other languages suggested below should be understood as rough approximations.

2.1.1 Pure vowels

Old Norse had nine basic vowel sounds, which might be long or short, nasal or oral, giving 36 potential distinctions. Nasality seems to have been lost in most people's speech by about 1200, and so is ignored here. Length is normally indicated by an acute accent. The relationship between spelling and sound is as follows.

á	as in English *father*	*ár* 'year'
a	the same sound, but short	*dagr* 'day'
é	as in French *été*, but longer	*él* 'storm'
e	as in French *été*	*ben* 'wound'
í	as in English *eat*	*lítr* 'looks [vb.]'
i	the same sound, but short	*litr* 'colour'
ó	as in French *eau*, but longer	*sól* 'sun'
o	as in French *eau*	*hof* 'temple'
ú	as in French *bouche*, but longer	*hús* 'house'
u	as in French *bouche*	*sumar* 'summer'
ý	as in French *rue*, but longer	*kýr* 'cow'
y	as in French *rue*	*yfir* 'over'
æ	as in English *pat*, but longer	*sær* 'sea'
œ	as in French *feu*, but longer	*œrr* 'mad'
ø	as in French *feu*	*døkkr* 'dark'
ǫ	as in English *hot*	*ǫl* 'ale'

Notes:

There is no short counterpart of *æ* or long counterpart of *ǫ*. Both sounds existed at one time, but in the kind of Old Norse on which the normalised spelling is based short *æ* had coalesced with *e* and *ǫ́* with *á*. The use of *œ* to denote the long equivalent of *ø* is an arbitrary convention, and in some works *ǿ* is found.

Most of these sixteen distinctive vowels occur exclusively in stressed syllables. In unstressed syllables there is no distinction of length and for the most part a basic three-way contrast is found between *a*, *i* and *u*. Some uncertainty exists about how these unstressed vowels were pronounced, but the student will be safe enough using the following.

a	as stressed *a*	*leysa* '[to] release'
i	as in English *city*	*máni* 'moon'
u	as in English *wood*	*eyru* 'ears'

2.1.1 Pure vowels — Exercise

1. Pronounce *á* and *a*. What is the difference?
2. Which are the long vowels of Old Norse?
3. How many unstressed vowels did Old Norse have, and what did they sound like?
4. Pronounce *o* and *ǫ*.
5. Pronounce the following words (use English equivalents for the consonants): *tál* 'deceit', *tal* 'talk', *sénn* 'seen [pp. nom. m. sg.]' (3.1.1, 3.1.2, 3.1.3), *senn* 'at the same time', *lítr* 'looks [vb.]', *litr* 'colour', *hól* 'praise', *hol* 'cavity', *dúra* '[to] doze', *dura* 'doorway [gen. pl.]', *flýtr* 'floats [vb.]', *flytr* 'conveys', *ær* 'ewe', *bær* 'farm', *gøra* '[to] make', *ǫl* 'beer', *gestir* 'guests [nom. pl.]', *gǫtur* 'paths [nom./acc. pl.]'.

2.1.2 Diphthongs

Diphthongs are vowel sounds that exhibit a change in quality within a single syllable, contrast English *beer* with a diphthong and *be early* with the same vowel qualities spread over two syllables. Diphthongs may be falling (where the first element is stressed and the second unstressed, the latter usually a semi-vowel like English *w* in *low* or *y* in *say*), rising (where the unstressed (semi)-vowel precedes the vowel as in English *with* or *yes*) or balanced (where both elements are given equal stress — as often in Faroese). Old Norse had three falling and a great many rising diphthongs. However, because rising diphthongs tend to be spelt with initial 'j' or 'v' in most forms of Scandinavian, they are often regarded simply as sequences of *j* (as in English *yes*) or *v* + vowel. This is more a theoretical than a practical question. Here only the three falling diphthongs are listed separately. They were all long and were pronounced as follows:

au	as in English *now*	*lauss* 'loose'
ei	as in English *bay*	*bein* 'bone'
ey	ON *e* + *y*	*hey* 'hay'

2.1.2 Diphthongs — Exercise

1. What is a diphthong?
2. What is the difference between a falling and a rising diphthong?
3. Which are the falling diphthongs of Old Norse?
4. Pronounce: *lauss*, *bein*, *hey*.

2.1.3 Consonants

Just as the vowels, so Old Norse consonants too may be long or short. Consonants with prolonged articulation are not a normal feature of English, but are heard in compounds, e.g. *la**k**e-**c**ountry*, *pe**n-kn**ife*, where the *k* and *n* sounds are extended. Consonant length in Old Norse is indicated by gemination (doubling). The relationship between spelling and sound is as follows.

b	as in English *b*uy	*bíta* '[to] bite'
bb	the same sound, but long	*gabb* 'mockery'
d	as in English *d*ay	*dómr* 'judgement'
dd	the same sound, but long	*oddr* 'point'

f	(1) as in English *f*ar	*fé* 'money'
	(2) as in English *v*ery	*haf* 'ocean'
ff	as in English *f*ar, but long	*offr* 'offering'
g	(1) as in English *g*oal	*gefa* '[to] give'
	(2) as in Scots lo*ch*	*lágt* 'low [nom./acc. n. sg.]'
	(3) as in Scots lo*ch*, but voiced	*eiga* '[to] own'
gg	(1) as in English *g*oal, but long	*egg* 'edge'
	(2) as in Scots lo*ch*	*glǿggt* 'clear [nom./acc. n. sg.]'
h	as in English *h*ave	*horn* 'horn'
j	as in English *y*ear	*jafn* 'even [adj.]'
k	as in English *c*all	*kǫttr* 'cat'
kk	the same sound, but long	*ekki* 'nothing'
l	as in English *l*eaf	*nál* 'needle'
ll	the same sound, but long	*hellir* 'cave'
m	as in English ho*m*e	*frami* 'boldness'
mm	the same sound, but long	*frammi* 'in front'
n	(1) as in English si*n*	*hrinda* '[to] push'
	(2) as in English si*ng*	*hringr* 'ring'
nn	as in English si*n*, but long	*steinn* 'stone'
p	as in English ha*pp*y	*ǿpa* '[to] shout'
pp	the same sound, but long	*heppinn* 'lucky'
r	rolled, as in Scottish English	*gøra* '[to] do'
rr	the same sound, but long	*verri* 'worse'
s	as in English *th*is	*reisa* '[to] raise'
ss	the same sound, but long	*áss* 'beam'
t	as in English *b*oat	*tǫnn* 'tooth'
tt	the same sound, but long	*nótt* 'night'
v	as in English *w*in	*vera* '[to] be'
þ	as in English *th*in	*þing* 'assembly'
ð	as in English *th*is	*jǫrð* 'earth'
x	two sounds, as in Scots lo*chs*	*øx* 'axe'
z	two sounds, as in English bi*ts*	*góz* 'property'

Notes:

f   Pronunciation (1) occurs in initial position (i.e. at the beginning of words), pronunciation (2) in medial and final position (i.e. in the middle or at the end of words).

g   Pronunciation (1) occurs in initial position and immediately after *n*, (2) immediately before *s* and *t*, (3) in all other positions ('voiced' means using the vocal cords, as, for example, in English *bill* versus *pill*; *b* is voiced, *p* unvoiced). (2) may alternatively be sounded as in English *act*.

gg Pronunciation (2) occurs immediately before *s* and *t*, (1) in all other positions. (2) may alternatively be sounded as in English *act*.

k Immediately before *s* and *t* this may alternatively be sounded as in Scots *loch*.

kk Ditto.

n Pronunciation (2) occurs immediately before *g* or *k*; note that in the combination *ng* the *g* is pronounced, as in some forms of northern English.

p Immediately before *s* and *t* this may alternatively be sounded as in English *far*.

pp Ditto.

s Never sounded as in English *rise*, always as in *goose*.

It will be seen that *h*, *þ*, *ð* and the semi-vowels *j* and *v* are always short.

2.1.3 Consonants — Exercise

1. How are long consonants denoted in Old Norse orthography?
2. Can all Old Norse consonants be both long and short? Give details.
3. Does Old Norse use any consonant letters not found in English? Give details.
4. What sounds do 'x' and 'z' stand for in Old Norse?
5. Pronounce the following words: *bjǫrn* 'bear', *gabba* '[to] mock', *dagr* 'day', *padda* 'toad', *fullr* 'full', *hof* 'heathen temple', *offra* '[to] make an offering', *gleði* 'joy', *sagt* 'said [pp.]', *sagði* 'said [3rd sg. past]' (3.6.1, 3.6.2), *steggi* 'he-bird', *hafa* '[to] have', *jǫrð* 'earth', *sekr* 'guilty', *sekkr* 'sack', *fela* '[to] hide', *fella* '[to] fell', *frami* 'boldness', *frammi* 'in front of', *men* 'necklace', *menn* 'men', *mengi* 'multitude', *krapi* 'slush', *krappi* 'narrow [weak nom. m. sg.]' (3.3.2), *vera* '[to] be', *verra* 'worse [n. sg.]', *áss* 'beam', *ás* 'beam [acc. sg.]', *nót* 'net', *nótt* 'night', *verða* '[to] become', *þjófr* 'thief', *ráð* 'advice', *vǫxtr* 'growth', *íslenzkr* 'Icelandic'.

2.1.4 Syllables

Because of the distribution of long and short vowels and consonants, stressed syllables in Old Norse were of four types (disregarding any consonants before the vowel):

1 — short: short vowel + short consonant, e.g. *bað* 'bath'.
2 — long: short vowel + long consonant or consonant cluster (i.e. a group of consonants), e.g. *rann* 'ran [1st/3rd sg. past]', *ǫnd* 'breath', 'spirit'.
3 — long: long vowel + short consonant or no consonant, e.g. *hús* 'house', *fé* 'money', *gnúa* '[to] rub'.
4 — overlong: long vowel + long consonant or consonant cluster, e.g. *nótt* 'night', *blástr* 'blowing'.

In simplex (i.e. non-compound) words of more than one syllable, it is customary to assume that the syllable division occurs immediately before a vowel, e.g. *far-a* '[to] go', *kall-a* '[to] call', *gǫrð-um* 'walls [dat.]', *gam-all-a* 'old [gen. pl.]', *kall-að-ar* 'called [pp. nom./acc. f. pl.]', *hundr-að-a* 'hundreds [gen.]'. In compound words the division comes at the point where the elements of the compound meet, e.g. *spá-maðr* 'prophet', *vápn-lauss* 'weaponless', *vík-ing-a-hǫfð-ing-i* 'viking chieftain' (with the division after -*a* marking the meeting point of the words *víkinga*- 'of vikings [gen. pl.]' and *hǫfðingi* 'chieftain'.

In Old Norse metrics (in which one long syllable is the equivalent of two short ones), length is sometimes measured differently. There, for example, all monosyllables (such as *bað*) count as long. This is not a matter that need concern the beginner, and the system of length described in 2.1.1, 2.1.2, and 2.1.3 should be adhered to.

2.1.4 Syllables — Exercise

1. How many syllable lengths are there in Old Norse?
2. What constitutes a short stressed syllable?
3. What constitutes a long syllable?
4. In words of more than one syllable, where does the division come?
5. Exemplify each of the following with two Old Norse words: short stressed syllable; long syllable; overlong syllable; unstressed syllable.

2.2 Modern Icelandic

Radical changes affected the sound system of Icelandic during the late medieval period. This means that normalised Old Norse orthography is not the best of guides to modern Icelandic pronunciation. Even so, the correspondence between the two is far more regular than between current spoken and written English.

Stress in modern Icelandic falls without exception on the initial syllable of a word; in compounds the first syllable of the second element has a strong secondary stress, e.g. *spákona* 'prophetess', with primary stress on *spá-*, secondary on *-kon-*. Intonation can only sensibly be learnt from listening to native speakers, or recordings of connected speech, and will not be described here. The equivalents of Icelandic sounds in other languages suggested below should be understood as rough approximations.

2.2.1 Vowels

The modern Icelandic vowel system is fundamentally different from that of Old Norse. What was originally a difference of length (e.g. between *á* and *a*) has become one of quality, and vowel length is regulated by the number of immediately succeeding consonants. In stressed syllables, a vowel before a single consonant, or no consonant at all, is long; a vowel before two or more consonants (including long consonants, which count as two) is short. The relationship between spelling and sound is as follows.

á	as in English *now*	*ár* 'year'
a	(1) as in French *mal*	*raf* 'amber'
	(2) as in English *now*	*langr* 'long'
	(3) as in English *my*	*hagi* 'pasture'
é	as in English *yes*	*léttr* 'light [adj.]'
e	(1) as in English *let*	*verri* 'worse'
	(2) as in English *bay*	*engi* 'no one'
í	as in English *eat*	*hlíð* 'hillside'
i	(1) as in English *pit*	*hlið* 'side'
	(2) as in English *eat*	*hringr* 'ring'
ó	as in American *roam*	*sól* 'sun'

o	(1) as in English l*aw*	h*o*f 'temple'
	(2) as in English b*o*y	b*o*gi 'bow'
ú	as in French b*ou*che	h*ú*s 'house'
u	(1) a sound between the vowels in French p*u* and p*eu*	s*u*mar 'summer'
	(2) as in French b*ou*che	*u*ngr 'young'
	(3) as in French h*ui*le	h*u*gi 'mind'
ý	as in English *ea*t	k*ý*r 'cow'
y	as in English p*i*t	*y*fir 'over'
æ	as in English m*y*	s*æ*r 'sea'
œ	the same sound	*œ*rr 'mad'
ø	as in French p*eu*r	d*ø*kkr 'dark'
ǫ	(1) as in French p*eu*r	*ǫ*l 'ale'
	(2) as in French *œi*l	l*ǫ*gin 'the law'
au	as in French *œi*l	l*au*ss 'loose'
ei	as in English b*ay*	b*ei*n 'bone'
ey	the same sound	h*ey* 'hay'

Notes:

a Pronunciation (2) occurs immediately before *ng*, (3) immediately before *gi*, (1) in all other positions.

e Pronunciation (2) occurs immediately before *ng*, *gi* and *gj*, (1) in all other positions.

i Pronunciation (2) occurs immediately before *ng* and *gi*, (1) in all other positions.

o Pronunciation (2) occurs immediately before *gi*, (1) in all other positions.

u Pronunciation (2) occurs immediately before *ng*, (3) immediately before *gi*, (1) in all other positions.

ǫ Pronunciation (2) occurs immediately before *ng* and *gi*, (1) in all other positions.

Although some of the above examples show long and others short realisations of the different sounds, all vowels (except the diphthongal variants of *o* and *u*, which are always short) may have either length. Corresponding to long *á* in *ár*, for example, we have short *á* in *árs* 'year [gen. sg.]' (and also in *langr*, although written 'a'); and corresponding to short *é* in *léttr* we have long *é* in *lét* 'let', 'caused' (1st/3rd sg. past of *láta*).

16   *Pronunciation and orthography*

As in Old Norse, the vowels of unstressed syllables are essentially three. All are short and are pronounced as follows:

a	as stressed *a*	*leysa* '[to] release'
i	as stressed *i*	*máni* 'moon'
u	as stressed *u*	*eyru* 'ears'

2.2.1 Vowels — Exercise

1. Where does stress fall in modern Icelandic?
2. In what positions do long vowels occur?
3. In what positions do short vowels occur?
4. Work through all the examples in 2.2.1, pronouncing each several times.

(Since modern Icelandic is a living language, access to native speech is available. Try to obtain an Icelandic pronunciation tape, or recordings of the spoken language. If you know an Icelander, get him or her to record the examples in 2.2 for you. Icelandic radio is now available on the internet, and a CD can be obtained from the Viking Society containing extracts I, II, IV, VIIB, VIII (b) and (e), IX and X from *NION* II read with Modern Icelandic pronunciation by Icelanders.)

2.2.2 Consonants

Consonants in modern Icelandic may be short or long, as in Old Norse (see 2.1.3). However, several of the long consonants of the medieval language have developed other pronunciations, although still spelt as geminates (double consonants). The relationship between spelling and sound is as follows. (On unvoiced sounds see the last paragraph of this sub-section.)

b	as in English *b*uy, but unvoiced	*bíta* '[to] bite'
bb	the same sound, but long	*gabb* 'mockery'
d	as in English *d*ay, but unvoiced	*dómr* 'judgement'
dd	the same sound, but long	*oddr* 'point'

f	(1) as in English *far*	*fé* 'money'
	(2) as in English *very*	*haf* 'ocean'
	(3) as in English *buy*, but unvoiced	*hefna* '[to] avenge'
ff	as in English *heifer*, but long	*offr* 'offering'
g	(1) as in English *goal*, but unvoiced	*gata* 'path'
	(2) as in English *geese*, but unvoiced and with English *y*-sound following	*gefa* '[to] give'
	(3) as in Scots *loch*	*lágt* 'low [nom./acc. n. sg.]'
	(4) as in Scots *loch*, but voiced	*eiga* '[to] own'
	(5) as in English *year*	*stigi* 'ladder'
gg	(1) as *g* (1), but long	*egg* 'edge'
	(2) as *g* (2), but long	*kleggi* 'haycock'
	(3) as *g* (3)	*gløggt* 'clear [nom./acc. n. sg.]'
h	(1) as in English *have*	*horn* 'horn'
	(2) as in English *huge*	*hjarta* 'heart'
	(3) as in English *call*	*hvass* 'sharp'
j	as in English *year*	*jafn* 'even [adj.]'
k	(1) as in English *call*	*kǫttr* 'cat'
	(2) as in English *keep*, but with English *y*-sound following	*kyrr* 'quiet'
	(3) as in Scots *loch*	*líkt* 'similar [nom./acc. n. sg.]'
kk	(1) as *k* (1), but preaspirated	*brekka* 'slope'
	(2) as *k* (2), but preaspirated	*ekki* 'nothing'
	(3) as *k* (3)	*skakkt* 'skew [nom./acc. n. sg.]'
l	as in English *leaf*	*nál* 'needle'
ll	(1) as in English *leaf*	*illt* 'bad [nom./acc. n. sg.]'
	(2) as in English *badly*	*hellir* 'cave'
m	as in English *home*	*frami* 'boldness'
mm	the same sound, but long	*frammi* 'in front'
n	(1) as in English *sin*	*hrinda* '[to] push'
	(2) as in English *sing*	*hringr* 'ring'
nn	(1) as in English *sin*, but long	*renna* '[to] run'
	(2) as in English *kidney*	*steinn* 'stone'
p	(1) as in English *happy*	*æpa* '[to] shout'
	(2) as in English *far*	*eptir* 'after'
pp	as *p* (1), but preaspirated	*heppinn* 'lucky'
r	(1) rolled, as in Scottish English	*gøra* '[to] do'
	(2) as *r* (1), but followed by *d*	*barn* 'child'

rr	as r (1), but long	*verri* 'worse'
s	as in English *this*	*reisa* '[to] raise'
ss	the same sound, but long	*áss* 'beam'
t	as in English *tug*	*tǫnn* 'tooth'
tt	the same sound, but preaspirated	*nótt* 'night'
v	as in English *very*	*vera* '[to] be'
þ	as in English *th*ink	*þing* 'assembly'
ð	as in English *th*is	*jǫrð* 'earth'
x	two sounds, as in Scots lo*chs*	*øx* 'axe'
z	as in English *this*	*góz* 'property'

Notes:

- *f* Pronunciation (1) occurs in initial position (i.e. at the beginning of words), pronunciation (2) in medial and final position (i.e. in the middle or at the end of words); (3) occurs immediately before *l* and *n* (except where a consonant follows, in which case *fl* may be pronounced as in English *flat* before a voiceless and as in English *naval* before a voiced consonant, and *fn* as *m* (e.g. *fíflt* 'seduced [pp.]', *fífldi* 'seduced [3rd sg. past]', *hefndi* 'avenged [3rd sg. past]').

- *g* Pronunciation (1) occurs initially before *á, a, ó, o, ú, u, ø, ǫ, au* and consonants, medially before *l* and *n* (e.g. *sigla* '[to] sail') and also between consonants and *a* or *u* (e.g. *saurga* '[to] dirty'), and finally after consonants (e.g. *þing*); pronunciation (2) occurs initially before *e, í, i, ý, y, æ, œ, ei, ey* and *j*, and medially between consonants and *i* or *j* (e.g. *helgi* 'holiness'); (3) occurs before *s* and *t* (e.g. *hugsa* '[to] think'); (4) occurs between vowels and *a, u, r* or *ð*, and finally after vowels; (5) occurs between vowels and *i* or *j*.

- *gg* Pronunciation (1) occurs between vowels and *a, u, r* or *v*, and in final position; (2) occurs between vowels and *i* or *j*; (3) occurs before *t*.

- *h* Pronunciation (2) occurs before *é* and *j*, (3) before *v*, (1) in all other positions.

- *k* Pronunciation (2) occurs before *e, í, i, ý, y, æ, œ, ei, ey* and *j*, (3) before *s* and *t*, (1) in all other positions.

- *kk* Pronunciation (2) occurs between a vowel and *i* or *j*, (3) before *s* and *t*, (1) in all other positions; preaspiration means that a

puff of air similar to the one expelled after *k*, *p* or *t* in (southern) English *keg*, *put* and *take* precedes the *kk*.
ll Pronunciation (1) occurs before consonants other than *n* and *r*, (2) between vowels and before *n* and *r*.
n Pronunciation (2) occurs before *g* and *k*, (1) in all other positions.
nn Pronunciation (2) occurs following all vowels with an acute accent (e.g. *á*), as well as *æ*, *œ* and the diphthongs *au*, *ei*, *ey*, (1) following other vowels.
p Pronunciation (2) occurs before *k*, *s* and *t*, (1) in all other positions.
pp Concerning preaspiration, see the note on *kk*.
r Pronunciation (2) occurs in the clusters *rl* and *rn* where they appear between vowels or in final position, (1) elsewhere.
s Never sounded as in English *rise*, always as in *goose*.
tt Concerning preaspiration, see the note on *kk*.

The pronunciation of modern Icelandic consonants involves many subtleties which it would be out of place to describe in a brief account such as this. The following may, however, be noted. (1) The voicelessness of *b*(*b*), *d*(*d*) and *g*(*g*) signifies that these consonants are pronounced much like their English equivalents (fairly laxly and with no following puff of air as with *p*, *t*, *k*), but without the use of the vocal cords. (2) There is a tendency to unvoice voiced consonants in voiceless environment (in particular when they immediately precede *k*, *p*, *s*, *t*: this is the norm in southern Icelandic pronunciation). (3) The clusters *hl*, *hn* and *hr* denote voiceless *l*, *n*, *r* (there is nothing like this in English: try pronouncing *l*, *n* and *r* without using the vocal cords). (4) Long consonants tend to be shortened when they occur immediately before another consonant (e.g. *þykkna* '[to] thicken', *brenndi* 'burnt [3rd sg. past]'). (5) Preaspiration (see above) occurs where *k*, *p* or *t* precede *l*, *m* or *n* as well as before *kk*, *pp* and *tt* (e.g. *vakna* '[to] awake', *ætla* '[to] intend'). (6) In clusters of more than two consonants, one or more may be altered or lost (e.g. *rigndi* 'rained [3rd sg. past]' is pronounced as though it were *ringdi* (the *g* not being sounded), *barns* 'child [gen. n. sg.]' as though it were *bass*).

2.2.2 Consonants — Exercise

1. Of the written geminates *bb*, *gg*, *ll*, *mm*, *nn*, *tt*, which always denote long consonants in modern Icelandic?
2. How many different sounds can *f* denote, and what are they?
3. How many different sounds can *g* denote, and what are they?
4. Work through all the examples in 2.2.2, pronouncing each several times.

(See the note following the exercise at the end of 2.2.1.)

2.2.3 Syllables

The fact that vowel length is regulated by the length of following consonants means that in modern Icelandic there are effectively only two types of stressed syllable, both long:

(1) short vowel + long consonant or consonant cluster, e.g. *blástr* 'blowing', *nótt* 'night', *rann* 'ran [1st/3rd sg. past]', *ǫnd* 'spirit'.
(2) long vowel + short consonant or no consonant, e.g. *bað* 'bath', *hús* 'house', *fé* 'money', *gnúa* '[to] rub'.

An exception to this pattern of distribution are clusters formed of *k*, *p*, *s*, or *t* + *j*, *r* or *v*, before which the vowel is always long. If both consonants are reckoned part of the syllable, it is clearly overlong, but conceivably only the first should be counted, so that in words like *vekja* '[to] wake', *daprar* 'sad [nom./acc. f. pl.]', *þysja* '[to] rush', *vǫkva* 'moisture', etc., the syllable boundary would be placed immediately after *k*, *p* and *s*. Syllable boundaries are otherwise as outlined in 2.1.4.

2.2.4 The epenthetic vowel

Also called the svarabhakti vowel, this intrusive *u*-sound began to develop towards the end of the Old Norse period. Because it did not originally form part of the words in which it is now found, and because of its relatively late arrival, the epenthetic vowel is not indicated in normalised Old Norse orthography. It develops between a consonant (other than *r*) and *r*, especially an *r* in final position. Thus ON *maðr* 'man [nom. m. sg.]', *dapr* 'sad [nom. m. sg.]', *eitr* 'poison [nom./acc. n. sg.]', *bindr* 'tie(s) [2nd/3rd sg. pres.]', for example, are pronounced *maður*, *dapur*, *eitur*, *bindur* (the first three with long stressed vowels because only a single consonant immediately follows) — and so written in modern Icelandic orthography.

2.2.3/2.2.4 Syllables/The epenthetic vowel — Exercise

1. What feature of length characterises stressed syllables in modern Icelandic?
2. What is the epenthetic vowel?
3. How does the occurrence of the epenthetic vowel affect the use of modern Icelandic pronunciation for Old Norse?

It should be stressed that section 2.2 is offered simply as an initial guide to help those learners who wish to pronounce Old Norse as a living language. For a detailed, if slightly old-fashioned, description of the sounds of modern Icelandic, see Stefán Einarsson 1945, 1–31; for a briefer but more recent analysis, see Höskuldur Thráinsson 1994, 142–52. As urged above, such accounts should preferably be studied in conjunction with recordings of spoken Icelandic.

3. Morphology and Syntax

Morphology deals with the form and structure of words, and syntax with the ways in which words are combined to form sentences. In section 3 we shall be concentrating on inflexional morphology (changes in word-form that express grammatical categories and relationships, sometimes called accidence) and the ways in which it interrelates with syntax. In dealing with a language like Old Norse, where grammatical categories such as **number**, **gender**, **case**, **person**, **tense** (see below and 3.2, 3.6.1, 3.6.2) are expressed by variation in word-form, it is unhelpful to divide the inflexions from the syntax, as has been common practice in earlier grammars. The student needs to appreciate from the outset that form and function are interlinked: the form has no purpose other than to express the function, and often the function cannot be expressed without the form.

3.1 Noun inflexions and their function

Nouns in Old Norse are inflected for **number** and **case**.

3.1.1 Number

Number in nouns is restricted to a difference between singular and plural, as in English *boy*, *foot* compared with *boys*, *feet*. Thus ON *hlíð* means 'slope', *hlíðir* 'slopes', *maðr* 'man', *menn* 'men'. (On the relationship between number in nouns and number in verbs, see 3.6.1.)

3.1.2 Case

Case is a much more complex matter than number. It is sometimes defined as a grammatical category that expresses the syntactic relationship between words in a sentence. While true as far as it goes, this definition is too abstract for our purposes. It gives no indication of how to recognise case. It does not explain *what* syntactic relations are, *how* they are, or may be, expressed, or *the nature of the link* between the means of expression and the thing expressed.

In modern English a few words change form according to their function in a sentence. Thus we say (as a complete sentence):

>   I saw him

but

>   He saw me

not:

>   *Me saw he

or

>   *Him saw I

This change of form between *I* and *me* and *he* and *him* according to function provides a clear example of what is traditionally called case: a particular form expresses a particular syntactic relation — in these examples subject (*I*, *he*; see pp. 31–2) or object (*me*, *him*; see pp. 32–3). For the most part, however, modern English expresses syntactic relationship by other means than changes in the form of words. We may say both:

>   John saw the cat

in which *John* is subject and *the cat* object, and:

>   The cat saw John

in which the roles are reversed, but it is the word-order that signals the function (as it does additionally in *I saw him* and *he saw me*) not the particular forms of the words involved, which do not change. Another common means of expressing syntactic relationship in English is by the use of function words (words which have little or no meaning on their own) such as *of*, *with*, *than*. In:

The king of England

for example, *of England* modifies *king*, in much the same way as would the addition of the adjective *English*. In:

He broke it with a stone

with a stone is an adverbial (3.5.4) expressing instrumentality (i.e. defining the 'tool' or 'instrument' used to cause the breakage). In:

My brother is taller than me

than me supplies the part of the comparative phrase that denotes the entity with which the comparison is made.

Where English uses word-order or function words to indicate syntactic relationship, Old Norse regularly uses changes of word-form instead or as well. This means that not only pronouns, but nouns and adjectives (and also verbs and adverbs, as to some extent in English), are likely to change form according to their relationship to other parts of the sentence. It is their form that — wholly or partly — specifies their grammatical role, as with *I/me* in English. English has traces of such a system in the *-'s* (singular) or *-s'* (plural) that may be added to nouns. Instead of saying (or writing) *the king of England* as above, for example, we may alternatively use *England's king*; instead of *the comfort of passengers*, *passengers' comfort*. However, the Old Norse system is vastly more complex than anything in English. Its heavy reliance on form to indicate a variety of functions means that a simple two-way distinction like that between English *I* and *me* or *England* and *England's* offers a wholly inadequate parallel.

Old Norse nouns, adjectives and pronouns exhibit four distinctive case-forms, known as **nominative**, **accusative**, **genitive** and **dative**. This means that a noun (or adjective or pronoun) potentially has eight different actual forms (four in the singular, four in the plural), but in reality most have fewer because the same form occurs in more than one case.

The number of functions expressed by these case-forms greatly exceeds four. This means that no case is uniquely associated with a particular function: each is used in a variety of ways. The accusative, for example, commonly marks the object of a verb (as English *him* in *I saw him*; see pp. 32–3), but among other functions it also expresses duration of, or point in, time, as well as occurring after a number of prepositions (see 3.7). The following sentences (each accompanied by a literal and an idiomatic English translation) illustrate these three possibilities (the words in the accusative form are in **bold**):

> Hann orti **vísu þessa**
> 'He made verse this'
> 'He made this verse' (object)
>
> Hann dvalðisk þar **mestan hluta** sumars
> 'He stayed-*sk* [see 3.6.5.3] there most part of-summer'
> 'He stayed there for most of the summer' (time)
>
> Þeir gengu á **skóg**
> 'They went into wood'
> 'They went into the wood' (after preposition *á*)

'Case-form' in relation to the nominative, accusative, genitive and dative has so far been used in an abstract sense. In reality, we are dealing not with one nominative, accusative, genitive or dative form, but with many (see the three examples just given). Thus to a question like: 'What is the nominative singular form of nouns in Old Norse?' there is no answer, only a return question: 'Which kind of noun do you have in mind?' Common nominative singular noun endings are *-r*, *-i*, *-a*, but there are others besides these, and a large group of nouns indicates this 'form' by exhibiting no ending at all.

It is time now to return to the starting point of the discussion: the definition of case. Three questions were thrown up by the definition initially suggested. (1) What are syntactic relations? (2) How are or may they be expressed? (3) What is the nature of the link between the means of expression and the thing expressed? In answer to the first question discussion and examples of common syntactic relations have been offered. In answer to the second it has been shown that change in word-form, word-order, and the use of function words are all important ways of expressing syntactic relations. The third question on the nature of the link between syntactic relations and the means by which they are expressed bears more directly on the understanding of case. There are two main issues. First, what can be usefully recognised as case, and what not? Second, in so far as case is identified primarily as the expression of syntactic relations by *changes in word-form*, where is case to be found — in the syntactic relations or in the differing word-forms?

Some have identified case in English sentences like *John saw the cat* or phrases like *the king of England*. This is either because they were arbitrarily transferring the rules of another language (as often as not Latin) to English, where the rules do not necessarily apply, or because they related case primarily to the level of meaning. Neither approach seems likely to be helpful in the learning of Old Norse. The rules of Old Norse must be derived from Old Norse itself, not from Latin or any other language, and seeing case in terms of meaning ignores the fact that in Old Norse form is also a crucial factor. For present purposes, therefore, case would seem a term best restricted to the expression of syntactic relations by changes in word-form. There are difficulties here, though, that have already been alluded to. Case as thus defined refers both to form and function and denotes entities — nominative, accusative, etc. — that have a variety of forms and a variety of functions. It can therefore be hard to see what the essence of a case is — leading to uncertainty about what one means by the term. Is the Old Norse accusative, for example, the sum of the inflexions by which certain syntactic relations are expressed or the sum of those syntactic relations? There is no clear answer to this question. Nevertheless it seems that most writers conceive of case in a language like Old Norse primarily as a morphological category: they prefer to think of the different inflexions a case may exhibit as varying realisations of a single underlying form than to think of its differing functions as somehow derived from a single abstract meaning — and indeed the latter idea does require considerably greater intellectual elasticity. We will therefore adopt the concept of morphological case here. We will consider, for example, the *-r*, *-i*, *-a* etc. endings of nouns in the nominative singular to be realisations of an underlying form NOM in its singular incarnation. The morphological category thus established as primary can then be seen as having a range of different functions.

The upshot of this discussion is that there are four cases in Old Norse: nominative, accusative, genitive and dative. The cases are regarded as relating primarily to form, although there is no single nominative, accusative, genitive or dative form as such. Each case expresses a range of syntactic relations. **The student's task is therefore twofold: to learn to recognise one case from another by mastering the essential inflexions, while simultaneously getting a grasp of the principal syntactic relations expressed by each case.**

3.1.3 Gender

As well as number and case, the role of gender in the inflexion of Old Norse nouns needs to be considered. Gender is an inherent category of the noun, that is, it is only when a noun is modified or referred to that its gender becomes manifest. There is, for example, nothing about the word *dalr* 'valley' to show that it is masculine rather than feminine or neuter, but if it is modified by an adjective, that adjective will appear in the appropriate masculine form, e.g. *djúpr dalr* 'deep valley' where *djúp-* is the root of the word and *-r* the nom. m. sg. ending (see 3.3.4). Similarly, if we wish to refer to a valley as 'it', it must be by the masculine form of the personal pronoun: *hann* 'he'.

While there is thus nothing gender-specific about any individual Old Norse noun in its dictionary form, it is nevertheless true that gender plays a part in the inflexional system of nouns, if only a minor one. Most masculines, for example, end in *-r* or *-i* in the nominative singular, and many feminines in *-a*; neuters are characterised in both singular and plural by a lack of distinction between nominative and accusative, and many have no specific nom./acc. pl. inflexion either (so that *kvæði* 'poem', for example, may be nom. or acc. sg. or pl.). However, given that none of the above features (except the nom./acc. sg./pl. identity of neuters) is totally restricted to one particular gender, they cannot be classed as gender markers in the same way as the forms of modifying adjectives or of anaphoric pronouns (pronouns that refer back to some previously expressed meaning, as, for example, *it* referring to *valley* above). What the features do offer is guidance about the *likely* gender of a noun — a useful insight since it can help (a) to see which words in a sentence belong together and (b) to predict what forms a given noun will have other than the particular one encountered.

3.1.1/3.1.2/3.1.3 Number/Case/Gender — Exercise

1. What does the grammatical category number refer to? Give examples from Old Norse.
2. What does the grammatical category case refer to? Give examples from Old Norse.
3. What does the grammatical category gender refer to? Give examples from Old Norse.
4. To what extent does case occur in English?
5. In what ways other than change in word-form can syntactic relations be expressed?
6. Which cases are found in Old Norse, and how do we recognise them?

3.1.4 Basic noun inflexions

In learning the inflexions of Old Norse it is important not to lose sight of the wood for the trees. This is not least true of the noun inflexions. If account were taken of every minor variation, it would be possible to list pages of paradigms (patterns of inflexion), as some grammars do, but that is likely to put the learner off and thus be counter-productive. Initially it is the essential patterns that need to be grasped. The small details can be added bit by bit. (Students keen to see the complete range of inflexions are recommended to consult one of the more traditional Old Norse grammars. In English there is Gordon 1957, in Norwegian Iversen 1973 and in German Noreen 1923. Less traditional grammars in Norwegian are Spurkland 1989 and Haugen 2001, the latter particularly systematic and lucid. An exhaustive account of modern Icelandic inflexions is given in Thomson 1987.)

Fundamentally there are two types of noun inflexion in Old Norse, traditionally known as **strong** and **weak**. The student should not look for any deep significance in these names. They have none. The two types could as well be called 'A' and 'B' or '1' and '2'. Strong nouns have a wider range of endings than the weak; weak nouns tend mostly to end in -*a*, -*i* or -*u*.

The strong and weak inflexional types can be sub-divided according to gender (cf. above). With three genders, masculine (m.), feminine (f.) and neuter (n.), this gives us six basic sets of endings. They are as follows (~ = zero, i.e. there is no ending, the form consisting of the root of the noun alone — e.g. *dal* 'valley', acc. m. sg.; ( ) = the ending does not always occur; actual paradigms are given in 3.1.8).

Strong masculine

Sg.	nom.	-r	Pl.	nom.	-ar/-ir
	acc.	~		acc.	-a/-i/-u
	gen.	-s/-ar		gen.	-a
	dat.	-(i)		dat.	-um

Weak masculine

Sg.	nom.	-i	Pl.	nom.	-ar
	acc.	-a		acc.	-a
	gen.	-a		gen.	-a
	dat.	-a		dat.	-um

Strong feminine

Sg.	nom.	~	Pl.	nom.	-ar/-ir
	acc.	~		acc.	-ar/-ir
	gen.	-ar		gen.	-a
	dat.	~		dat.	-um

Weak feminine

Sg.	nom.	-a	Pl.	nom.	-ur
	acc.	-u		acc.	-ur
	gen.	-u		gen.	-na
	dat.	-u		dat.	-um

	Strong neuter				
Sg.	nom.	~	Pl.	nom.	~
	acc.	~		acc.	~
	gen.	-s		gen.	-a
	dat.	-i		dat.	-um

	Weak neuter				
Sg.	nom.	-a	Pl.	nom.	-u
	acc.	-a		acc.	-u
	gen.	-a		gen.	-na
	dat.	-a		dat.	-um

Certain regularities and patterns will be observed in these endings.

(1) The dat. pl. always ends in -*um*.
(2) The gen. pl. always ends in -*a*, in the case of the weak feminines and neuters preceded by -*n*-.
(3) There are no distinct case-forms in the weak sg. except in the nom. masculine and feminine.
(4) The strong nom. sg. ends in -*r* or has no ending.
(5) The strong acc. sg. is characterised by the absence of an inflexional ending.
(6) The strong gen. sg. ends in -*s* or -*ar*.
(7) The strong dat. sg. ends in -*i* or has no ending.
(8) The masculine and feminine nom. pl. end in -*a*, -*i* or -*u* + *r*.
(9) The masculine acc. pl. ends in -*a*, -*i* or -*u*, and the feminine acc. pl. in -*a*, -*i* or -*u* + *r*.

These are the essentials of noun inflexion in Old Norse. It is by no means the whole story, but all other noun inflexions can be seen as variations on this basic pattern. It is vitally important that the student masters the above sets of endings before proceeding to the finer detail.

3.1.4 Basic noun inflexions — Exercise

1. Where is a difference between the nom. and acc. pl. to be found?
2. How many endings does the gen. pl. exhibit?
3. What characterises the singular inflexions of strong feminines?
4. What characterises the singular inflexions of weak masculines and feminines?
5. In what way do the plural inflexions of strong neuter nouns differ from those of strong masculines and feminines?
6. What are the different nom. sg. endings?
7. What are the different gen. sg. endings?
8. What are the different dat. sg. endings?

3.1.5 Examples of noun usage

To assist in the task of learning, examples will now be given of a selection of the different noun case-forms in function. The relevant inflexions are in **bold** (or the whole word where there is no difference from the root form). Two translations are normally provided, the first literal for a better understanding of the structure of the Old Norse sentence, the second idiomatic. Notes explain the relationship between form and function. Compare the case-forms used with those set out on pp. 29–30. Observe, too, the differences between Old Norse and English phraseology and sentence formation.

(1) Gerðisk Eiríkr þá konungsmaðr
'Made-*sk* [see 3.6.5.3] Eiríkr then king's-man'
'Eiríkr then became a king's man'

Eiríkr (strong nom. m. sg.) is the subject, *konungsmaðr* (strong nom. m. sg.) the subject complement; for both subject and subject complement the nominative is almost always the case used. Subject is an extremely hard concept to get to grips with; it is sometimes loosely defined as 'what the sentence is about'; where the verb denotes an action, the subject is often the agent, or 'doer' of the action. However, such definitions relate chiefly to meaning. Syntactically subjects may be defined both in English and Old Norse as the first noun phrase of a sentence in unmarked word-order (where 'noun phrase' means a noun or pronoun with or without accompanying modifiers — e.g. *John, she, the white-bearded old man* — and 'unmarked word-order' word-order not deliberately altered for emphasis). The subject complement is *Y* in constructions like: *X is Y, X becomes Y* or *X is called Y*.

(2) Var bardag**i** milli þeira
     'Was battle between them'
     'There was a battle between them'

Bardagi (weak nom. m. sg.) is the subject, the first noun phrase in the sentence.

(3) Kon**ur** tvær vǫkðu yfir leið**inu**
     'Women two watched over tomb-the'
     'Two women kept a vigil over the tomb'

Konur (weak nom. f. pl.), modified by *tvær*, is the subject; it is the first noun phrase in the sentence and the women perform the action denoted by the verb *vǫkðu*. *Leiðinu* (strong dat. n. sg. + def. art. — see 3.1.9) does not function here as a noun phrase, but is part of the preposition phrase *yfir leiðinu*, in which the noun is governed (i.e. has its case determined) by the preposition *yfir* (see 3.7, 3.7.4).

(4) **Vápn** bíta ekki á hann
     'Weapons bite not on him'
     'Weapons make no impression on him'

Vápn (strong nom. n. pl.) is the subject, the first noun phrase in the sentence; whether the weapons are seen as the agent, or 'doer', of the action, will depend partly on the wider context, partly on the analysis; normally a human agent wields weapons and the weapons are thus the instrument, but they can also be portrayed as agent.

(5) Hann tekr eigi **mat** né **drykk**
     'He takes not food nor drink'
     'He takes neither food nor drink'

Mat and *drykk* (both strong acc. m. sg.) are objects of the verb *tekr*. Like subject, object is a hard concept to define; traditionally a distinction is made between 'direct object', the goal of an action, and 'indirect object' the beneficiary, as in: *I sent Peter* (indirect object) *a letter* (direct object), but such definitions have to do with meaning rather than syntax. Syntactically objects may be defined both in English and Old Norse as the second and third noun phrases of a sentence in unmarked word-order, with the accusative commonly marking the direct and the dative regularly marking the indirect object in Old Norse, second position the indirect and third position the direct object (by and large) in English. *Mat* and *drykk* are both direct objects: they are the goal of the action, and whereas direct objects regularly appear unaccompanied by indirect objects, the reverse is very uncommon (cf. the impossibility of English *I gave him). The direct objects appear here in the accusative, the most common case for this function.

(6) Þeir báru þar reið**a** allan af skip**i**nu
    'They bore there tackle all off ship-the'
    'There they carried all the tackle off the ship'

Reiða (weak acc. m. sg.), modified by *allan*, is the second noun phrase in the sentence and the direct object of the verb *báru*. *Skipinu* (strong dat. n. sg. + def. art.) does not function here as a noun phrase, but as part of the preposition phrase *af skipinu*, and its case is determined by the preposition *af* (see 3.7.3).

(7) Hann átti margar orrust**ur** í Englandi
    'He had many battles in England'

Orrustur (weak acc. f. pl.), modified by *margar*, is the second noun phrase in the sentence and the direct object of the verb *átti*. *Englandi* (strong dat. n. sg.) is part of the preposition phrase *í Englandi*, and its case is determined by the preposition *í* (see 3.7.4).

(8) Þeir drukku þar of dag**a** í skál**a** miklum
    'They drank there during days in hall big'
    'They drank there by day in a big hall'

Daga (strong acc. m. pl.) is governed by the preposition *of*, *skála* (weak dat. m. sg.), + its modifier *miklum*, by the preposition *í*.

(9) Lát þér þat ekki í aug**u** vaxa
    'Let to-you that not into eyes grow'
    'Don't make a mountain of it'

This is an idiomatic phrase, of which Old Norse has its fair share. *Augu* (weak acc. n. pl.) is governed by the preposition *í*, which requires the accusative here because a sense of motion is involved (contrast examples 7 and 8).

(10) Dvalðisk Brúsi litla **hríð**
'Stayed-*sk* [see 3.6.5.3] Brúsi little while'
'Brúsi stayed for a short time'

Brúsi (weak nom. m. sg.) is the subject; it is the first noun phrase in the sentence and the man bearing the name performs the action denoted by the verb *dvalðisk*. *Hríð* (strong acc. f. sg.), modified by *litla*, is an adverbial phrase expressing duration of time (it answers the question: 'How long?').

(11) Hann hefndi dráp**s** Þorgrím**s**
'He avenged killing of-Þorgrímr'
'He avenged the killing of Þorgrímr'

Dráps (strong gen. n. sg.), the second noun phrase of the sentence, is the direct object of the verb *hefndi*; *hefna* is one of the few verbs that take a direct object in the genitive. *Þorgríms* (strong gen. m. sg.) is an objective genitive, that is, it corresponds to English 'of Þorgrímr' and presents Þorgrímr as the object or goal of an action (cf. 'NN killed Þorgrímr').

(12) Hann sendi þá vestr at leita ǫndvegissúl**na** sinnar
'He sent them west to seek high-seat-posts REFL. POSS.'
'He sent them west to look for his high-seat posts'

Ǫndvegissúlna (weak gen. f. pl.), modified by *sinna*, is the direct object of the verb *leita*. It comes in an infinitive clause (i.e., we have the infinitive *at leita* 'to seek', but only an implied subject). A full sentence might run: *þeir leituðu ǫndvegissúlna* 'they sought the high-seat posts', in which the direct object would be the second noun phrase.

(13) Gunnar**r** var eina **nótt** at Sigríð**ar**, frændkon**u** sinnar
'Gunnarr was one night at Sigríðr's, kinswoman's REFL. POSS.'
'Gunnarr stayed one night at Sigríðr's, his kinswoman's'

Gunnarr (strong nom. m. sg.), the first noun phrase in the sentence, is the subject; he does the staying. *Nótt* (strong acc. f. sg.), modified by *eina*, is an adverbial phrase expressing duration of time. *Sigríðar* (strong gen. f. sg.) and *frændkonu* (weak gen. f. sg.) + *sinnar* are subjective (possessive) genitives, that is, they correspond to English '-'s' and present Sigríðr, the kinswoman, as the owner of the house where Gunnarr stayed (cf. 'NN owns the house'); note that 'house' is not expressed in the Old Norse sentence, paralleling English usage as above or in, e.g., *I am at Peter's*.

(14) Ingólf**r** var frægastr allra landnámsmann**a**
'Ingólfr was most-famous of-all settlers'
'Ingólfr was most famous of all the settlers'

Ingólfr (strong nom. m. sg.) is the subject, the first noun phrase in the sentence and what it is about. *Landnámsmanna* (strong gen. m. pl.), modified by *allra*, is a genitive of type, that is, it corresponds to English 'of the settlers' and presents *landnámsmenn* as a type of which Ingólfr is a representative.

(15) Hann bar hann til vatn**s** nǫkkurs
'He bore him to lake some'
'He carried him to a certain lake'

Vatns (strong gen. n. sg.), modified by *nǫkkurs*, is governed by the preposition *til*.

(16) Eigi leyna aug**u** ef ann kon**a** mann**i**
'Not hide eyes if loves woman man'
'The eyes do not hide it if a woman loves a man'

This is an adage, consisting of two sentences. *Augu* (weak nom. n. pl.), the first (and only) noun phrase in sentence 1, is the subject of the verb *leyna*; the eyes fail to perform the action denoted by the verb. *Kona* (weak nom. f. sg.) is the subject of the verb *ann*, the first noun phrase in sentence 2 and what it is about. *Manni* (strong dat. m. sg.) is the direct object of *ann*, the second noun phrase; a good many verbs take a direct object in the dative.

(17) Hon skyldi bera **ǫl** víking**um**
'She should bear beer to-vikings'
'She was to serve beer to the vikings'

Ǫl (strong acc. n. sg.) is the direct object of the verb *bera*; it is the goal of the action and the second noun phrase in the sentence. *Víkingum* (strong dat. m. pl.) is the indirect object of *bera*; it denotes the beneficiary of the action and is the third noun phrase. In English the indirect object may be expressed by a preposition phrase ('to the vikings') or word-order ('She was to serve the vikings beer' — indirect object before direct); in Old Norse the indirect object appears in the dative.

(18) Þeir hétu Rǫgnvald**i** traustri **fylgð**
'They promised Rǫgnvaldr firm support'

Rǫgnvaldi (strong dat. m. sg.) is the indirect, *fylgð* (strong dat. f. sg.), modified by *traustri*, the direct object of *hétu*. As noted in connection with (16), many verbs take a direct object in the dative, and *heita* 'promise' is among these.

(19) Þeir ljá jarl**i** líf**s**
 'They grant earl life'
 'They spare the earl's life'

Jarli (strong dat. m. sg.) is the indirect, *lífs* (strong gen. n. sg.) the direct object of *ljá*. As noted in connection with (11), a few verbs take a direct object in the genitive, and *ljá* 'grant' is among these.

(20) Hann kastar bein**um** smám um þvert **gólf**it
 'He throws bones small over crossways floor-the'
 'He throws small bones across the floor'

Beinum (strong dat. n. pl.), modified by *smám*, has instrumental sense; in Old Norse people are conceived as throwing *with* something (cf. the close semantic relationship between English: *He threw water onto the ground* and *He splashed the ground with water*). Instrumentality in Old Norse is expressed either by the dative on its own or by the preposition *með* 'with' + dat. *Gólfit* (strong acc. n. sg. + def. art.), modified by *þvert*, is governed by the preposition *um*.

(21) Hon var hverri kon**u** fríðari
 'She was than-every woman more-beautiful'
 'She was more beautiful than any other woman'

Konu (weak dat. f. sg.), modified by *hverri*, is the second proposition in a comparative construction — the proposition denoting the entity with which the comparison is made (i.e., taking every other woman as the basis — the standard by which 'she' is to be judged — 'she' is more beautiful); in Old Norse the basis of the comparison may be expressed either by the dative, as here, or by the conjunction *en* 'than' (3.8, 3.8.2.4) + the appropriate case.

(22) Váru d**yrr** á end**a**
 'Was doorway on end'
 'There was a doorway at the end'

Dyrr (nom. f. pl.) is the first noun phrase in the sentence and the subject. It has only plural forms, although it corresponds to the English singular 'doorway'.

These forms are also in part irregular (see 3.1.7.2, 3.1.7.4), and the nom. f. pl. is indicated by other means than the adding of -*a*, -*i* or -*u* + *r* to the root. *Enda* (weak dat. m. sg.) is governed by the preposition *á*.

3.1.5 Examples of noun usage — Exercise

1. What are the principal functions of the nominative case in Old Norse?
2. What cases are used to denote the direct object?
3. What role do prepositions play in the assignment of case?
4. Account for the use of all the genitives in the above examples.
5. What case is used to denote the indirect object?
6. How is instrumentality expressed?
7. What is the role of the dative case in comparative constructions?
8. Where may the accusative be found other than as a marker of the direct object?

3.1.6 Difficulties in recognising noun inflexions and ways of overcoming them

Unfortunately it is not enough just to learn the endings listed in the tables in 3.1.4. For one thing, Old Norse nouns ring the changes on a relatively small number of endings. We find little other than the vowels -*a*, -*i*, -*u* or the consonants -*r*, -*s* on their own, or -*a*, -*i*, -*u* in conjunction with the consonants -*m*, -*n*, -*r*. This parsimony has the effect that the same ending may be found in a variety of different cases. While -*s* clearly signals the genitive singular, and -*um* the dative plural, for example, -*ar* may be genitive singular or nominative or accusative plural, and -*a* can denote any case in the singular as well as accusative and genitive plural.

Very often the context can determine which number and case a particular form represents. It will be clear from the overall sense of the sentence and the passage of which it forms a part — and usually, too, from the forms of words dependent on the noun: their number, and regularly their case and gender as well. Thus in the example sentence (4):

Vápn bíta ekki á hann

we know that *vápn* is plural because the verb-form *bíta*, dependent on the number of the subject (see 3.6.1), is also plural (cf. English *dogs bite* as opposed to *John bites*). Since *vápn* has no plural ending we may further deduce that it is neuter — though this deduction is in itself no help in gauging the role of the noun in the sentence, since we have already established that it is the subject and plural. In sentence (10):

> Dvalðisk Brúsi litla hríð

we can tell from the agreement between the noun form *hríð* and the adjective form *litla* that we are dealing with the accusative feminine singular. 'Agreement' means that there is a formal relationship between the two words, expressed by their having the same case, gender and number (see further 3.3.1), and since *litla* can only be acc. f. sg. or acc. m. pl. (see 3.3.9, paradigm 9), and *hríð* cannot be acc. m. pl., the case, gender and number they have in common must be acc. f. sg. Having established that, we may further deduce that accusative case in conjunction with a verb meaning 'stayed' (*dvalðisk*) — and given the sense of *hríð* ('while' 'short time') — indicates duration of time. In (6):

> Þeir báru þar reiða allan af skipinu

it is the form of the agreeing adjective, *allan* 'all', which shows that of the various cases *reiða* might be, singular or plural, it is in fact accusative singular, the adjective ending *-an* denoting acc. m. sg. alone (see 3.3.4). That it is accusative means it is likely to be the direct object of the verb *báru* 'carried' (examination of the other words in the sentence and their forms will in fact show that to be the only possible analysis). That it is singular is of little consequence, since *reiði* does not normally appear in the plural (any more than 'tackle' in English). That it is masculine is of importance to the extent that when used with a function that requires accusative case, the agreeing adjective will show the case, gender and number unambiguously.

3.1.6 Difficulties in recognising noun inflexions and ways of overcoming them — Exercise

1. Why may it sometimes be difficult to recognise the case and number of nouns in Old Norse?
2. What means can we use to help deduce their case and number?

3.1.7 Important variations in noun inflexion

A further problem for the learner of Old Norse is that the endings listed so far are by no means the whole story (cf., e.g., *dyrr*, nom. f. pl., in example sentence 22). To be reasonably sure of recognising a particular case-form for what it is, the student needs to be aware of additional features that play their part in noun inflexion. These will now be examined.

3.1.7.1 Labial mutation

Mutation, sometimes known by the German term *Umlaut*, occurs where the vowel of a stressed syllable adopts one or more of the features of the vowel or semi-vowel of the immediately following unstressed syllable. The vowel *u* and the semi-vowel *w* (the latter written 'v' in standardised Old Norse spelling) are labial sounds, that is, they are pronounced with rounded lips. Rounding is thus one of the features that characterise them. This feature is regularly adopted by a preceding stressed *a*, so instead of appearing as *a* it takes the form *ǫ*, i.e. it is pronounced like *a* with lip-rounding (see 2.1.1). In fact, it is a rule of Old Norse that *a* cannot appear before *u* or *v* in the next syllable. A noun with *a* in the root will therefore always change that *a* to *ǫ* when the ending consists of or contains a *u*. Thus, the dative plural of the nouns *maðr* 'man', *bardagi* 'battle', and *vatn* 'lake', which appear in the example sentences, is *mǫnnum*, *bardǫgum*, *vǫtnum* (see paradigms 2, 9, 26 below). A weak feminine noun like *saga* 'story' has root *a* only in the nominative singular and genitive plural; the remaining forms are *sǫgu* (acc./gen./dat. sg.), *sǫgur* (nom./acc. pl.) and *sǫgum* (dat. pl., see paradigm 23). Likewise, the weak neuter *hjarta* 'heart' has the nom./acc. pl. forms *hjǫrtu* and dat. *hjǫrtum*.

The rule that root *a* changes to *ǫ* before *u* should not cause the learner problems, **as long as s/he remembers that an unknown word with *ǫ* in the root and *u* in the ending must be looked up in a dictionary as though it had root *a* if it cannot be found there with root *ǫ*.** For example, *stjǫrnur* (nom./acc. pl.), *fjǫru* (acc./gen./dat. sg.), *dǫlum*, *grǫnnum* (both dat. pl.) will be found not under *stjǫ-*, *fjǫ-*, *dǫ-*, *grǫ-*, but under *stjarna* 'star', *fjara* 'shore', *dalr* 'valley', *granni* 'neighbour'.

Somewhat greater difficulties are caused for the learner by the fact that strong feminine and neuter nouns may exhibit root *ǫ* in certain forms even though no *u* or *v* follows. The reason for the occurrence of *ǫ* here is the presence of a following *u* at an earlier stage of the language. This *u* caused *a* to develop to *ǫ* and was subsequently lost (e.g. nom./acc. n. pl. **landu > lǫnd* 'countries'). The forms concerned are: nominative, accusative and dative feminine singular and nominative and accusative neuter plural. In addition, a small group of masculine nouns (several of them very common) has root *ǫ* in the nominative and accusative singular. If the feminine or masculine nouns are met with in forms with root *ǫ*, no problem arises for the learner, since the nominative singular is also the entry form in dictionaries. **For neuter plurals with root *ǫ*, however, root *a* must be substituted before the word is sought in a dictionary**, e.g. *fjǫll* 'mountains', *lǫnd* 'countries' will be found under *fjall*, *land* (see paradigm 26).

Difficulties with masculines and feminines of this type occur where a form other than one with root *ǫ* is encountered. The bulk of the feminines are the least troublesome: in the genitive singular, nominative, accusative and genitive plural these have root *a*, so the process of looking such words up is simply the reverse of that which applies in the case of those like *stjǫrnur*, *fjǫru*, *dǫlum*, or *grǫnnum*. For example, *kvalar* (gen. sg. or nom./acc. pl.), *hafnar* (gen. sg.), *hafnir* (nom./acc. pl.), *kvala*, *hafna* (gen. pl.) will be found not under **kval* or **hafn*, but under *kvǫl* 'torment', and *hǫfn* 'harbour' (see paradigm 12). The residual feminines and the masculines with original root *a* present a more complex picture in that it is only in the genitive singular and plural that *a* appears. In the remaining forms, where there is or has been no *u* in the endings (automatically triggering *a > ǫ*, cf. above), i.e., dative singular and nominative (also analogically accusative) plural masculine, nominative and accusative plural feminine, we most often find root *e*, though sometimes *i* (see 3.1.7.2). Thus *vallar* (gen. sg.), *valla* (gen. pl.), *velli* (dat. sg.), *vellir* (nom. pl.) should all be looked up under *vǫllr* 'field', m., *fjarðar* (gen. sg.), *fjarða* (gen. pl.), *firði* (dat. sg.), *firðir* (nom. pl.) under *fjǫrðr* 'fjord', m., *strandar* (gen. sg.), *stranda* (gen. pl.), *strendr* (nom./acc. pl.) under *strǫnd* 'beach', f. (see paradigms 4, 5, 18).

U-mutation affects unstressed as well as stressed syllables. In unstressed syllables, however, it results in *u*, thus enabling the mutation to spread further. The strong masculine noun *fǫgnuðr* 'joy', for example, comes ultimately from **fagnaðuz* via the intermediate forms, first **fagnǫðuz* and then **fagnuðuz*. The *u*-mutated forms — nom. and acc. sg. and dat. pl.: *fǫgnuðr, fǫgnuð, fǫgnuðum* — thus contrast markedly with the other parts of the paradigm whose root is *fagnað*- (see paradigm 6). A strong neuter noun like *sumar* 'summer' has nom. and acc. pl. *sumur* (< **sumuru* < **sumǫru* < **sumaru*) (paradigm 27).

3.1.7.1 Labial mutation — Exercise

1. What does the term 'mutation' ('*Umlaut*') refer to?
2. In what circumstances does root *a* change to *ǫ* in Old Norse?
3. Look up the following nouns in an Old Norse dictionary or in the Glossary in *NION* III and write down the entry forms you find: *nǫfnum* (n.), *gǫtur* (f.), *vǫku* (f.), *ǫrmum* (m.).
4. In which cases, genders and numbers can we expect to find root *ǫ* where no *u* follows in the next syllable?
5. Look up the following nouns in an Old Norse dictionary or in the Glossary in *NION* III and write down the entry forms you find: *gjǫld* (n.), *lǫmb* (n.), *raddar* (f.), *sagnir* (f.), *hatta* (m.), *vaxtar* (m.).

3.1.7.2 Front mutation

Front mutation, in common with its labial counterpart, mainly concerns the adoption by the vowel of a stressed syllable of a feature of the vowel or semi-vowel of the immediately following unstressed syllable. Here, however, the principal conditioning factors were the front vowel *i* and the front semi-vowel *j*. So-called 'palatal *r*' (or *z*, as in **kūz/*kūʀ*, which developed to *kýr*, see below), and the combined influence of earlier *-gē*, *-kē* (as in *dagē, which became *degi*, see below) — as well as analogical levelling (the restructuring of forms by the force of analogy) — also played their part in this process. All the conditioning sounds are likely to have been pronounced with the front of the tongue raised close to its maximum height, and their presence had the effect of turning a preceding back vowel (one pronounced with the back of the tongue raised or lowered) into its front counterpart. Thus *ó*, for example, which is a mid-high back vowel (the back of the tongue is raised to above mid-height, but not to its full extent), became *œ*, a mid-high front vowel, when an *i*, *j* or other 'conditioner' followed. That is why the masculine noun *fótr* 'foot' and the feminine *bók* 'book' have nominative plurals *fœtr*, *bœkr* respectively (see paradigms 7 and 19).

As these introductory remarks and examples suggest, front mutation, unlike the labial variety, is very much a historical process (it is also common to most Germanic languages, cf. English *foot* — *feet*, *man* — *men*, German *Fuß* — *Füße*, *Mann* — *Männer*). It occurred at a stage of Scandinavian language development that preceded Old Norse, and had ceased to be productive some time before the Old Norse period. This has two important consequences for the recognition of inflexions. First, we find an unstressed *i* that does not cause front mutation because it arose after the period when mutation was taking place, e.g. dat. m. sg. *armi* 'arm' (< *armē). This circumstance makes it impossible to formulate a hard-and-fast rule (like $a > \varrho$ before *u*, *v*) stating which stressed vowels we can expect to find immediately preceding *i*. Second, the *i*, *j* or other conditioner triggering the fronting may no longer be present (very often it is not — cf. *fœtr* and *bœkr* above, earlier forms of which were *fōtiz, *bōkiz). This latter situation is parallel to the loss of *u* in forms such as *fjǫll* 'mountains', *hǫfn* 'harbour', noted in 3.1.7.1.

With such complications, what the learner of Old Norse needs to know are the front mutation products of the back vowels affected, so that s/he may recognise that *fótr* — *fœtr* or *bók* — *bœkr*, for example, are different forms of the same lexical item. It is further useful to know where in different paradigms to expect front-mutated root vowels.

The back : front correspondences arising from front mutation, together with examples (contrasting nom. sg. with nom. pl. unless otherwise stated), are as follows:

a —— e	(dagr —— degi	'day', nom. and dat. m. sg.)
á —— æ	(tá —— tær	'toe', f.)
o —— ø	(hnot —— hnøtr	'nut', f.)
ó —— œ	(bóndi —— bœndr	'farmer', m.)
u —— y	(dura —— dyrr	'doorway', gen. and nom. f. pl.)
ú —— ý	(mús —— mýss	'mouse', f.)
au —— ey	(aurar —— eyrir	'ounce', nom. m. pl. and sg.)

Occasionally o (from an earlier u) and ó (from an earlier lengthened a) can correspond to y and æ respectively (e.g. sonr —— synir 'son', m.; nótt —— nætr 'night', f.).

The places where front mutation forms are to be expected in noun paradigms are:

(1) nom., acc., gen. sg. of words (all masculine) ending in -ill (e.g. lykill 'key' — dat. sg. lukli, pl. forms all with root lukl-; see paradigm 3).

(2) dat. sg. of certain masculines (notably those with root vowel ǫ in the nom. sg., e.g. hetti — nom. sg. hǫttr 'hood'; birni — nom. sg. bjǫrn 'bear' (not strictly mutation, but often counted as such, see 3.1.7.3); fœti — nom. sg. fótr 'foot'; see paradigms 4, 5 and 7).

(3) nom. pl. of a good many masculines (again, notably those with root vowel ǫ in the nom. sg.) and feminines (e.g. kettir — nom. m. sg. kǫttr 'cat'; þættir — nom. m. sg. þáttr 'strand', 'short story'; feðr — nom. m. sg. faðir 'father'; hendr — nom. f. sg. hǫnd 'hand'; bœtr — nom. f. sg. bót 'compensation'; kýr — acc. f. sg. kú 'cow' (see (5) below); paradigms 5, 8, 18, 19, 21).

(4) acc. pl. of a few masculines (and, in later texts, of most of those with root vowel ǫ in the nom. sg.) and all feminines included under (3) (e.g. fœtr — nom. m. sg. fótr 'foot'; velli (as alternative to vǫllu) — nom. m. sg. vǫllr 'field' 'ground'; feðr, hendr, bœtr, kýr — as under (3); paradigms 5, 7, 8, 18, 19, 21).

Additional cases of front mutation in nouns, affecting only a few words, but often very common ones, are:

(5) nom. and gen. sg. of the feminines kýr 'cow'; sýr 'sow'; ær 'ewe' (contrast acc. and dat. sg., gen. and dat. pl. of, e.g., kýr: kú, kú, kúa, kúm; paradigm 21).

(6) gen. sg. of certain feminines (e.g. bœkr — nom. sg. bók 'book'; nætr — nom. sg. nátt 'night'; the genitives of these feminines can also be found without mutation and with the more usual ending -ar; paradigm 19).

(7) dat. sg., gen. and dat. pl. of four nouns of relationship: *faðir* 'father', m.; *bróðir* 'brother', m.; *móðir* 'mother', f.; *dóttir* 'daughter', f. (e.g. *feðr*, dat. sg., *feðra*, gen. pl., *feðrum*, dat. pl.; *mæðr*, dat. sg., *mæðra*, gen. pl., *mæðrum*, dat. pl.; the dative singular of these nouns can also be found with the ending *-ur*, causing labial rather than front mutation in *faðir*; paradigms 8, 22).

It is further worth noting a small group of weak masculines consisting of root + *-and-* suffix. These have front mutation in the nom. and acc. pl., but it affects the suffix only (e.g. *dómandi* 'judge', nom. and acc. pl. *dómendr*; with contraction of the suffix: *bóndi* (< *búandi*) 'farmer', nom./acc. pl. *bændr*; paradigm 10).

3.1.7.2 Front mutation — Exercise

1. Which front-mutated vowels correspond with which back vowels?
2. In which parts of noun paradigms are front-mutated vowels to be expected?
3. Does front mutation ever affect other syllables than the initial?
4. Look up the following nouns in an Old Norse dictionary or in *NION* III and write down the entry forms you find: *strendr* (f.), *rætr* (f.), *mætti* (m.), *brýr* (f.), *tugli* (m.), *erni* (m.), *eigendr* (m.), *katlar* (m.).

3.1.7.3 Breaking

Like front mutation, breaking is a historical phenomenon. Its causes are disputed, but it results in a diphthong where earlier there was a single vowel sound, cf. ON *jafn* 'even [adj.]', *hjǫrð* 'herd', f., with the English and German counterparts *even*, *eben* and *herd*, *Herde*. Though there are many nouns in ON with a broken (diphthongised) root vowel, there are only a few where this alternates with unbroken varieties within the paradigm, causing difficulties of recognition for the learner. In a small group of masculine nouns conditions have favoured breaking in all cases except the dat. sg. and nom. pl., where the root vowel *i* (from earlier *e*) is found. While the acc. and gen. sg. and acc., gen. and dat. pl. of *skjǫldr* 'shield' are thus *skjǫld*, *skjaldar*, *skjǫldu*, *skjalda*, *skjǫldum* respectively, the dat. sg. and nom. pl. are *skildi*, *skildir* (see paradigm 4). All such nouns have root vowel *jǫ* in the nom. sg.

3.1.7.4 Deviations from the basic endings

Certain endings occur that do not accord with those given on pp. 29–30. We have already seen in 3.1.7.1 and 3.1.7.2 above that the nom. and acc. pl. of a number of common masculine and feminine nouns end in -*r* rather than -*a*, -*i* or -*u* + *r*. Other deviations which may cause problems of recognition are:

(1) Nominative masculine singulars that lack the -*r* ending. These are due to the assimilation of *r* to an immediately preceding *l*, *n*, *s* (e.g. *lykill* 'key', m. (< *lykilr); *hrafn* 'raven', m. (< *hrafnn < *hrafnr); *áss* 'god', m. (< *ásr); see paradigms 3, 5). *Hrafn* exemplifies a general rule that consonant + geminate (double) consonant is simplified to consonant + single consonant (thus also in nouns with consonant + root *r*; compare, e.g., nom. and acc. m. sg. *vetr* 'winter', the former from earlier *vetrr). Nominative and accusative plural -*r* can be assimilated in the same way as nom. sg. when the pl. ending does not contain a vowel (e.g. *mús* 'mouse', f. — nom. and acc. pl. *mýss*).

(2) A small group of strong feminines that has -*r* in the nom. sg., just as most strong masculines, and -*i* in the acc. and dat. sg. (e.g. *heiðr*, *heiði*, *heiði* 'moor'; see paradigm 17).

(3) Strong feminines with the suffix -*ing* or -*ung*, as well as a few others, that have -*u* in the dat. sg. (e.g. *dróttning* 'queen', dat. sg. *dróttningu*; *sól* 'sun', dat. sg. (usually) *sólu*; see paradigm 14).

(4) A small group of weak feminines that has -*i* throughout the singular (e.g. *gleði* 'joy'; see paradigm 24). These nouns denote abstract concepts and have no plural form.

(5) A few nouns with root *nn* that have -*ðr* in the nom. sg. (e.g. *muðr* 'mouth', m., acc. sg. *munn*; *forkuðr* 'strong desire', f., gen. sg. *forkunnar*).

3.1.7.5 Minor irregularities

The inflexions of ON nouns exhibit yet other deviations from the basic pattern, but these are less likely to cause the learner problems of recognition.

(1) The unstressed syllables of many disyllabic nouns lose their vowel when an inflexional ending is added which itself consists of a syllable (e.g. *þistill* 'thistle', m. — dat. sg. *þistli*, nom., acc., gen., dat. pl. *þistlar*,

þistla, þistla, þistlum; *hirðir* 'shepherd', m. — dat. sg. *hirði* (not **hirðii*), nom., acc., gen., dat. pl. *hirðar, hirða, hirða, hirðum*; *sumar* 'summer', n. — dat. sg. *sumri*, gen., dat. pl. *sumra, sumrum*; *kvæði* 'poem', n. — dat. sg. *kvæði* (not **kvæðii*), gen., dat. pl. *kvæða, kvæðum*; see paradigms 3, 27; note also 28).

(2) The vowels of inflexional endings tend to be dropped when they immediately follow a long vowel of the same or similar quality (e.g. *á* 'stream', f. — gen. sg. *ár*, nom., acc., gen., dat. pl. *ár, ár, á, ám*; *kné* 'knee', n. — dat. sg. *kné*; see paradigms 16, 29).

(3) Where stressed *é* is followed by unstressed *a* or *u*, the stress tends to be shifted onto the latter (with resultant vowel lengthening and occasionally vowel change), the *é* becoming the semi-vowel *j* (e.g. *kné* 'knee', n. — gen. pl. *knjá* (< **knéa*), dat. pl. *knjám* or *knjóm* (< **knéum*); paradigm 29).

(4) In some nouns *j* is inserted before inflexional endings consisting of or beginning in *a* or *u*; in others *v* is inserted before endings consisting of or beginning in *a* or *i* (e.g. *erfingi* 'heir', m. — acc., gen., dat. sg. *erfingja*, nom., acc., gen., dat. pl. *erfingjar, erfingja, erfingja, erfingjum*; *ey* 'island', f. — gen., dat. sg. *eyjar, eyju*, nom., acc., gen., dat. pl. *eyjar, eyjar, eyja, eyjum*; *sker* 'skerry', n. — gen., dat. pl. *skerja, skerjum*; *sǫngr* 'song', m. — dat. sg. *sǫngvi*, nom., acc., gen. pl. *sǫngvar, sǫngva, sǫngva*; *ǫr* 'arrow', f. — gen. sg. *ǫrvar*, nom., acc., gen. pl. *ǫrvar, ǫrvar, ǫrva*; see paradigm 15).

3.1.7.3/3.1.7.4/3.1.7.5 Breaking/Deviations from the basic endings/ Minor irregularities — Exercise

1. Look up the following nouns in an Old Norse dictionary or in the Glossary in *NION* III and write down the entry forms you find: *birni* (m.), *skildir* (m.), *djǫful* (m.), *sveinar* (m.), *byrði* (f.).
2. Which group of strong nouns have *-u* in the dative singular?
3. What is unusual about the inflexion of the noun *gleði* and of other feminines in *-i*?
4. Look up the following nouns in an Old Norse dictionary or in *NION* III and write down the entry forms you find: *himnar* (m.), *hersar* (m.), *gamni* (n.), *erendum* (n.), *gjár* (f.), *benjar* (f.), *hǫggvi* (n.).

3.1.8 Examples of noun inflexion

Having established the basic pattern of noun inflexions (pp. 29–30), and discussed the principal variations, we can now proceed to flesh out this skeleton with complete paradigms of individual nouns. These follow below.

It is customary when presenting nouns in Old Norse grammars to provide an example of every or virtually every inflexional type and to divide this wealth of data into classes and sub-classes, based often on features that had died out before the Old Norse period began. This does not help the learner much, and here instead an example is given of each of the basic patterns of noun inflexion, augmented by such others as will assist in the recognition of the majority of forms likely to be encountered in Old Norse texts. These examples should be studied in conjunction with the guidance given in 3.1.4, 3.1.6 and 3.1.7. Each pattern or paradigm is numbered for ease of reference.

Strong masculine (basic pattern)

		(1) *hestr* 'horse'			
Sg.	nom.	hest**r**	Pl.	nom.	hest**ar**
	acc.	hest		acc.	hest**a**
	gen.	hest**s**		gen.	hest**a**
	dat.	hest**i**		dat.	hest**um**

		(2) *staðr* 'place'			
Sg.	nom.	staðr	Pl.	nom.	stað**ir**
	acc.	stað		acc.	stað**i**
	gen.	stað**ar**		gen.	stað**a**
	dat.	stað		dat.	stǫð**um**

Strong masculine (other patterns)

		(3) *ketill* 'kettle' 'pot'			
Sg.	nom.	keti**ll**	Pl.	nom.	katl**ar**
	acc.	ketil		acc.	katla
	gen.	ketil**s**		gen.	katla
	dat.	**katli**		dat.	kǫtl**um**

(4) *skjǫldr* 'shield'

Sg.	nom.	skjǫld**r**	Pl.	nom.	sk**i**ld**ir**
	acc.	skjǫld		acc.	skjǫld**u**
	gen.	skjald**ar**		gen.	skjald**a**
	dat.	sk**i**ld**i**		dat.	skjǫld**um**

(5) *ǫrn* 'eagle'

Sg.	nom.	ǫrn	Pl.	nom.	**e**rn**ir**
	acc.	ǫrn		acc.	ǫrn**u**/**e**rn**i**
	gen.	**a**rn**ar**		gen.	**a**rn**a**
	dat.	**e**rn**i**		dat.	ǫrn**um**

(6) *fǫgnuðr* 'joy'

Sg.	nom.	fǫgnuð**r**	Pl.	nom.	f**a**gn**a**ð**ir**
	acc.	fǫgnuð		acc.	f**a**gn**a**ð**i**
	gen.	f**a**gn**a**ð**ar**		gen.	f**a**gn**a**ð**a**
	dat.	f**a**gn**a**ð**i**		dat.	fǫgnuð**um**

(7) *fótr* 'foot'

Sg.	nom.	fót**r**	Pl.	nom.	f**œ**tr
	acc.	fót		acc.	f**œ**tr
	gen.	fót**ar**		gen.	fót**a**
	dat.	f**œ**t**i**		dat.	fót**um**

(8) *faðir* 'father'

Sg.	nom.	faðir	Pl.	nom.	f**e**ðr
	acc.	f**ǫ**ð**ur**		acc.	f**e**ðr
	gen.	f**ǫ**ð**ur**		gen.	f**e**ðr**a**
	dat.	f**e**ðr/f**ǫ**ð**ur**		dat.	f**e**ðr**um**

Weak masculine (basic pattern)

(9) *bardagi* 'battle'

Sg.	nom.	bardag**i**	Pl.	nom.	bardag**ar**
	acc.	bardag**a**		acc.	bardag**a**
	gen.	bardag**a**		gen.	bardag**a**
	dat.	bardag**a**		dat.	bard**ǫ**g**um**

Weak masculine (other pattern)

(10) *eigandi* 'owner'

Sg.	nom.	eigand**i**	Pl.	nom.	eig**e**nd**r**
	acc.	eigand**a**		acc.	eig**e**nd**r**
	gen.	eigand**a**		gen.	eigand**a**
	dat.	eigand**a**		dat.	eig**ǫ**nd**um**

Strong feminine (basic pattern)

(11) *laug* 'bath'

Sg.	nom.	laug	Pl.	nom.	laug**ar**
	acc.	laug		acc.	laug**ar**
	gen.	laug**ar**		gen.	laug**a**
	dat.	laug		dat.	laug**um**

(12) *mǫn* 'mane'

Sg.	nom.	mǫn	Pl.	nom.	m**a**n**ar**
	acc.	mǫn		acc.	m**a**n**ar**
	gen.	m**a**n**ar**		gen.	m**a**n**a**
	dat.	mǫn		dat.	mǫn**um**

(13) *hlíð* 'slope' 'hillside'

Sg.	nom.	hlíð	Pl.	nom.	hlíð**ir**
	acc.	hlíð		acc.	hlíð**ir**
	gen.	hlíð**ar**		gen.	hlíð**a**
	dat.	hlíð		dat.	hlíð**um**

Strong feminine (other patterns)

(14) *kerling* 'old woman'

Sg.	nom.	kerling	Pl.	nom.	kerling**ar**
	acc.	kerling		acc.	kerling**ar**
	gen.	kerling**ar**		gen.	kerling**a**
	dat.	kerling**u**		dat.	kerling**um**

(15) *ey* 'island'

Sg.	nom.	ey	Pl.	nom.	eyjar
	acc.	ey		acc.	eyjar
	gen.	eyjar		gen.	eyja
	dat.	eyju		dat.	eyjum

(16) *á* 'stream'

Sg.	nom.	á	Pl.	nom.	ár
	acc.	á		acc.	ár
	gen.	ár		gen.	á
	dat.	á		dat.	ám

(17) *heiðr* 'heath'

Sg.	nom.	heiðr	Pl.	nom.	heiðar
	acc.	heiði		acc.	heiðar
	gen.	heiðar		gen.	heiða
	dat.	heiði		dat.	heiðum

(18) *strǫnd* 'shore'

Sg.	nom.	strǫnd	Pl.	nom.	strendr
	acc.	strǫnd		acc.	strendr
	gen.	strandar		gen.	stranda
	dat.	strǫnd		dat.	strǫndum

(19) *bók* 'book'

Sg.	nom.	bók	Pl.	nom.	bœkr
	acc.	bók		acc.	bœkr
	gen.	bœkr/bókar		gen.	bóka
	dat.	bók		dat.	bókum

(20) *tá* 'toe'

Sg.	nom.	tá	Pl.	nom.	tær
	acc.	tá		acc.	tær
	gen.	tár		gen.	tá
	dat.	tá		dat.	tám

Noun inflexions and their function

		(21) *kýr* 'cow'			
Sg.	nom.	kýr	Pl.	nom.	kýr
	acc.	kú		acc.	kýr
	gen.	kýr		gen.	kúa
	dat.	kú		dat.	kúm

		(22) *dóttir* 'daughter'			
Sg.	nom.	dóttir	Pl.	nom.	dœtr
	acc.	dóttur		acc.	dœtr
	gen.	dóttur		gen.	dœtra
	dat.	dœtr/dóttur		dat.	dœtrum

Weak feminine (basic pattern)

		(23) *saga* 'story'			
Sg.	nom.	saga	Pl.	nom.	sǫgur
	acc.	sǫgu		acc.	sǫgur
	gen.	sǫgu		gen.	sagna
	dat.	sǫgu		dat.	sǫgum

Weak feminine (other pattern)

		(24) *reiði* 'anger'
Sg.	nom., acc., gen., dat.	reiði

Strong neuter (basic pattern)

		(25) *orð* 'word'			
Sg.	nom.	orð	Pl.	nom.	orð
	acc.	orð		acc.	orð
	gen.	orðs		gen.	orða
	dat.	orði		dat.	orðum

		(26) *vatn* 'water','lake'			
Sg.	nom.	vatn	Pl.	nom.	vǫtn
	acc.	vatn		acc.	vǫtn
	gen.	vatns		gen.	vatna
	dat.	vatni		dat.	vǫtnum

		(27) *sumar* 'summer'			
Sg.	nom.	sumar	Pl.	nom.	sumur
	acc.	sumar		acc.	sumur
	gen.	sumars		gen.	sumra
	dat.	sumri		dat.	sumrum

		(28) *erindi* 'message', 'speech'			
Sg.	nom.	erindi	Pl.	nom.	erindi
	acc.	erindi		acc.	erindi
	gen.	erindis		gen.	erinda
	dat.	erindi		dat.	erindum

Strong neuter (other pattern)

		(29) *kné* 'knee'			
Sg.	nom.	kné	Pl.	nom.	kné
	acc.	kné		acc.	kné
	gen.	knés		gen.	knjá
	dat.	kné		dat.	knjám/knjóm

Weak neuter (basic pattern)

		(30) *auga* 'eye'			
Sg.	nom.	auga	Pl.	nom.	augu
	acc.	auga		acc.	augu
	gen.	auga		gen.	augna
	dat.	auga		dat.	augum

Noun inflexions and their function 53

The learner who has conscientiously mastered the above should be in a position to recognise the forms of virtually all the Old Norse nouns with which s/he is confronted in a text. It should further be possible to deduce the nominative singular form of unfamiliar nouns, so that these can be looked up in a dictionary. (The amount of help offered by dictionaries varies, but in addition to the nominative singular, the genitive singular and nominative plural are usually noted, as well as (other) forms that cannot easily be predicted.)

3.1.8 Examples of noun inflexion — Exercise

Identify the case, gender, number, syntactic function and semantic role of the nouns printed in **bold** in the following passage (adapted from *Hrafnkels saga Freysgoða* 'The Saga of Hrafnkell, Priest of Freyr'). Where a noun appears in a case other than the nominative singular, give the nominative singular — the dictionary entry — form. In the case of compound nouns, give the case, gender, number, function and role of the last element only (e.g., in *Breiðdal*, analyse *-dal*, in *Hallfreðarstǫðum*, *-stǫðum* and in *fjárskiptis*, *-skiptis*).

Þat var á **dǫgum Haralds konungs** ins hárfagra, **Hálfdanar sonar** ins svarta, at sá **maðr** kom **skipi** sínu til **Íslands** í **Breiðdal**, er **Hallfreðr** hét.

> It was in days-of-Haraldr king the hairfair, Hálfdan's son the black, that that man came with-ship REFL. POSS. to Iceland into Breiðdalr, who Hallfreðr was-called.

> It was in the days of King Haraldr fairhair, son of Hálfdan the black, that a man called Hallfreðr brought his ship to Iceland, to Breiðdalr.

Þar var á **skipi kona** hans ok **sonr**, er **Hrafnkell** hét. Hann var fimmtán **vetra** gamall. **Hallfreðr** setti **bú** saman.

> There was on ship wife his and son, who Hrafnkell was-called. He was fifteen of-winters old. Hallfreðr put dwelling together.

> On board the ship was his wife and son, who was called Hrafnkell. He was fifteen years old. Hallfreðr established a farmstead.

En um várit fœrði **Hallfreðr bú** sitt norðr yfir **heiði** ok gerði **bú** þar, sem heitir í **Geitdal**.

> But in spring-the moved Hallfreðr dwelling REFL. POSS. north over moor and made dwelling there that is-called in Geitdalr.

> But in the spring Hallfreðr moved his dwelling northwards across the moor and made a dwelling in the place called Geitdalr.

Ok eina **nótt** dreymði hann, at **maðr** kom at honum ok mælti: 'Þar liggr þú, **Hallfreðr**, ok heldr óvarliga. Fœr þú á brott bú þitt ok vestr yfir **Lagarfljót**. Þar er **heill** þín ǫll.'

> And one night dreamt him that man came to him and said: 'there lie you, Hallfreðr, and rather unwarily. Move you a(-)way dwelling your and west over Lagarfljót. There is fortune your all.'

> And one night he dreamt that a man came to him and said: 'There you lie, Hallfreðr, and rather unwarily. Move your dwelling away and westwards across Lagarfljót. There is where all your good fortune lies.'

Eptir þat vaknar hann ok fœrir bú sitt út yfir **Rangá** í **Tungu**, þar sem síðan heitir á **Hallfreðarstǫðum**, ok bjó þar til **elli**.

> After that wakes he and moves dwelling REFL. POSS. out over Rangá into Tunga, there that later is-called at Hallfreðarstaðir, and lived there till old-age.

> After that he wakes up and moves his dwelling out across Rangá to Tunga, to the place which has since been called Hallfreðarstaðir, and lived there into his old age.

En honum varð þar eptir **geit** ok **hafr**. Ok inn sama **dag**, sem Hallfreðr var í brott, hljóp **skriða** á húsin, ok týndusk þar þessir **gripir**, ok því heitir þat síðan í Geitdal.

> But to-him came-to-be there behind she-goat and billy-goat. And the same day that Hallfreðr was a(-)way, ran landslide onto houses-the, and lost-*sk* [see 3.6.5.3] there these animals, and therefore is-called it since in Geitdalr.

> But it turned out he left a she-goat and a billy-goat there. And the same day as Hallfreðr moved away, a landslide fell onto the buildings and these animals perished there, and for that reason the place has since been called Geitdalr.

Hrafnkell lagði þat í **vanða** sinn at ríða yfir á **heiðar** á sumarit. Þá var **Jǫkulsdalr** albyggðr upp at **brúm**.

> Hrafnkell laid that in custom REFL. POSS. to ride over onto moors in summer-the. Then was Jǫkulsdalr fully-settled up to bridges.

> Hrafnkell made it his practice to ride up onto the moors in the summer. At this time Jǫkulsdalr was fully settled right up to the (rock) bridges.

Hrafnkell reið upp eptir **Fljótsdalsheiði** ok sá, hvar eyðidalr gekk af **Jǫkulsdal**. Sá **dalr** sýndisk **Hrafnkatli** byggiligri en aðrir **dalir**.

> Hrafnkell rode up along Fljótsdalsheiðr and saw where empty-valley went from Jǫkulsdalr. That valley showed-*sk* to-Hrafnkell more-habitable than other valleys.

> Hrafnkell rode up over Fljótsdalsheiðr and saw an uninhabited valley leading off from Jǫkulsdalr. The valley seemed more habitable to Hrafnkell than other valleys.

En er Hrafnkell kom heim, beiddi hann **fǫður** sinn **fjárskiptis**, ok sagðisk hann **bústað** vilja reisa sér.

> But when Hrafnkell came home, asked he father REFL. POSS. for-division-of-property, and said-*sk* he dwelling-place want raise for-self.

> And so when Hrafnkell came home, he asked his father for a division of the property, and said he wanted to build a dwelling for himself.

Þetta veitir **faðir** hans honum, ok hann gerir sér **bœ** í **dal** þeim, ok kallar á **Aðalbóli**.

> This grants father his to-him, and he makes for-self farm in valley that and calls at Aðalból.

> His father grants him this, and he makes himself a farm in that valley and calls it Aðalból.

Hrafnkell fekk **Oddbjargar Skjǫldólfsdóttur** ór **Laxárdal**. Þau áttu tvá **sonu**.

> Hrafnkell got Oddbjǫrg Skjǫldólfsdóttir from Laxárdalr. They had two sons.

> Hrafnkell married Oddbjǫrg Skjǫldólfsdóttir from Laxárdalr. They had two sons.

3.1.9 The suffixed definite article

As in the Scandinavian languages in general, the definite article — the word for 'the' — may be suffixed to the noun. That is to say, it takes the form of an ending. Like the noun itself, the definite article is inflected for number and case. In addition, it is inflected for gender, i.e. it has different forms for masculine, feminine and neuter.

The forms of the suffixed article in Old Norse are as follows.

		Masculine			
Sg.	nom.	-(i)nn	Pl.	nom.	-(i)nir
	acc.	-(i)nn		acc.	-(i)na
	gen.	-(i)ns		gen.	-nna
	dat.	-(i)num		dat.	-num

		Feminine			
Sg.	nom.	-(i)n	Pl.	nom.	-nar
	acc.	-(i)na		acc.	-nar
	gen.	-(i)nnar		gen.	-nna
	dat.	-(i)nni		dat.	-num

		Neuter			
Sg.	nom.	-(i)t	Pl.	nom.	-(i)n
	acc.	-(i)t		acc.	-(i)n
	gen.	-(i)ns		gen.	-nna
	dat.	-(i)nu		dat.	-num

The presence or absence of the initial *-i* (in some texts *-e*) is unlikely to cause the learner serious problems of recognition. In the example sentences in 3.1.5 we had on the one hand (3), (6) *leiðinu, skipinu*, with dat. n. sg. *-i* noun ending + *-nu*, and on the other (20) *gólfit* with acc. n. sg. zero noun ending + *-it*, all of them unambiguously combinations of noun and definite article (cf. also *vár-it, sumar-it* (both acc. n. sg.) and *hús-in* (acc. n. pl.) in the extract from *Hrafnkels saga* above). Contrastive examples with and without *-i*, based on the list of noun paradigms in 3.1.8, are:

hestr-inn	—	*bardagi-nn*	(nom. m. sg.)
staðar-ins	—	*eiganda-ns*	(gen. m. sg.)
menn-inir	—	*skildir-nir*	(nom. m. pl.)
hlíð-ina	—	*sǫgu-na*	(acc. f. sg.)
strǫnd-inni	—	*á-nni*	(dat. f. sg.)
kné-in	—	*erindi-n*	(nom./acc. n. pl.)

The most general rule governing the occurrence of initial *-i* in the def. art. is that it is found in conjunction with words of one syllable and omitted elsewhere (contrast the left and right-hand lists above). However, there are several exceptions to this.

The *-i* is omitted after the following monosyllabic forms.
(1) Nom./acc. m./f. pl. (cf. *fœtr-nir* (nom. m. pl.), *fœtr-na* (acc. m. pl.) *dœtr-nar* (nom./acc. f. pl.)); an exception to the exception is represented by *menn-inir*, *menn-ina* (nom. and acc. m. pl. respectively), though this is a rare type.
(2) Those ending in a vowel, but only where the article is disyllabic (contrast *kné-in* with *á-nni* above).
(3) Dative masculine singulars that lack the usual *-i* ending (cf. *stað-num*).

The *-i* is retained after genitive singulars in *-ar* (cf. *staðarins* above, further *eyjarinnar* (gen. f. sg.)).

Note that in the dative plural, the noun ending *-(u)m* loses its *m* and the article is suffixed onto the *u* or stressed vowel (cf. *kǫtlunum*, *sǫgunum*, *orðunum*, *knjánum*).

As with the nouns, certain regularities will be observed in the definite article paradigms. It will also be noticed that there are various points of similarity between noun and article endings.
(1) The dat. pl. always ends in *-um* (as with nouns).
(2) The gen. pl. always ends in *-a* (as with nouns).
(3) It is only in the f. sg. and m. pl. there is a difference between nom. and acc. forms.
(4) The gen. m. and n. sg. ends in *-s*, the gen. f. sg. in *-ar* (as with most nouns, though some masculine genitives end in *-ar*).
(5) The nom. m. pl. ends in *-ir*, the acc. m. pl. in *-a*, and the nom./acc. f. pl. in *-ar* (cf. the pattern for nouns: nom. m. pl. and nom./acc. f. pl. = vowel + *r*, acc. m. pl. = vowel alone).

As well as the *-(i)nn* suffix dealt with here, Old Norse has a free-standing definite article. However, since its use is closely bound up with that of the adjective, it is dealt with in 3.3.5, following the description of adjective inflexions.

It should be noted that the definite article is used more sparingly in Old Norse than in modern English. It is regularly omitted, for example, from nouns that denote something familiar to writer and reader. Thus *konungr* may mean 'a king' or 'the king' depending on the context. Contrast:

> Fornjótr hefir konungr heitit
> 'Fornjótr has king been-called'
> 'There was a king called Fornjótr'

> Konungr varð reiðr mjǫk
> 'King became angry very'
> 'The king became very angry'

3.1.9 The suffixed definite article — Exercise

Identify the case, gender, number, syntactic function and semantic role of the definite nouns printed in **bold** in the following sentences, and insert a hyphen between noun and article. Where the noun appears in a case other than nominative singular, give the nominative singular definite form.

(1) **Brúðrin** var heldr dǫpr
'The bride was rather sad'

(2) Illugi kippði inn aptr **vǫrusekkunum**
'Illugi snatched in again the sacks of wares'

(3) Þeir kómu til **boðsins**
'They came to the feast'

(4) Tekr Skrýmir **nestbaggann**
'Skrýmir takes the provision-bag'

(5) **Konan** þakkaði honum vel **gjǫfina**
'Woman-the thanked to-him well gift-the'
'The woman thanked him well for the gift'

(6) Þá sendi hann **gestina** út eptir þeim
     'Then he sent the retainers out after them'

(7) Þeir kómu þá til **borgarinnar**
     'They came then to the castle'

(8) **Berserkrinn** leit aptr yfir **ána**
     'The berserk looked back across the river'

(9) Þá smugu þeir milli **spalanna**
     'Then they slipped between the bars'

(10) Lítil var gleði manna at **boðinu**
     'Little was joy of-men at feast-the'
     'Men were not very joyful at the feast'

(11) Jarl kom út í **eyjarnar**
     'The earl came out to the islands'

(12) Þorsteinn lagði fæð á **Austmanninn**, ok fór hann á brott um **sumarit**, ok er hann nú ór **sǫgunni**
     'Þorsteinn laid coldness on easterner-the, and went he a(-)way in summer-the, and is he now out-of story-the'
     'Þorsteinn was cold towards the Norwegian, and in the summer he left, and now he is out of the story'

(13) Þeir eru vanir at halda til móts við **hǫfðingjana**
     'They are accustomed to hold a(-)gainst towards chieftains-the'
     'They are accustomed to offer resistance to the rulers'

(14) Í **hellinum** var féván mikil, ok **kaupmenninir** réðu til ok gengu **hellinn**
     'In cave-the was treasure-hope great, and merchants-the set about and walked cave-the'
     'There was great hope of finding treasure in the cave, and the merchants had a go and explored the cave'

(15) Þeir lǫgðu saman **skipin**
     'They laid together ships-the'
     'They laid the ships alongside each other'

3.2 Pronoun inflexions and their function

Pronouns are sometimes defined as words that stand in place of nouns. A more accurate definition is that they are words that occupy the same position in sentences as noun phrases. What this means is that in English, for example, noun phrases such as (1) *the old man with the long white beard*, (2) *my colleague, who works at the university*, (3) *all the people*, (4) *not the tiniest little bit* are reducible to single words like (1) *he*, (2) *she*, (3) *everyone*, (4) *none*. Of course, a noun phrase will often consist of just one word, e.g. *John, moonlight*, and these too may be replaced by pronouns (*he, it*), but a definition of pronoun that looks no further than this is clearly inadequate.

Many pronouns in addition to replacing noun phrases may be used adjectivally, i.e. as modifiers of noun phrases, like English *this* and *some* in *this man, some particularly interesting ideas*. Although arguably function should determine word class, it is impractical in a basic learners' grammar such as this to operate with both pronominal and adjectival *this, some* etc. Section 3.2 therefore deals with words that regularly function as pronouns, irrespective of how else they may be used.

The personal pronouns *I, you, he, she, it, we, they*, together with the demonstratives *this, that*, the indefinites *some, any*, the negatives *no one, nothing, none* and the interrogatives *who, what*, are among the most commonly occurring words in English, and the same is true of their Old Norse equivalents. **It is therefore clearly essential to learn the (often somewhat idiosyncratic) inflexions of these words as quickly as possible.**

Since pronouns occupy the same position in sentences as noun phrases, it is no surprise to find that, like nouns, they are inflected for number and case in Old Norse, and that the function of the inflexions is in general the same as for nouns (cf. 3.1.1, 3.1.2). In addition, because pronouns 'stand for', i.e. take their reference from, noun phrases, many of them are also inflected for gender. Personal pronouns distinguish 'person', that is, the choice of pronoun depends on the perspective from which the participants in a situation are viewed. Old Norse, like English, has a three-way contrast: 1st person, in which a speaker or writer refers to him/herself (English *I*) or a group of which s/he is a part (Eng. *we*), 2nd person, in which a speaker/writer refers to a person or persons s/he is addressing (Eng. *you*, sg. or pl.), 3rd person, in which a person or persons other than the speaker/writer him/herself or the one/those s/he is addressing are referred to (Eng. *he*, *she*, *it*, *they*).

3.2.1 Personal pronouns: form

1st person: 'I [sg.]', 'we two [dual]', 'we [pl.]'						
nom.	Sg.	ek	Dual	vit	Pl.	vér
acc.		mik		ok(k)r		oss
gen.		mín		okkar		vár
dat.		mér		ok(k)r		oss

2nd person: 'you [sg.]', 'you two [dual]', 'you [pl.]'						
nom.	Sg.	þú	Dual	(þ)it	Pl.	(þ)ér
acc.		þik		yk(k)r		yðr
gen.		þín		ykkar		yð(v)ar
dat.		þér		yk(k)r		yðr

3rd person singular: 'he', 'she', 'it'			
nom.	hann	hon	þat
acc.	hann	hana	þat
gen.	hans	hennar	þess
dat.	honum	henni	þ(v)í

3rd person plural: 'they'						
nom.	m.	þeir	f.	þær	n.	þau
acc.		þá		þær		þau
gen.		þeir(r)a		þeir(r)a		þeir(r)a
dat.		þeim		þeim		þeim

Reflexive, 3rd person only: '-self'	
nom.	—
acc.	sik
gen.	sín
dat.	sér

Various features of these paradigms are worthy of note.

(1) No distinction of gender is found in the first and second person, or in the third person reflexive. Observe, though, that, unlike English, Old Norse employs a masculine, feminine or neuter form of 'they' depending on the gender of the entity referred to. Where more than one gender is involved, the neuter plural is used.

(2) The three-way distinction: singular (used of one entity) — dual (used of two) — plural (used of more than two), occurs only in the first and second person.

(3) A separate reflexive pronoun is found only in the third person. The same forms are used whether the entity referred to by the pronoun is singular or plural, masculine, feminine or neuter. The only distinction made is of case, and then only between accusative, genitive and dative. No nominative form exists since reflexives are normally coreferential with (i.e. refer to the same entity as) the subject (cf. English: *John hurt himself*, but not **heself hurt John*). In the first and second person, the accusative, genitive and dative forms function both as non-reflexives and reflexives (thus *mik*, for example, means 'me' or 'myself', *yðr* 'you [pl.]' or 'yourselves').

Beyond this, the student will observe certain regularities in the paradigms, and similarities with other inflexions. The accusative, genitive and dative of the first and second person singular and of the reflexive vary only in the initial consonant. There is also minimal variation between the first and second person dual. First and second person dual and plural do not distinguish accusative and dative, and all have a genitive ending in *-r* (*-ar* except for *vár*). The third person endings, especially in the singular, will be seen to correspond quite closely to those of the suffixed definite article, while the masculine and neuter genitive singular in *-s* and the feminine in *-ar*, the nominative masculine and nominative/accusative feminine plural in *-r*, the accusative masculine plural in a vowel, the genitive plural in *-a* and the dative plural in *-m* show a marked similarity to noun inflexions as well. Finally, it should be noted that the nominative forms *ek* and *þú* can sometimes be found suffixed to the verb, in which case *ek* loses its vowel (e.g. *hafðak* < *hafða ek* 'I had', *kannk* < *kann ek* 'I can'), while the *þ* of *þú* undergoes partial or complete assimilation with the immediately preceding consonant (e.g. *heyrðu* < *heyr þú* 'hear you [i.e. listen!]', *fórtu* < *fórt þú* 'you went', *seldu* < *sel þú* 'hand you [i.e. hand over!]'). Occasionally other of the personal pronoun forms may be suffixed in this way, but the student is unlikely to come across them in straightforward prose texts.

3.2.2 Demonstrative pronouns: form

		sá 'that', 'those'		
		m.	**f.**	**n.**
Sg.	nom.	sá	sú	þat
	acc.	þann	þá	þat
	gen.	þess	þeir(r)ar	þess
	dat.	þeim	þeir(r)i	þ(v)í
Pl.	nom.	þeir	þær	þau
	acc.	þá	þær	þau
	gen.	þeir(r)a	þeir(r)a	þeir(r)a
	dat.	þeim	þeim	þeim

The neuter singular and all the plural forms of this pronoun will be seen to be identical with those of the personal pronoun, third person, given in 3.2.1. In fact we are dealing with one and the same word. The change in meaning from, for example, 'those female beings' or 'those feminine objects' to 'they [f.]' is very small. Indeed, the same development can be observed in many languages (French *il* 'he', *elle* 'she', for example, come from the Latin pronoun *ille* 'that'), and on occasion Old Norse *sá*, *sú* are found in place of *hann*, *hon*.

Although there is considerable irregularity in the paradigm, compare the acc., gen., dat. m. sg. endings *-nn*, *-ss*, *-m* and the acc., gen., dat. f. sg. *-á*, *-ar*, *-i* with those of the corresponding forms of the suffixed definite article (3.1.9) and of *hinn* immediately below.

		hinn 'that' 'the other', 'those' 'the others'		
		m.	f.	n.
Sg.	nom.	hinn	hin	hitt
	acc.	hinn	hina	hitt
	gen.	hins	hinnar	hins
	dat.	hinum	hinni	hinu
Pl.	nom.	hinir	hinar	hin
	acc.	hina	hinar	hin
	gen.	hinna	hinna	hinna
	dat.	hinum	hinum	hinum

The student will observe the close similarity between the forms of this pronoun and those of the suffixed definite article (though note the *-tt* in the nom./acc. n. sg.). There is in fact a strong likelihood that the suffixed article is a reduced form of *hinn*. Not only does the similarity of form suggest this, the development: demonstrative pronoun > definite article is quite widely attested (cf., for example, French *le, la* — like *il, elle*, though by a different route — from Latin *ille* 'that'). On the relationship between *hinn* and *(h)inn*, the free-standing definite article of Old Norse, see 3.3.5.

		sjá, þessi 'this', 'these'		
		m.	f.	n.
Sg.	nom.	sjá/þessi	sjá/þessi	þetta
	acc.	þenna	þessa	þetta
	gen.	þessa	þessar/þessar(r)ar	þessa
	dat.	þessum/þeima	þessi/þessar(r)i	þessu/þvísa
Pl.	nom.	þessir	þessar	þessi
	acc.	þessa	þessar	þessi
	gen.	þessa/þessar(r)a	þessa/þessar(r)a	þessa/þessar(r)a
	dat.	þessum	þessum	þessum

In this paradigm the number of alternative forms is noteworthy, but few are likely to cause problems of recognition. The nominative singulars *sjá* and *þessi* are both common, but dat. m. sg. *þeima* and dat. n. sg. *þvísa* are much less so. The genitive and dative feminine singular and the genitive plural can be thought of as *þessar*, *þessi*, *þessa* respectively, basic forms which are sometimes expanded by suffixes (*þessar-(r)ar*, *þessa-r(r)a*), or infixes (*þess-ar(r)-i*). Although the forms of this pronoun may appear anomalous, similarities with other paradigms can still be found. The endings of the plural in particular are very close to those of *hinn* (above), and even in the singular we notice the characteristic *-a* and *-ar* endings in the feminine accusative and genitive, and *-um*, *-i*, *-u* in the masculine, feminine and neuter dative respectively. Some of the remaining forms also show characteristic features, though not in the endings — observe the *n*, *t* and *s* of acc. m. *-nn-*, nom./acc. n. *-tt-* and gen. m. and n. *-ss-*.

3.2.3 Indefinite pronouns: form

By far the most common indefinite pronoun in Old Norse is *nǫkkurr* (in some texts with *o* for *ǫ*: *nokkurr*, *nokkut*, etc.) 'some(one/thing)' 'any(one/thing)' '(a) certain'. Its endings are almost identical to those of a strong adjective (see 3.3.4), and very close to those of *hinn* (above). The difference between the inflexions of *nǫkkurr* and *hinn* is largely determined by the final consonant of the root: the *n* of *hin-* assimilates a following *r*, and so we get forms like nom. m. sg. *hinn*, dat. f. sg. *hinni*, gen. pl. *hinna* (instead of *hinr, *hinri, *hinra).

		m.	f.	n.
Sg.	nom.	nǫkkurr	nǫkkur	nǫkkut
	acc.	nǫkkurn	nǫkkura	nǫkkut
	gen.	nǫkkurs	nǫkkurrar	nǫkkurs
	dat.	nǫkkurum	nǫkkurri	nǫkkuru
Pl.	nom.	nǫkkurir	nǫkkurar	nǫkkur
	acc.	nǫkkura	nǫkkurar	nǫkkur
	gen.	nǫkkurra	nǫkkurra	nǫkkurra
	dat.	nǫkkurum	nǫkkurum	nǫkkurum

In the oldest sources many of the forms of this pronoun appear with root *nakkvar-*.

Other indefinite pronouns are *einnhverr* 'some(one/thing)', and *sumr* 'some'. The former consists of an invariable *ein-*, except in the nom./acc. m. and n. sg. (*einn-*, *eitt-* respectively), and occasionally the gen. m. and n. sg. (*eins-*), + *hverr*, the inflexions of which are described below. The latter inflects like a strong adjective (see 3.3.4).

3.2.4 Negative pronouns: form

Of the sundry negative pronouns of Old Norse the only one the learner will encounter regularly is *engi* 'no one' 'nothing' 'none' 'no'. The various forms of the other negatives, *manngi* 'no one', *vættki* 'nothing', *hvárigr* or *hvárgi* 'neither', will, when met with, be well enough understood from the glosses and examples given in Old Norse dictionaries.

		m.	f.	n.
Sg.	nom.	engi	engi	ekki
	acc.	engan/engi	enga	ekki
	gen.	enskis	engrar	enskis
	dat.	engum	engri	engu
Pl.	nom.	engir	engar	engi
	acc.	enga	engar	engi
	gen.	engra	engra	engra
	dat.	engum	engum	engum

The paradigm presented here gives the most common forms of *engi*. A complete list of attested forms will be found in Noreen 1923 (p. 323). Virtually all of these are easily deducible, however, as long as it is known (1) that the root of the word may be *eing-* or *øng-* as well as *eng-*, and (2) that *-v-* may be added before endings beginning with *-a* (e.g. nom./acc. f. pl. *øngvar*, *engvar*) and before the *-ir* of the nom. m. pl. (e.g. *øngvir*, *engvir*).

The inflexions of *engi* present a familiar enough pattern (observe, however, nom./acc. n. sg. *ekki*, from *eitt-ki < *eitt-gi). The student should compare the endings given above with those of *hinn* and *nǫkkurr*, especially the latter, and make a note of where they coincide. Only forms peculiar to *engi* need be learnt specially.

3.2.5 Interrogative and distributive pronouns: form

The two principal pronouns in this category are *hverr* 'who' 'what' 'which', 'each' 'every', and *hvárr* 'which of two', 'each of two' (sg.), 'which of two groups', 'each of two groups' (pl.). With the exception of the acc. m. sg. forms, *hvern* and *hvárn*, both decline like strong adjectives (see 3.3.4). In common with some adjectives *hverr* inserts a -*j*- between root and endings beginning with -*a* or -*u*; *hvárr* does not. For ease of overview, the complete paradigm of *hverr* is now given.

		m.	f.	n.
Sg.	nom.	hverr	hver	hvert
	acc.	hvern	hverja	hvert
	gen.	hvers	hverrar	hvers
	dat.	hverjum	hverri	hverju
Pl.	nom.	hverir	hverjar	hver
	acc.	hverja	hverjar	hver
	gen.	hverra	hverra	hverra
	dat.	hverjum	hverjum	hverjum

In addition to *hverr* and *hvárr* we have *hvat* 'what', 'each (thing)' 'every(thing)', *hvatki* 'each thing', and *hvatvetna* 'everything'. None of these occurs with anything like a complete set of forms; indeed, apart from odd relics of a masculine equivalent of *hvat*, they are neuter singular only. Even then, except in the case of *hvatvetna* (gen. *hversvetna*, dat. *hvívetna*), the paradigms are defective. For although *hvess* and *hví* are often quoted as the genitive and dative form of *hvat*, they tend to function as separate words (*hví*, for example, occurs mostly in the sense 'why?'). And while a genitive *hves(s)kis* and dative *hvígi* of neuter singular *hvatki* are indeed found, the meaning, 'whatsoever', is somewhat removed from that of *hvatki*.

3.2.1/3.2.2/3.2.3/3.2.4/3.2.5 Personal pronouns: form/Demonstrative pronouns: form/Indefinite pronouns: form/Negative pronouns: form/Interrogative and distributive pronouns: form — Exercise

1. Which of the personal pronouns are inflected for gender?
2. Which of the personal pronouns distinguish three numbers (singular, dual and plural)?
3. Give the forms of the 3rd person reflexive pronoun and explain why there is no nominative.
4. What regularities can be observed in the forms of the personal pronouns?
5. What similarities are there between the endings of *hinn* and *sjá/þessi*?
6. In what respects do the endings of *hinn*, *nǫkkurr* and *engi* differ?
7. Give the full paradigm of *hvárr* and compare its endings with those of *hverr*.
8. In what sense is the paradigm of *hvat* defective?

3.2.6 Examples of pronoun usage

As was done for nouns, examples will now be given of pronouns in function. With the wide range of pronominal words and forms that exists, nothing like a comprehensive survey can be provided; the aim is rather to illustrate typical usage. The exemplification follows the same pattern as for nouns (see the preamble on p. 31). Note in particular that the ending or word-form being illustrated is printed in bold type. Compare the endings and word-forms used with those set out and discussed on pp. 61–67. Observe, too, the differences between Old Norse and English phraseology and sentence formation. Definitions of basic concepts that have already been given are not repeated; if in doubt, the student should consult the individual commentaries that accompany each of the examples of noun function.

(1) Eigi sagða **ek þér þat**
'Not said I to-you that'
'I did not tell you that'

Ek (1st person sg. nom.) is the subject; 'I' is the agent or 'performer' of the action and the first noun phrase in the sentence. *Þér* (2nd sg. dat.) is the indirect object; 'you' is the beneficiary of the action and the second noun phrase. *Þat* (3rd. sg. n. acc.) is the direct object, the goal of the action (i.e. what is said) and the third noun phrase.

(2) Þá skutu **þeir** spjótum inn at **þeim**
'Then they threw spears in at them'

The subject is *þeir* (3rd pl. m. nom.), the agent and first noun phrase in the sentence. *Þeim* (3rd pl. dat.) does not function here as a noun phrase, but is part of the preposition phrase *at þeim*, in which the pronoun is governed (i.e. has its case determined) by the preposition *at* (see 3.7, 3.7.3).

(3) Vil**tu** nǫkkut liðsinni **okkr** veita?
'Will-you any help to-us-two give?'
'Will you give us two any help?'

The subject is *-tu* (2nd sg. nom., suffixed to the verb); it is the agent and first noun phrase in the sentence. *Nǫkkut* is part of the direct object. The second noun phrase and the goal of the action consists of the noun *liðsinni* (acc. n. sg.) modified by the pronoun *nǫkkut* (which since it appears here in the role of modifier functions adjectivally; see 3.2). As a modifier *nǫkkut* appears in the same case (acc.), gender (n.) and number (sg.) as its head word (*liðsinni*). This formal relationship between the two (whereby the head word determines the form of its modifier) is known as grammatical agreement or concord and is a regular phenomenon in Old Norse (see 3.3.1). *Okkr* (1st dual dat.) is the indirect object; it denotes the beneficiary of the action and is the third noun phrase in the sentence.

(4) Þórhildr lagði yfir **hann** skikkjuna, ok gekk **hann** út á meðal **þeira**
'Þórhildr put the cloak over him, and he went out between them'

This example consists of two sentences. *Hann* (3rd sg. m. acc.) in sentence 1 is part of the preposition phrase *yfir hann*, and its case is determined by the preposition *yfir* (see 3.7, 3.7.4). *Hann* (3rd sg. m. nom.) in sentence 2 is subject, the first noun phrase and the agent. *Þeira* (3rd pl. gen.) is part of the preposition phrase *meðal þeira*, and its case is determined by the preposition *meðal* (see 3.7.2).

(5)   Hefn **þú vár**, en **vér** skulum **þín**, ef **vér** lifum eptir
'Avenge you us, but we shall you, if we live afterwards'
'Avenge us, and we shall (avenge) you, if we survive'

This example consists of three sentences. *Þú* (2nd sg. nom.) in sentence 1 is the subject (of an imperative verb, cf. 3.6.3, 3.6.5.1), the first noun phrase and the agent; *vár* (1st pl. gen.) is the direct object of the verb (*hefn*) and the second noun phrase. *Vér* (1st pl. nom.) in sentence 2 is subject, the first noun phrase and agent (of the understood verb *hefna*); *þín* (2nd sg. gen.) is the direct object of the (understood) verb and the second noun phrase. *Vér* (1st pl. nom.) in sentence 3 is subject, not so much agent here, rather the 'experiencer', denoting those who (may) experience survival.

(6)   **Þau** væntu **sér** af **honum** nǫkkurs trausts
'They expected for-self of him some support'
'They expected (for themselves) some support from him'

Þau (3rd pl. n. nom., referring to persons of more than one gender) is subject, the first noun phrase and the experiencer. *Sér* (refl. dat.) is the indirect object, the second noun phrase and the intended beneficiary; it is coreferential with the subject (i.e. both subject and indirect object refer to the same entity; see 3.2.1). *Honum* (3rd sg. m. dat.) is part of the preposition phrase *af honum*, and its case is determined by the preposition *af* (see 3.7.3). *Nǫkkurs* is part of the direct object: the third noun phrase, denoting what is experienced (the goal of the experiencing), consists of the noun *trausts* (gen. n. sg.) modified by the pronoun *nǫkkurs*, which has the same case, gender and number as its head word (see example (3) above).

(7)   **Því** skal**tu** heita **mér**, at koma aptr til **mín** at ǫðru hausti
'That shall-you promise to-me, to come back to me at second autumn'
'You must promise me to come back to me next autumn'

Því (3rd sg. n. dat.) is the anticipatory direct object: the thing promised is 'to come back ... ', but the infinitive clause — the equivalent of a noun phrase — is postponed and its place filled by the pronoun *því*. The unmarked position for the direct object would be somewhere after the subject and the finite verb (*skaltu*), but here it has been moved to the front of the sentence for emphasis. The subject is *-tu* (2nd sg. nom., suffixed to the verb); it is the agent, and — the fronted *því* apart — the first noun phrase in the sentence. *Mér* (1st sg. dat.) is the indirect object, the beneficiary (the person to whom the promise is made), and the second or third noun phrase. *Mín* (1st sg. gen.) is part of the preposition phrase *til mín*, and its case is governed by the preposition *til* (see 3.7.2).

(8) Takið **hana** ok haldið **henni**
'Take her and hold her'

This example contains two sentences, each with its finite verb in the imperative ('take!', 'hold!'; see (5) above, but also 3.6.3). The subject is left unexpressed, as generally happens with imperatives in English too. *Hana* and *henni* (3rd sg. f. acc. and dat. respectively) are both direct objects, the goals of the actions; their case is determined by the verb they are object of (*taka* 'take' normally has a direct object in the accusative, *halda* in the sense 'hold fast' 'restrain' has its direct object in the dative).

(9) Meguð **þér** vel bíða **þess**, er eldrinn vinnr **þá**
'Can you well await that, that fire-the overcomes them'
'You can easily wait for the fire to overcome them'

This example consists of two sentences. *Þér* (2nd pl. nom.) is the subject of sentence 1, the agent and the first noun phrase. *Þess* (3rd sg. n. gen.) is the anticipatory direct object (see (7) above): the thing being waited for is 'that the fire overcomes them', but this dependent sentence — the equivalent of a noun phrase — is postponed and its placed filled by the pronoun *þess*. *Þá* is the direct object of (the dependent) sentence 2, the goal of the 'action' and the second noun phrase (the first — the subject — being *eldrinn*).

(10) **Þær** hvíla **sik** þar nǫkkur**ar** nætr
'They rest self there some nights'
'They rest themselves there for a few nights'

Þær (3rd pl. f. nom., referring to women) is subject, the first noun phrase in the sentence and the agent. *Sik* (refl. acc.) is the direct object, the goal of the action and the second noun phrase; it is coreferential with the subject (see (6) above). *Nǫkkurar* is part of the adverbial phrase *nǫkkurar nætr* (acc. f. pl.), which expresses duration of time; *nǫkkurar* modifies the head word *nætr*, and so appears in the same case, gender and number.

(11) Hver**s** þykkir **yðr sá** verðr, er **þetta** ráð gaf til?
'Of-what seems to-you that-man worthy who this advice gave towards [a solution of the problem]?'
'What do you think the man who proffered this advice deserves?'

This example consists of an interrogative sentence, followed by an elliptical infinitive clause (3.9.5.2) and a dependent sentence. *Hvers* (gen. n. sg.) is an interrogative pronoun, and as such is moved out of an unmarked position after *verðr* (*sá er verðr X* 'that person is worthy of X') to the front of the sentence (cf. the identical movement in English); its case is determined by the adjective *verðr* (cf. English *worthy/deserving of something*), and its neuter gender by the fact that it does not refer to anything of specifically masculine or feminine gender. In traditional analysis *yðr* (2nd pl. dat., but used here as a singular honorific, like French *vous* — the person being addressed is the king) would be classed as the indirect object (the recipient or experiencer of the 'seeming', cf. 'to-you'), but recently claims have been made for the existence of a class of 'oblique' (i.e. non-nominative) subjects into which *yðr* here would fall (note that with *þyk(k)ir* 'seems' the person to whom something seems is normally always the first noun phrase in the sentence; see further 3.9.3). *Sá* (nom. m. sg.) is the subject of the elliptical infinitive clause (*sá* [*vera*] *verðr* 'that man [to be] worthy') — what the clause is about. *Þetta ráð* (acc. n. sg.), with *þetta* modifying *ráð*, is the direct object of the dependent sentence, the goal of the action (the words refer to the thing given or proffered); it is the only noun phrase in the sentence, the subject being subsumed into the relative particle or complementiser *er*, which is best regarded as being outside the sentence (see 3.8, 3.8.2.1).

(12) **Hin** vistin fœðir likaminn, **sjá** fœðir sálina
 'That sustenance feeds the body, this feeds the soul'

This example consists of two sentences. In sentence 1, *hin vistin* (nom. f. sg.), with *hin* modifying *vist-in* (noun + def. art.), is the subject; it is the 'performer' of the action and the first noun phrase. In sentence 2, *sjá* (nom. f. sg.) is also the subject, fulfilling on its own the same function as *hin vistin* in sentence 1. Notice how *hin* contrasts with *sjá*: 'that other one' as opposed to 'this one'.

(13) **Hon** virði **þenna** meira en hin**n**
 'She valued this more than that'
 'She held this one in higher esteem than the other'

Hon (3rd sg. f. nom.) is the subject, the agent and the first noun phrase in the sentence. *Þenna* (acc. m. sg., referring to an entity — person, animal or object — of masculine gender) is the direct object (what is valued) and the second noun phrase. *Hinn* (acc. m. sg., likewise referring to an entity of masculine gender) is part of a comparative phrase; this can be understood as 'more than [she valued] the other', and *hinn* taken as a direct object too.

(14) Nú verðr **hann** varr þess**ara** tíðinda
 'Now becomes he aware of-these tidings'
 'Now he becomes aware of these events'

Hann (3rd sg. m. nom.) is the subject, not the agent here but the experiencer, and the first noun phrase in the sentence. The noun phrase *þessara tíðinda* (gen. pl.), with *þessara* modifying *tíðinda*, has its case determined by the adjective *varr* (cf. English *aware of something*).

(15) Sum**ir** váru drepnir ok sum**ir** flýðu ór landi
 'Some were killed and some fled from (the) country'

This example consists of two sentences, in both of which *sumir* (nom. m. pl.) is subject, the first noun phrase and, in sentence 2, the agent. In sentence 1 with its passive verb phrase (*váru drepnir* 'were killed', see 3.6.4) the subject is the recipient or goal of the action (a typical feature of passive constructions).

(16) **Engi** er svá lítill drykkjumaðr, at . . .
 'None is so little drinking-man that . . . '
 'No one is so feeble a drinker that . . . '

Engi (nom. m. sg.) is the subject (the X in an *X is Y* construction, see 3.1.5, sentence 1) and the first noun phrase in the sentence.

(17) **Hon** svarar eng**u**
 'She answers nothing'

Hon (3rd sg. f. nom.) is subject, the agent and first noun phrase in the sentence. *Engu* (dat. n. sg.) can be construed as the direct object of *svarar* (what is answered), but in origin it probably had instrumental sense (the idea of answering with something, cf. 3.1.5, sentence 20).

(18) **Engi** skip skulu sigla burt
 'No ships shall sail away'

Engi skip (nom. n. pl.), with *engi* modifying *skip*, is subject, the (potential) 'performer' of the action and the only noun phrase in the sentence.

(19) Hver**ju** skal launa kvæðit?
 'With-what shall reward poem-the?'
 'What shall one reward the poem with?'

Hverju (dat. n. sg.) as an interrogative pronoun is moved out of an unmarked position after the verb *launa* (*X launar kvæðit Y*, where Y represents the dative phrase) and fronted (cf. (11) above); the sense is instrumental, hence the use of the dative. It will be observed that (19) is without a subject (i.e. there is no element that corresponds to *X* in the abstraction above); although rare in English, subjectless sentences are a regular feature of Old Norse (see 3.9.3).

(20) Hvár**r ykkar** hefir drepit dýrit?
      'Which (of the two) of you two has killed the animal?'

Hvárr (nom. m. sg.) is an interrogative pronoun ('which of two?'), but unlike *hverju* in the preceding example it is the subject of its sentence and thus stands in its unmarked position as the first noun phrase (cf. *X hefir drepit dýrit* where *X* is the agent). *Ykkar* (2nd dual gen.) has partitive sense: 'you two' is the whole of which one is the part (cf. English: *five of the students* (*five* = part, *students* = whole), *the south of the country* (*the south* = part, *country* = whole)).

(21) **Hvat** sýnisk þér ráð?
      'What shows-*sk* to-you plan?'
      'What seems to you a good plan/advisable?'

Hvat (nom. n. sg.) is an interrogative pronoun; traditionally it would be analysed as subject and *þér* as indirect object (the recipient or experiencer of the 'seeming'), but more recent approaches (cf. (11) above) would class *þér* as (an oblique) subject and *hvat* as direct object (notwithstanding the latter is nominative, cf. 3.1.2 and 3.1.5, sentences 1 and 5), in which case the interrogative must be deemed to have moved from its unmarked position to the front of the sentence (cf. *mér sýnisk þat ráð* 'to-me shows-*sk* that plan [i.e. that seems to me advisable/I think that advisable]', where *þat* (nom.) is the putative object). Note that the pronoun *hvat* normally only occurs in the nominative and accusative neuter singular (cf. 3.2.5).

(22) Nú forvitnar **mik** at vita, hver**ja ek** hefi hér fóstrat, eðr hver**rar** ættar **þit** eruð
      'Now interests me to know whom I have here fostered, or of-what family you-two are'
      'Now I am curious to know whom I have been fostering here, or what family you two belong to'

This example consists of three sentences and an infinitive clause (*at vita*). Sentence 1 is what is traditionally called 'impersonal', by which is meant that it has no nominative subject; such an analysis would class *mik* (1st sg. acc.) as direct object. More recent approaches would see *mik* as an oblique subject (cf.

(11) and (21) above), the experiencer and first (and only) noun phrase. *Hverja* (acc. m. pl.) in sentence 2 is the direct object — the goal of the action — but since it takes the form of an interrogative pronoun, it is fronted from its unmarked position after subject and finite or non-finite verb (cf. *ek hefi fóstrat hann* or *ek hefi hann fóstrat*). *Ek* (1st sg. nom.) is the subject of sentence 2, the agent and, apart from the fronted interrogative, the first noun phrase. In *hverrar ættar* (gen. f. sg.) in sentence 3, with *hverrar* modifying *ættar* and the whole phrase fronted because of the presence of the interrogative, the genitive has a defining or connective sense (note that once again the Old Norse genitive can correspond to English *of*). *Þit* (2nd dual nom.) is the subject: the *X* of an *X is Y* construction, and, the fronted interrogative apart, the first noun phrase.

(23) **Hann** er hver**jum** manni betr vígr
'He is than-every man better able-to-fight'
'He is a more able fighter than anyone else'

Hann (3rd sg. m. nom.) is subject: the *X* of an *X is Y* construction and the first noun phrase. *Hverjum manni* (dat. m. sg.), with *hverjum* modifying *manni*, is the second proposition in a comparative construction — the proposition denoting the entity with which the comparison is made (cf. 3.1.5, sentence 21); the dative phrase is the equivalent of the noun phrase *X* (in whatever case is appropriate) that follows *en* 'than' in a comparative adjective + *en* construction (e.g. *fleiri en X* 'more than X').

(24) Þá skyldu ein manngjǫld koma fyrir hver**n** hin**na**
'Then should single compensation come for each of-the-others'
'Then there was to be single compensation for each of the others'

Hvern (acc. m. sg.) does not function here as a noun phrase, but is part of the preposition phrase *fyrir hvern*, and its case is determined by the preposition *fyrir* (see 3.7.4). *Hinna* (gen. pl.) has partitive sense: 'the others' is the whole of which each individual is a part (cf. (20) above).

3.2.6 Examples of pronoun usage — Exercise

1. What is the principal grammatical function of pronouns?
2. What does it mean that pronouns may be used 'adjectivally'? Give two Old Norse examples of such usage.
3. Explain the difference between singular, dual and plural function. Give one example of each from Old Norse.
4. How are the reflexive forms *sik*, *sín*, *sér* used?
5. *Þau* can refer to a plural entity of neuter gender. What else may it refer to?
6. What is the difference in function between *hann*/*hon* on the one hand and *sá*/*sú* on the other?
7. In what sense is the pronoun *hinn* contrastive? Give two examples of the way in which it is used.
8. What is the difference in meaning between *hverr* and *hvárr*?
9. Give the case and, where appropriate, the gender and number of the pronouns (printed in bold) in the following sentences, and explain their syntactic function and semantic role:

   (a) Váru **þeir** með **honum þann** vetr
   'They were with him that winter'
   (b) Sel **mér** fé **nǫkkut** at láni
   'Give me some money on loan'
   (c) **Þessu** skulu **engi** undirmál fylgja
   'No deceit is to accompany this'
   (d) **Hverr yðar** skal fá **okkr** eyri silfrs
   'Each of you is to give us two an ounce of silver'
   (e) **Hann** vildi hefna **sín**
   'He wanted to avenge himself'

3.3 Adjective inflexions and their function

The principal function of adjectives is to modify nouns, and to a lesser extent pronouns. Adjectives may occur as part of a noun phrase — attributive function — or as the complement of a noun phrase — predicative function. English examples, using the adjective *yellow*, are: *a yellow car* or *the yellow car* (attributive), and *the car is yellow* or *he painted the car yellow* (predicative). In addition, adjectives are sometimes used in place of nouns, as in English *the old and the new* or *good and evil*. The fact that nouns, pronouns and adjectives all occur in noun phrases either alone or in conjunction with other words indicates that the three word classes have much in common.

Like nouns and pronouns, adjectives in Old Norse are inflected for number and case. In common with many but not all pronouns, they are also inflected for gender. In addition they are inflected for definiteness and degree. **This variety of adjectival inflexion means it is particularly important for the student to be able to distinguish one form from another and understand what function any particular form has.**

3.3.1 Number, case and gender

Definitions and exemplification of number, case and gender have been given in 3.1.1, 3.1.2 and 3.1.3. What the student needs to grasp about adjectival inflexion for these categories is that it is determined by the noun or pronoun being modified by the adjective. That is to say, there is a formal relationship between the two whereby the form of the noun/pronoun requires a corresponding form of the adjective. E.g. *góðr* (nom. m. sg.) is the appropriate form of 'good' when modifying *maðr* (nom. m. sg.), *góð* (nom. f. sg.) when modifying *kona* (nom. f. sg.), *gott* (nom./acc. n. sg.) when modifying *skip* (nom./acc. n. sg.), *góðir* (nom. m. pl.) when modifying *menn* (nom. m. pl.), etc. This relationship is known as (grammatical) agreement or (grammatical) concord. It operates more widely than simply between noun/pronoun and adjective (see especially 3.6.1), but is particularly important in the noun/pronoun~adjective context because it governs much of adjectival inflexion in Old Norse. Furthermore, it is very often in the grammatical agreement between an adjective and a noun that the gender of the noun is manifested (see 3.1.3).

3.3.2 Definiteness

In Old Norse, as in all Germanic languages originally, there were two types of adjective inflexion, known traditionally as **strong** and **weak**. We saw (3.1.4) that the terms themselves had no particular significance when applied to the noun, and the same is true of the adjective.

The weak adjective shares formal similarities with the weak noun. In the singular the two have identical endings, and overall, just as with the nouns, the weak paradigm exhibits much less variety than the strong (cf. that in the plural weak adjectives end either in *-u* (nom., acc., gen.) or *-um* (dat.)).

In terms of use the weak noun and weak adjective have little in common. The weak noun, as we have seen, is an inflexional type and nothing more: a noun is either strong or weak, and remains so, however it is used. Adjectives can inflect according to both the strong and the weak pattern. Choice of form depends on function: strong adjectives by and large have indefinite function, weak adjectives definite.

What this means in practice is that strong adjectives chiefly occur in noun phrases without determiners, e.g. **ríkr** *konungr* 'a powerful king', *maðr* **gamall** 'an old man', *strendr* **langar** 'long beaches' (with attributive *ríkr*, *gamall* and *langar*); *konungr varð* **reiðr** *mjǫk* 'the king became very angry', *fǫgr er hlíðin* 'beautiful is the hillside' (with predicative *reiðr* and *fǫgr*, which belong to different noun phrases from *konungr* and *hlíðin*, cf. English: *the king* [NP1] *became a beggar* [NP2]; because of their function, predicative adjectives are almost always strong — but cf. 3.3.6, sentence 24). Where strong adjectives do appear in conjunction with determiners, these are usually indefinite, e.g. *nǫkkurri* **mannligri** *mynd* (dat. f. sg.) 'any human shape'.

Weak adjectives typically occur in noun phrases with determiners: the definite article (3.3.5 below), demonstratives (3.2.2) and possessives (3.3.4 below), the latter two commonly in conjunction with the definite article, e.g. *hinna* **ríku** *konunga* (gen. pl.) 'the powerful kings', *sjá hinn* **ungi** *maðr* 'this the young man [i.e. this young man]', *þeim* **helga** *manni* (dat. m. sg.) 'that holy man [i.e. that saint]', *hinn* **yngsta** *son þinn* (acc. m. sg.) 'the youngest son your [i.e. your youngest son]'. Sometimes where used as an epithet a weak adjective may occur without a determiner, e.g. *Eiríkr **rauði*** 'Eiríkr the red'; here the adjective alone carries the definite sense 'the red'.

3.3.3 Degree (comparison)

Adjectives in Old Norse, together with adverbs, are inflected for degree. There are three degrees: positive, comparative and superlative, corresponding in form to English: *big — bigger — biggest*. As in English, the positive degree has no special inflexion, and therefore the form of an adjective in the positive is simply its root plus the appropriate inflexion to indicate number, case, gender and definiteness. The comparative and superlative degrees are normally marked by the suffixes -(*a*)*r*, -(*a*)*st* respectively; to the superlative suffix is added the appropriate strong or weak ending just as in the positive, to the comparative suffix a limited range of endings that indicate number, case and gender (see 3.3.4 below). Comparative and superlative forms of the adjective are thus double-inflected, e.g. *hvass-ar-i* (comp. nom. m. sg., f. sg., nom./acc./gen. pl.) 'sharper', *dýr-r-a* (comp. acc./gen./dat. m. sg., n. sg.) 'dearer' 'more precious', *hvass-ast-ar* (sup. strong nom./acc. f. pl.) 'sharpest', *dýr-st-a* (sup. strong acc. f. sg., acc. m. pl., weak acc./gen./dat. m. sg., nom. f. sg., n. sg.) 'dearest' 'most precious'.

3.3.1/3.3.2/3.3.3 Number, case and gender/Definiteness/Degree — Exercise

1. For what grammatical categories are adjectives inflected in Old Norse?
2. What does the term grammatical agreement (or grammatical concord) mean, and how does it apply to the adjective in Old Norse?
3. What governs the choice between strong and weak adjectives in Old Norse?
4. What does it mean that adjectives are inflected for degree?
5. Analyse the following words into root, comparative or superlative suffix and grammatical ending: *sterkastir*, *sæmri*, *sannara*, *reiðasti*.

3.3.4 Basic adjective inflexions

Just as in the case of noun inflexion (see 3.1.4), it is the basic patterns the student needs to grasp. Minor variations — to the extent they cause problems of understanding — can be noted and learnt when they are encountered.

From 3.3.2 and 3.3.3 above it will be clear that — the comparative and superlative suffixes and comparative endings apart — there are two distinct types of adjective inflexion in Old Norse, strong and weak. Both types, as already observed, inflect for number, case and gender. With two numbers, four cases and three genders, there is thus a possible total of twice twenty-four different inflexions. In fact, because the same form may occur in different parts of the paradigm, the total is much smaller: fundamentally, there are thirteen different strong adjective forms and just four weak. They are as follows (~ = zero, i.e. there is no ending, the form consisting of root alone — e.g. *rík* 'powerful', strong nom. f. sg.; actual paradigms are given in 3.3.9).

Strong masculine					
Sg.	nom.	-r	Pl.	nom.	-ir
	acc.	-an		acc.	-a
	gen.	-s		gen.	-ra
	dat.	-um		dat.	-um

Weak masculine					
Sg.	nom.	-i	Pl.	nom.	-u
	acc.	-a		acc.	-u
	gen.	-a		gen.	-u
	dat.	-a		dat.	-um

Strong feminine					
Sg.	nom.	~	Pl.	nom.	-ar
	acc.	-a		acc.	-ar
	gen.	-rar		gen.	-ra
	dat.	-ri		dat.	-um

Adjective inflexions and their function

			Weak feminine			
Sg.	nom.	-a	Pl.	nom.	-u	
	acc.	-u		acc.	-u	
	gen.	-u		gen.	-u	
	dat.	-u		dat.	-um	

			Strong neuter			
Sg.	nom.	-t	Pl.	nom.	~	
	acc.	-t		acc.	~	
	gen.	-s		gen.	-ra	
	dat.	-u		dat.	-um	

			Weak neuter			
Sg.	nom.	-a	Pl.	nom.	-u	
	acc.	-a		acc.	-u	
	gen.	-a		gen.	-u	
	dat.	-a		dat.	-um	

Certain regularities will be observed in these paradigms.

(1) The dat. pl. always ends in *-um*.
(2) Apart from the dat., the weak pl. ends in *-u* throughout.
(3) There are no distinct case-forms in the weak sg. except in the nom. masculine and feminine.
(4) The strong gen. pl. always ends in *-ra*.
(5) There is no difference between the neuter nom. and acc., sg. or pl., weak or strong.
(6) The strong feminine nom. and acc. pl. have the same ending.
(7) The strong masculine and neuter gen. sg. have the same ending.

As well as observing these regularities, the student will notice that adjectival and noun inflexion have much in common. Attention has already been drawn to the complete identity between the singular forms of weak nouns and adjectives. Other instances where the forms are identical or closely similar (all in the strong declension bar (10), which applies to both strong and weak) are as follows.

(1) Nom. m. sg. in -*r*.
(2) Gen. m. and n. sg. in -*s*.
(3) Nom. f. sg. with zero ending.
(4) Gen. f. sg. in -*ar* (noun), -*rar* (adj.).
(5) Nom. m. pl. in vowel + *r*.
(6) Acc. m. pl. in vowel.
(7) Nom./acc. f. pl. in vowel + *r*.
(8) Nom./acc. n. pl. with zero ending.
(9) Gen. pl. in -*a* (noun), -*ra* (adj.).
(10) Dat. pl. in -*um*.

The student should further observe the close similarity between the strong adjectival endings and those of pronouns such as *hinn*, *nǫkkurr*, *engi*, *hverr* (cf. 3.2.2, 3.2.3, 3.2.4, 3.2.5). The similarity becomes even clearer when the many adjectives with an -*in* suffix are added to the equation and the comparison is extended to certain of the possessive adjectives and the suffixed definite article (probably a reduced form of *hinn*, cf. 3.2.2).

Adjectives in -*in* inflect according to the tables above, but with three distinct deviations (see the example *kominn*, 3.3.9, paradigm 7). (1) Where the tables show an ending in or beginning with -*r*, adjectives in -*in* have -*n* instead, e.g. -*inn* (strong nom. m. sg.), -*inni* (strong dat. f. sg.). This is because an earlier *r* has assimilated to the *n* (-*inn* < *-*inr*, -*inni* < *-*inri*, cf. *hinn* < *hinr, 3.2.3). (2) The *n* of the suffix disappears in the strong nom./acc. n. sg. ending, giving -*it* (the end result of the development *-*int* > *-*itt* > -*it*, cf. *hitt*, nom./acc. n. sg. of *hinn* (3.2.2)). (3) The strong acc. m. sg. has the same form as the nom., ending in -*inn*. It should also be noted that the -*i*- of the -*in* suffix is dropped when the inflexional ending consists of an additional syllable, except in the strong gen. and dat. f. sg. and the strong gen. pl., e.g. -*nir* (strong nom. m. pl.), -*ni* (weak nom. m. sg.), -*inna* (strong gen. pl.). This is not unlike what happens to the suffixed definite article (see 3.1.9), although the pattern is not wholly identical. Most two-syllable adjectives, in fact, drop the unstressed vowel of the second syllable according to the pattern of those in -*in*. A great many of these have an -*al*, -*il*, or -*ul* suffix (see the example *gamall*, 3.3.9, paradigm 8), and, just as with the *n* of -*in*, the immediately following *r* of the inflexional endings is assimilated to the *l*, giving -*ll*(-) instead of the expected *-*lr*(-), e.g. -*all* (strong nom. m. sg.), -*allar* (strong gen. f. sg.).

The possessive adjectives of the first and second person and the third person reflexive possessive (i.e., words corresponding to English 'my', 'our', etc. and, with pronominal function, 'mine', 'ours', etc.) inflect according to one or other of the strong adjective patterns just discussed. *Minn* 'my' (see 3.3.9, paradigm 21), *þinn* 'your [sg.]', *sinn* 'his/her/its/their own' go for the most part like adjectives in *-in* (but without loss of the *i* at any point since in the possessives it is part of the root syllable). It is worth noting, however, that in having the nom./acc. n. sg. forms *mitt*, *þitt*, *sitt*, they parallel even more closely the paradigm of the pronoun *hinn*, the only difference between the two being that the root vowel of the possessives is long before everything except a geminate consonant, e.g. *minn* (nom. m. sg.), *míns* (gen. m. or n. sg.). *Várr* 'our [pl.]' is inflected according to the strong pattern of the tables above, except that, as with certain pronouns, the acc. m. sg. ends in *-n* (*várn*). *Okkarr* 'our [dual]', *ykkarr* 'your [dual]' and *yð(v)arr* 'your [pl.]' parallel *várr* (acc. m. sg. *okkarn*, *ykkarn*, *yð(v)arn*), but as two-syllable words drop the unstressed vowel of the second syllable according to the pattern of the two-syllable adjectives discussed above (giving, for example, acc. f. sg. *okkra*, *ykkra*, *yðra*).

It remains to list the adjective endings that follow the comparative suffix.

			Masculine		
Sg.	nom.	-i	Pl.	nom.	-i
	acc.	-a		acc.	-i
	gen.	-a		gen.	-i
	dat.	-a		dat.	-um

			Feminine		
Sg.	nom.	-i	Pl.	nom.	-i
	acc.	-i		acc.	-i
	gen.	-i		gen.	-i
	dat.	-i		dat.	-um

		Neuter			
Sg.	nom.	-a	Pl.	nom.	-i
	acc.	-a		acc.	-i
	gen.	-a		gen.	-i
	dat.	-a		dat.	-um

This minimal set of endings is also the one used with present participles, e.g. *sofandi* (nom. m. sg., f. sg., nom./acc./gen. pl.) 'sleeping' (see 3.3.9, paradigm 19).

These are the essentials of adjectival inflexion in Old Norse. It is not the whole story, but all other adjective inflexions can be seen as variations on this basic pattern. It is vitally important that the student masters the endings set out and discussed on pp. 80–84 before proceeding to the finer detail.

3.3.4 Basic adjective inflexions — Exercise

1. How many different endings do the strong masculine, the weak neuter, and the comparative adjective exhibit respectively?
2. Is there a difference between the strong and weak dat. pl. forms?
3. Where is a difference between the nom. and acc. pl. to be found?
4. Enumerate the gen. sg. endings.
5. Enumerate the acc. pl. endings.
6. What characterises the nom. and acc. of neuter adjectives?
7. Where is there (1) identity and (2) close similarity between noun and adjective endings?
8. Compare the principal adjective inflexions as given on pp. 80–81 with the paradigm of *hinn*. What similarities and differences between their inflexions can be observed?

3.3.5 The free-standing definite article

Before examples of adjective usage are given, it will be helpful to expand on what was said about definite function in 3.3.2, and show

how the definite article manifests itself in noun phrases that include adjectives.

As will have been apparent from certain of the examples in 3.3.2, Old Norse has a free-standing definite article in addition to the suffixed variety (just as in the modern Scandinavian languages). The free-standing article occurs where a definite noun is modified by an adjective (the adjective normally always being weak), e.g. (*h*)*inn blindi maðr* 'the blind man'. It is also used where an adjective with definite function (once again weak) is 'substantivised', i.e. used without a noun and thus, in a sense, in its place, e.g. (*h*)*inir auðgu* 'the rich [pl.]'. (The inflexional forms of (*h*)*inn* are the same as those of the demonstrative pronoun *hinn* given in 3.2.2, except for the nom./acc. n. sg. which is (*h*)*it* with a single *t*. Note that in some texts instead of (*h*)*inn*, (*h*)*it*, (*h*)*inir*, etc. we get *enn*, *et*, *enir*, i.e., no initial *h-* and root vowel *e*.)

In Old Norse prose neither of the constructions just illustrated is in fact particularly common except where something or someone is being distinguished from another or others of the same type or name, e.g.: *hin síðasta orrosta* 'the last battle', *hinna gǫmlu skálda* 'the old poets [gen. pl.]' (as opposed to the new ones), *hendi inni hægri* 'the right hand [dat. f. sg.]', *Óláfr inn helgi* 'Óláfr the saint', *hit síðara* 'the latter', *hinn þriði* 'the third'. (Observe that the free-standing article and its accompanying weak adjective may be found either before or after the noun).

To express the equivalent of English *the* + adj. ± noun Old Norse employs a variety of other constructions. In prose a much more common rendering of the definite article than (*h*)*inn* on its own is (*h*)*inn* together with the demonstrative pronoun *sá* (see 3.2.2), giving phrases of the type: *sá* (*h*)*inn blindi maðr* 'that the blind man', *maðr sá* (*h*)*inn blindi* 'man that the blind', or, less commonly, *sá maðr* (*h*)*inn blindi* 'that man the blind', i.e. (in all three cases) 'the blind man'. (Note the possible variations in word-order, and that *sá* and (*h*)*inn* agree with, i.e. always appear in the same case, gender and number as, adjective and noun — here nom. m. sg.; see 3.3.1.) Occasionally (*h*)*inn* may be omitted, and we then get the phrase-type: *sá blindi maðr* or *maðr sá blindi*, where *sá* alone renders 'the'. In Norwegian sources in particular, the suffixed article may be used in addition to its free-standing counterpart, or the demonstrative *sá*, or both together, giving phrases like *hinn hvíti bjǫrninn* 'the white bear-the' (literally), *hǫndin sú hægri* 'hand-the that right', *sá hinn þǫgli maðrinn* 'that the silent man-the', *vápnin þau in góðu* 'weapons-the those the good', all equivalents of English *the* + adj. + noun. (Note that the phrase-types without *hinn*, e.g. *sá blindi maðr*, *hǫndin sú hægri*, sometimes have greater deictic emphasis, i.e. the pronoun is closer in meaning to 'that' than 'the'.)

Observe the fundamental identity of (*h*)*inn* and the suffixed definite article, the former of which certainly and the latter probably derive from demonstrative *hinn* (see above and 3.2.2). Additional notes on word-order in noun phrases will be found in 3.9.2.

3.3.5 The free-standing definite article — Exercise

Identify the case, gender, number, syntactic function and semantic role of the definite noun phrases printed in **bold** in the following sentences.

(1) **Inn blindi maðr** kom í húsit
    'The blind man came into the house'

(2) Gekk hann þegar fram fyrir **þá kristnu hǫfðingja**
    'Went he immediately forward before the Christian rulers'
    'He at once went forward in front of the Christian rulers'

(3) Hann skipaði lǫgunum með ráði **hinna vitrustu manna**
    'He organised the laws with the advice of the wisest men'

(4) Þrándr fór til Nóregs með **kaupmǫnnum þeim hinum norrœnum**
    'Þrándr went to Norway with the Norwegian merchants'

(5) Engi maðr mátti nefna hann annan veg en **jarl hinn illa**
    'No man might call him another way than earl the bad'
    'No man might call him anything other than "the bad earl"'

(6) En **þau hin stóru skip**, er áðr hǫfðu siglt, ok þeir hugðu at Ormrinn væri, þat var **hit fyrra** Tranan, en **hit síðara Ormr hinn skammi**
    'But those the big ships which before had sailed, and they thought that Ormrinn were, that was the former Tranan but the latter Ormr hinn skammi'

'But as for the big ships which had sailed previously and which they thought were "The Serpent", the former was "The Crane" and the latter "The Short Serpent"'

(7) Þá minntisk hann þess er **mærin sú hin mikilláta** hafði mælt til hans
'Then he remembered that which the proud girl had said to him'

(8) Þeir snúa þegar at **hinni miklu hǫllinni**
'They turn immediately to the big hall'

(9) Konungr hét þar fyrir Óláfi **hinum mestum afarkostum**
'King promised there for to-Óláfr the greatest hard-treatments'
'The king promised Óláfr in return the harshest treatment'

3.3.6 Examples of adjective usage

As was done for nouns and pronouns, examples are now given of adjectives in function. With the wide range of adjectival functions and inflexions that exists, only a selection can be illustrated, with the emphasis on the most common types. As far as is practicable, the examples are ordered as follows: (a) strong adjectives; (b) weak adjectives; (c) substantivised adjectives (strong and weak); (d) superlatives (strong and weak); (e) comparatives — though some sentences contain examples of more than one type. In other respects, the exemplification follows the same pattern as for nouns (see the preamble on p. 31). Note that the adjectival inflexions being illustrated (or the whole word where there is no difference from the root form) are printed in bold type. To underline the grammatical relations involved, bold is also used for the noun or pronoun with which the adjective agrees. Compare the inflexions used below with those set out and discussed in 3.3.4. Observe, too, the differences between Old Norse and English phraseology and sentence formation. Definitions of basic concepts that have already been given are not repeated; if in doubt the student should consult the individual commentaries that accompany each of the examples of noun function in 3.1.5.

(1) Því var **hann** skakk**r** kallað**r**
'Therefore was he crooked called'
'For that reason he was called crooked'

Skakkr and *kallaðr* are nom. m. sg., agreeing with *hann*, the subject. *Skakkr* is used predicatively (see 3.3), as the subject complement (i.e. as *Y* in: *X is/becomes/is called Y*); it has indefinite function and therefore strong inflexion. *Kallaðr* is the past participle of the verb *kalla* '[to] call' which together with *var* forms a passive phrase (see 3.6.4); in such phrases the past participle (which itself functions not unlike a subject complement) inflects as a strong adjective.

(2) Þar verðr **orrosta** bæði **mikil** ok hǫr**ð**
'There happens battle both great and hard'
'There a great and hard battle ensues'

Mikil and *hǫrð* are nom. f. sg., agreeing with *orrosta* (f.), the subject. They are attributive adjectives (see 3.3), occurring in an indefinite noun phrase and therefore having strong inflexion. Although *hǫrð* as a nom. f. sg. strong adjective is without ending, the root vowel has *u*-mutation, just as the nom. sg. of strong feminine nouns (see 3.1.7.1 and 3.3.8.1).

(3) Eigi mun **þat** kauplaus**t**
'Not will that chargeless'
'That will not be free of charge'

Kauplaust is nom. n. sg., agreeing with *þat*, the subject. It is the subject complement; it has indefinite function and therefore strong inflexion. *Eigi mun þat kauplaust* is elliptical for *Eigi mun þat kauplaust vera* (see 3.9.5.2).

(4) **Þeir** lágu bún**ir** at sigla til Suðreyja
'They lay ready to sail to the Hebrides'

Búnir is nom. m. pl., agreeing with *þeir*, the subject. It is the subject complement; it has indefinite function and therefore strong inflexion.

(5) Þau váru skamm**a hríð** ásamt
'They were short while together'
'They were together for only a short while'

Adjective inflexions and their function

Skamma is acc. f. sg., agreeing with *hríð* (f.), which is accusative because it functions as a time adverbial (see 3.1.2 and 3.1.5, sentence 10). The adjective is used attributively, and, occurring in an indefinite noun phrase, has strong inflexion.

(6)   Þeir fengu í Dynrǫst **strauma** váðvæ**na**
      'They got in Dynrǫst currents dangerous'
      'They encountered dangerous currents in Sumburgh Roost'

Váðvæna is acc. m. pl., agreeing with *strauma* (m.), which is the direct object. The adjective is used attributively, and, occurring in an indefinite noun phrase, has strong inflexion.

(7)   Konungsmenn gerðu **jarl** handtekin**n**
      'King's-men made earl captured'
      'The king's men seized the earl'

Handtekinn is acc. m. sg., agreeing with *jarl* (m.), which is the direct object. The adjective is used predicatively, as the object complement; it has indefinite function and therefore strong inflexion.

(8)   Hann bað þá vinda **segl** sín
      'He bade them hoist sails REFL. POSS.'
      'He told them to hoist their sails'

Sín is acc. n. pl., agreeing with *segl* (n.), which is the direct object of the infinitive clause. Note that though the reflexive possessive agrees with *þá* (the subject of *vinda*, cf. 3.9.4) in person (both are 3rd), it agrees with *segl* in case, gender and number. Possessives have only strong forms: they are themselves determiners, not part of what is determined or defined.

(9)   Því næst heyrðu þeir út til **hǫggva** stór**ra**
      'To-that next heard they out to blows big'
      'Thereupon they heard the sound of great blows outside'

Stórra is gen. pl., agreeing with *hǫggva* (n.), the noun of the preposition phrase *til hǫggva stórra*. The case of the noun is governed by the preposition *til* (see 3.7, 3.7.2). The adjective is used attributively, and, occurring in an indefinite noun phrase, has strong inflexion.

(10) Oss er ván snarplig**rar orrostu**
'To-us is expectation of-hard battle'
'We can expect a hard battle'

Snarpligrar is gen. f. sg., agreeing with *orrostu* (f.), which is an objective genitive, that is, it corresponds to English 'of . . . ' and presents the battle as the object of the expectation (cf. the idiomatic translation above). The adjective is used attributively, and, occurring in an indefinite noun phrase, has strong inflexion.

(11) Nú skuluð þér taka ǫmbun **verka** yðvar**ra**
'Now shall you [pl.] take reward of-works your [pl.]'
'Now you shall reap the reward of your deeds'

Yðvarra is gen. pl., agreeing with *verka* (n.), which is an objective genitive, that is, it corresponds to English 'of . . . ' and presents the deeds as being rewarded (cf. 'X rewarded the deed'). Note that though the possessive adjective (here functioning as a reflexive, cf. 3.2.1) agrees with *þér* in person (they are both 2nd pl.), it agrees with *verka* in case and number (gender is not marked in the gen. pl.). (On the strong inflexion of *yðvarra*, see (8) above.)

(12) Þeir dvǫlðusk þar í allgóð**um fagnaði**
'They stayed-*sk* [see 3.6.5.3] there in very-good hospitality'
'They stayed there with excellent hospitality'

Allgóðum is dat. m. sg., agreeing with *fagnaði* (m.), the noun of the preposition phrase *í allgóðum fagnaði*. The case of the noun is governed by the preposition *í*. The adjective is used attributively, and, occurring in an indefinite noun phrase, has strong inflexion.

(13) **Aðils** konungr var mjǫk kær**r** at góð**um hestum**
'King Aðils was very fond of good horses'

Kærr is nom. m. sg., agreeing with *Aðils* (m.), the subject. It is the head word of the subject complement; it has indefinite function and therefore strong inflexion. *Góðum* is dat. pl., agreeing with *hestum* (m.), the noun of the preposition phrase *at góðum hestum*. The case of the noun is governed by the preposition *at*. The adjective is used attributively and has indefinite function and therefore strong inflexion. The preposition phrase modifies the adjective *kærr*.

(14) Hverr er þessi **maðr** hinn drengilig**i**?
'Who is this man the valiant?'
'Who is this valiant man?'

Drengiligi is nom. m. sg., agreeing with *maðr* (m.), the subject (cf. *who is X? X is Y*, where *X* is the subject). The adjective is used attributively, and, occurring in a definite noun phrase, has weak inflexion.

(15) Erlingr jarl lét drepa **Eindriða** ung**a**
'Erlingr earl let kill Eindriði ungi'
'Earl Erlingr had Eindriði the young killed'

Unga is acc. m. sg., agreeing with *Eindriða* (m.), the direct object. It is used as a 'defining' epithet (Eindriði 'the young' as opposed to any other Eindriði); as such it is part of a definite noun phrase and therefore has weak inflexion. Observe that definite function in itself is enough to trigger weak inflexion, there being no determiners in the noun phrase in question.

(16) Hann var sonr **Óláfs** ins hvít**a** ok **Auðar** innar djúpúðg**u**.
'He was the son of Óláfr the white and Auðr the deep-minded'

Hvíta is gen. m. sg., agreeing with *Óláfs* (m.), and *djúpúðgu* gen. f. sg., agreeing with *Auðar* (f.); both nouns are subjective (possessive) genitives (Óláfr and Auðr have 'him' as their son). As in (15), the adjectives are used as 'defining' epithets, but here in conjunction with the free-standing article (*h*)*inn*. Both are part of definite noun phrases and therefore have weak inflexion.

(17) Hann bauð **ambótt** si**nni** þeirri þrœnzk**u** at hon skyldi . . .
'He ordered bondwoman REFL. POSS. that Throndish that she should . . .'
'He ordered his bondwoman from Þrœndalǫg to . . .'

Sinni and *þrœnzku* are dat. f. sg., agreeing with *ambótt* (f.), which is the indirect object of *bauð* (cf. that he gave an order *to* the bondwoman). Note that though the reflexive possessive agrees with *hann* in person (both are 3rd), it agrees with *ambótt* in case, gender and number. *Þrœnzku* is used attributively, and, occurring in a definite noun phrase, has weak inflexion (on the strong inflexion of *sinni*, see (8) above).

(18) Þá sendi hann braut ena gauzk**u** **menn**
'Then he sent away the Gautish (= from Gautland) men'

Gauzku is acc. m. pl., agreeing with *menn* (m.), the direct object. It is used attributively, and, occurring in a definite noun phrase, has weak inflexion.

(19) Því munu fá**ir** trúa
'That will few [pl.] believe'
'Few will believe that'

Fáir is nom. m. pl. (masculine is the default gender where the reference is to people in general). The adjective stands on its own without a noun and forms the subject. It has indefinite function and therefore strong inflexion.

(20) Hann lét jafn**a** **refsing** hafa rík**an** ok órík**an**
'He let equal punishment have mighty [sg.] and unmighty [sg.]'
'He gave both mighty and unmighty equal punishment'

Jafna is acc. f. sg., agreeing with *refsing* (f.), which is the direct object of *hafa*. The adjective is used attributively, and, occurring in an indefinite noun phrase, has strong inflexion. *Ríkan* and *óríkan* are acc. m. sg. They stand on their own without a noun — but referring to individual males — and form the direct object of *lét*. They have indefinite function and therefore strong inflexion. The construction here is what is known as an accusative and infinitive: the accusative objects of *lét*, 'mighty and unmighty', are in a sense also the subjects of *hafa* (see 3.9.4).

(21) Snústu frá ill**u** ok ger g**ott**
'Turn from evil and do good'

Illu is dat. n. sg. It stands on its own without a noun and is part of the preposition phrase *frá illu*, its case being determined by the preposition. *Gott* is acc. n. sg., and it, too, stands on its own without a noun. It is the direct object of the verb *ger*. Both adjectives have indefinite function and therefore strong inflexion. They are neuter because they do not refer to an entity of masculine or feminine gender. (Note that *snústu* is a contracted form of *snúsk þú*: -*sk* verb (see 3.6.5.3) + the personal pronoun *þú* (literally 'turn you'). *Gott* is an irregular nom./acc. n. sg. form (see 3.3.8.4), nom. m. sg. *góðr*.)

(22) Sýn þik þessum enum nýkomna
'Show yourself to-this the newly-come'
'Show yourself to this newly arrived one'

Nýkomna is dat. m. sg. It stands on its own without a noun — but referring to a male animal — and forms the head of the indirect object phrase *þessum enum nýkomna*. Determined by *þessum enum*, it has definite function and therefore weak inflexion.

(23) **Sveinn** var all**ra manna** skygn**astr**
'Sveinn was of-all men most-sharp-sighted'
'Sveinn was the most sharp-sighted of men'

Skygnastr is nom. m. sg. sup., agreeing with *Sveinn* (m.), the subject. The adjective is the subject complement; it has indefinite function and therefore strong inflexion (which follows the superlative *-ast* suffix). (Note that the superlative here is what is known as absolute, i.e. it denotes not the highest but a very high degree.) *Allra* is gen. pl. of *allr* 'all', which has only strong forms; it agrees with *manna*, a genitive of type: *menn* are presented as a type of which Sveinn is a particularly sharp-sighted member (see 3.1.5, sentence 14).

(24) Varð þessi **ferð** in fræg**sta**
'Became this expedition the most-famous'
'This expedition became most famous'

Frægsta is nom. f. sg. sup., agreeing with *ferð* (f.), the subject. It is the subject complement; it has definite function and therefore weak inflexion (which follows the superlative *-st* suffix). (Note that here too the superlative is absolute (see (23)) — notwithstanding the definiteness of the noun phrase.)

(25) Meðan hann var á létt**asta aldri**, hafði hann hvert sumar leiðangr úti
'While he was at lightest age, had he each summer levy out'
'While he was at the most active age, he made naval expeditions each summer'

Léttasta is dat. m. sg. sup., agreeing with *aldri* (m.), the noun of the preposition phrase *á léttasta aldri*. The case of the noun is governed by the preposition *á*. The adjective is used attributively and has definite function and therefore weak inflexion (which follows the superlative *-ast* suffix). On the occurrence of weak inflexion in the absence of determiners, cf. (15).

(26) Sá mun þér hinn be**zti**
'That will to-you the best'
'That will be the best one (i.e. option) for you'

Bezti is nom. m. sg. sup. It stands on its own without a noun and forms the subject complement. It has definite function and therefore weak inflexion. *Bezt-* and the comparative *betr-* are suppletive forms (i.e. they have a different root from other parts of the word, cf. positive *góð-*; see further 3.3.8.3); 'z' denotes the sounds *ts* (cf. 2.1.3), so what we have is in effect **bet-st-*. The phrase *hinn bezti* is elliptical for *hinn bezti kostr* 'the best choice/option'.

(27) Ok svá var, því at **jarl** var þess fús**ari**
'And thus was, therefore that earl was of-that keener'
'And thus it was, because the earl was more in favour of it'

Fúsari is nom. m. sg. comp., agreeing with *jarl* (m.), the subject of the second sentence. The adjective is the subject complement. Following the comparative suffix *-ar*, we get the appropriate comparative inflexion, which remains the same whether the function is indefinite or definite.

(28) Þar gekk Rǫgnvaldr jarl af skipum ok all**t** it gǫfg**ara lið** þeira
'There went Rǫgnvaldr earl off ships and all the more-noble force their'
'There Earl Rǫgnvaldr and all the more noble of their force left the ships'

Allt is nom. n. sg. of *allr* 'all', which has only strong forms. Together with *gǫfgara* (nom. n. sg.) it agrees with *lið* (n.), one of the two subjects. Both adjectives are used attributively. In *gǫfgara*, following the comparative suffix *-ar*, we get the appropriate comparative inflexion (see (27)). The comparative and superlative forms *gǫfgar-*, *gǫfgast-* show loss of an unstressed vowel: the positive root is *gǫfug-* (see 3.3.8.5 point (1)).

(29) Hin **yngri skáld** hafa ort eptir dœmum hinna gǫml**u skálda**
'The younger poets have composed following the examples of the old poets'

Yngri is nom. n. pl. comp., agreeing with *skáld* (n.), the subject. The adjective is used attributively. Following the comparative suffix *-r*, we get the appropriate comparative inflexion (see (27)). The comparative and superlative forms *yngr- yngst-* have a different root vowel from the positive *ung-* (because of front mutation, see 3.3.8.2). *Gǫmlu* is gen. pl., agreeing with *skálda* (n.), a possessive genitive (the examples, in a sense, 'belong to' the old poets). The adjective is used attributively, and, occurring in a definite noun phrase, has weak inflexion. The form *gǫmlu* has suffered loss of the second, unstressed, syllable, and its root vowel has undergone *u*-mutation (strong nom. m. sg. *gamall*; cf. 3.3.4, 3.3.8.5 point (1), 3.1.7.1, 3.3.8.1).

(30) Þeir lǫgðu á þat hit me**sta kapp**, hverr bet**ri hesta** átti
 'They laid on that the most contest, who better horses owned'
 'They made it a matter of the greatest rivalry who owned the better horses'

Mesta is acc. n. sg. sup., agreeing with *kapp* (n.), the direct object of *lǫgðu*. The adjective is used attributively; it has definite function and therefore weak inflexion (which follows the superlative *-st* suffix). The comparative and superlative forms *meir-*, *mest-* are suppletive (positive *mikil-*; see (26)). *Betri* is acc. m. pl. comp., agreeing with *hesta* (m.), the direct object of *átti*. The adjective is used attributively. Following the comparative suffix *-r*, we get the appropriate comparative inflexion (see (27)). Like the superlative *bezt-*, *betri* is a suppletive form (cf. (26)).

3.3.6 Examples of adjective usage — Exercise

1. In which of the above examples do comparative forms occur? List all that you find.
2. In which of the above examples are adjectives used predicatively? List all that you find together with the nouns or pronouns with which they agree.
3. In which of the above examples are adjectives used with definite function? List all that you find.
4. In which of the above examples do possessive adjectives occur? List all that you find and explain which other words in their respective sentences they agree with and in what way.
5. Explain the following forms (i.e. state what inflexion or inflexions they have and, where possible, the reason for the inflexion(s)): *kauplaust* in example (3), *handtekinn* (7), *djúpúðgu* (16), *gauzku* (18), *ríkan* (20), *léttasta* (25), *gǫfgara* (28).

3.3.7 Difficulties in recognising adjective inflexions and ways of overcoming them

As in the case of nouns (cf. 3.1.6), the learner may initially experience some difficulty in recognising which adjective inflexions are which.

The strong endings are by and large distinctive, and even where an ending recurs in different parts of the paradigm there are unlikely to be serious problems of understanding. Although the genitive masculine and neuter singular, for example, both end in -*s*, they clearly signal the genitive singular, just as -*ra* is an unambiguous sign of the genitive plural. The identity between nominative and accusative in the neuter singular and feminine and neuter plural may be problematic, but very often their function and therefore their case will be apparent from the context.

It is when confronted with the minimal distinctions of the weak and comparative systems of endings — and their overlap with certain strong endings — that the learner will regularly have to rely on the presence or absence of other words in the noun phrase, and, where appropriate, their forms, to determine the case, gender and number of the adjective. Fortunately, as we have seen, it is the way of adjectives, and weak adjectives in particular, to be accompanied by words with which they exhibit grammatical agreement. In sentence (17), for example:

> Hann bauð ambótt sinni þeirri þrœnzku at hon skyldi . . .

it can be shown that *þrœnzku* is dat. f. sg., even though one strong and eleven other weak forms have the -*u* ending, because of the presence of *sinni* and *þeirri*. These words determine the noun that *þrœnzku* modifies, which means (a): the function of the adjective is definite and the form weak, and (b): *þrœnzku* will have the same case, gender and number as *sinni* and *þeirri* since all three agree with the noun *ambótt*. Given that *sinni* and *þeirri* are unambiguously dat. f. sg., we can thus deduce that *þrœnzku* represents the same combination of case, gender and number. Similarly, in sentence (22):

> Sýn þik þessum enum nýkomna

it can be shown that *nýkomna* is dat. m. sg., even though two strong and seven other weak forms have the *-a* ending. Here the noun phrase lacks a noun with which the adjective can agree, but there is agreement with the determiners *þessum enum*. Their presence indicates the phrase is definite and the adjective therefore weak, and although *þessum enum* can represent the dat. m. sg. or dat. pl., in combination with *nýkomna* the pair can only be dat. m. sg. since the dat. pl. adjective ending (weak and strong) is *-um*. In sentence (27):

> Ok svá var, því at jarl var þess fúsari

it is clear that *fúsari* is nom. m. sg. even though a total of fourteen comparative forms share the *-i* ending. *Jarl*, with which *fúsari* agrees, is masculine and singular, and the only masculine singular comparative form ending in *-i* is the nominative.

Sometimes direct pointers may be lacking. In sentence (15):

> Erlingr jarl lét drepa Eindriða unga

unga might represent the strong acc. f. sg. or acc. m. pl., or the weak acc., gen. or dat. m. sg. or n. sg. (any case). The only word with which *unga* can agree, *Eindriða*, is masculine singular. That excludes the possibility of feminine or neuter gender, or masculine plural, but given that weak nouns have exactly the same forms in the singular as weak adjectives, it does not help determine whether *unga* is acc., gen. or dat. (m. sg.). Here one has to rely on function. The verb *drepa* takes a direct object in the accusative, and since its *-r* ending shows *Erlingr* to be nominative and thus subject, and there are no other noun phrases in the sentence, *Eindriða unga* must be the direct object and therefore accusative.

3.3.7 Difficulties in recognising adjective inflexions and ways of overcoming them — Exercise

1. Why may it sometimes be difficult to recognise the case, gender and number of adjectives in Old Norse?
2. What means can we use to help us deduce their case and number?

3.3.8 Important variations in adjective inflexion

Adjectives in Old Norse are not subject to as much inflexional variation as nouns (cf. 3.1.7). Nevertheless, they exhibit a wider range of forms than those described in 3.3.4 (cf., e.g., the comparative *yngri* and the weak pl. *gǫmlu* in (29)). The significant variations will now be examined.

3.3.8.1 Labial mutation

The basics of labial mutation were discussed in 3.1.7.1. Since, as pointed out there, it is a rule of Old Norse that *a* cannot appear before *u* or *v*, it is clear that adjectives with *a* in the root, just as nouns, will change that *a* to *ǫ* whenever an ending is applied that consists of or contains a *u*. Thus, the strong dat. m. sg. and dat. pl. of *harðr* 'hard' is *hǫrðum*, and the strong dat. n. sg., weak acc., gen., dat. f. sg. and weak nom., acc., gen. pl. *hǫrðu* (see paradigms 2 and 14 in 3.3.9).

This rule should not cause the learner problems, **as long as s/he remembers that an unknown word with *ǫ* in the root and *u* in the ending must be looked up in the dictionary as though it had root *a* if it cannot be found there with root *ǫ*** (for an example of the latter type, cf. *fǫlr* 'pale' — paradigm 6 below). Just as *hǫrðum* and *hǫrðu* will be found under *harðr*, so *grǫnnum* or *grǫnnu* must be looked up under *grannr* 'thin', *lǫngum* or *lǫngu* under *langr* 'long', *snǫrpum* or *snǫrpu* under *snarpr* 'keen', 'hard', etc.

Like certain noun forms, adjectives may have *ǫ* in the root even where no *u* or *v* follows in the next syllable. The cause is the same: the presence of a following *u* at an earlier stage of the language. We have seen (pp. 81–2) how closely adjective inflexions parallel those of nouns, and it is therefore no surprise (and of some help to the student) to learn that it is in part in the same forms that root *ǫ* is encountered in adjectives. The forms concerned are: strong nom. f. sg. and strong nom./acc. n. pl. The strong nom. f. sg. and nom./acc. n. pl. of *harðr* is thus *hǫrð* (< *harðu; cf. sentence (2)), of *grannr grǫnn*, of *langr lǫng*, etc. (see paradigm 2 below). In these cases, too, an unknown word with root *ǫ* must be looked up in a dictionary as though it had root *a* if it cannot be found there with root *ǫ*.

Adjective inflexions and their function 99

U-mutation in adjectives affects unstressed as well as stressed syllables, just as with nouns. In adjectives, too, it results in *u* in the unstressed syllable, and the mutation can then spread further (for the historical process, see p. 41). The superlative suffix *-ast*, for example, appears as *-ust* when a *-u* or *-um* ending follows. Thus *skygnastr* of sentence (23) and *léttasta* of (25) become *skygnustu, léttustu, skygnustum, léttustum* in the appropriate forms; adjectives with root *a*, e.g. *harðr*, exhibit *u* in the superlative suffix and *ǫ* in the root: *hǫrðustu, hǫrðustum* (see paradigms 12, 17 below). Adjectives with two-syllable stems are also affected: *spurall* 'inquisitive', *ykkarr* 'your [dual]', for example, become *spurul, ykkur* in the (strong) nom. f. sg. and nom./acc. n. pl., and *gamall* 'old', with root *a*, has strong nom. f. sg. and nom./acc. n. pl. *gǫmul* (< *gamalu*) (see paradigms 8, 22). Present participles are a partial exception in that the *-and-* suffix by which they are formed becomes *-ǫnd-* in the dat. pl., e.g., *sofǫndum* 'sleeping' (paradigm 19); this is because the suffix has secondary stress.

3.3.8.1 Labial mutation — Exercise

1. In which forms of the adjective does root *a* change to *ǫ*?
2. Explain the differences in vowel quality (a) between the strong nom. m. sg. sup. *spakastr* and the dat. pl. sup. *spǫkustum* 'wisest', and (b) between the strong nom. m. sg. *atall* and the strong nom. f. sg. *ǫtul* 'fierce'.
3. Look up the following adjectives in an Old Norse dictionary or in the Glossary in *NION* III and write down the entry forms you find: *sǫnnu, glǫð, spǫkurum, þǫgul, vitrustu*.

3.3.8.2 Front mutation

The basics of front mutation were discussed in 3.1.7.2. The only parts of adjectival inflexion affected by this process are certain comparative and superlative forms. Those adjectives that form the comparative with the *-r* and the superlative with the *-st* suffix undergo front mutation of back root vowels. We find the following back : front correspondences (the examples contrast the strong nom. m. sg. pos. form with the nom. m. sg. comp.):

a —— e	(langr —— lengri	'long', 'longer')
á —— æ	(lágr —— lægri	'low', 'lower')
ó —— œ	(stórr —— stærri	'big', 'bigger')
u —— y	(ungr —— yngri	'young', 'younger')
ú —— ý	(djúpr —— dýpri	'deep', 'deeper')
ǫ —— ø	(þrǫngr —— þrøngri	'narrow', 'narrower')

Observe the loss of *j* in *dýpri*. The corresponding superlative forms (strong nom. m. sg.) are: *lengstr, lægstr, stærstr, yngstr, dýpstr, þrøngstr*.

If the learner is confronted by what appears to be a comparative or superlative form with one of the above front vowels, and s/he is unable to find the word in a dictionary, it should be looked up substituting the appropriate back vowel. No entry *fegr will be found, for example, so the learner puzzled by the word *fegrstu* in the phrase *enir fegrstu litir* 'the fairest colours' should try under *fagr*.

3.3.8.3 Suppletive forms

As will have become clear from certain of the examples in 3.3.6, a few comparative and superlative forms (mostly very common) are suppletive, i.e. they have a completely different root from that of their positive counterpart. There are unfortunately no rules or guide-lines here and the student will simply have to learn the positive and the suppletive forms as separate items. Some help is to be had from the fact that many of the suppletives also occur in English, cf. the following list (featuring the (strong) nom. m. sg. positive, comparative and superlative forms):

gamall —— ellri —— elztr		'old', 'older', 'oldest' (cf. elder, eldest)
góðr —— betri —— beztr		'good', 'better', 'best'
illr —— verri —— verstr		'bad', 'worse', 'worst'
lítill —— minni —— minnstr		'little', 'smaller', 'smallest'
margr —— fleiri —— flestr		'many a', 'more', 'most'
mikill —— meiri —— mestr		'big', 'bigger', 'biggest'

Observe that in *minni* (< *minri) the *r* of the comparative suffix assimilates to the *n* of the root (cf. 3.3.8.4 below). *Fleiri, flestr* are used of entities that can be counted, e.g. *í flestum lǫndum* 'in most countries'; for non-count entities, *meiri*, *mestr* are employed in the sense 'more', 'most', e.g. *meira fé* 'more wealth'.

3.3.8.4 Deviations from the basic endings

Certain endings occur that do not accord with those given in 3.3.4. We have already seen there that consonantal assimilations affect adjectives with the *-in* and *-al*, *-il*, *-ul* suffixes as well as the possessives *minn*, *þinn*, *sinn*, and that the *-in*-suffix adjectives and the possessives have an acc. m. sg. in *-n* rather than *-an* (see paradigms 7, 8, 21, 22). Other deviations that may cause problems of recognition are:

(1) Consonantal assimilations in monosyllabic adjectives that follow the pattern of the disyllabic types and the possessives just mentioned. In some monosyllabic adjectives whose root ends in *l*, *n*, *s*, an immediately following *r* (in the strong nom. m. sg., gen. and dat. f. sg. and gen. pl. endings, and in comparatives with an *-r* suffix) assimilates to the *l*, *n* or *s* (e.g. *háll* 'slippery' (< **hálr*); dat. f. sg. *heilli* 'whole', 'healthy', (< **heilri*); gen. f. sg. *vænnar* 'hopeful', 'beautiful' (< **vænrar*); dat. pl. comp. *hreinnum* 'purer' (< **hreinrum*); *jafn* 'equal', 'even' (< **jafnn* < **jafnr*); *frjáls* 'free' (< **frjálss* < **frjálsr*); see paradigms 3, 4, 20). *Jafn* and *frjáls* exemplify the general rule that consonant + geminate consonant is simplified to consonant + single consonant (thus also in adjectives with consonant + *r* in the root: contrast, for example, strong nom. f. sg. *fǫgr* 'beautiful' (< **fagru*) with strong nom. m. sg. *fagr* (< **fagrr*), strong gen. pl. *fagra* (< **fagrra*)).

(2) Consonantal assimilations that result in the loss or alteration of root *-d* or *-ð* before the strong nom./acc. n. sg. *-t* ending (e.g. *óðr* 'furious' — nom./acc. n. sg. *ótt* (< **óðt*); *vandr* 'difficult' — nom./acc. n. sg. *vant* (< **vandt*, with simplification of *-ntt* to *-nt*, cf. above); *kallaðr* 'called' (pp.) — nom./acc. n. sg. *kallat* (< **kallatt* < **kallaðt*, with simplification of geminate *tt* in unstressed position); see paradigms 2, 11).

(3) A miscellaneous group of very common adjectives with irregular forms.

(a) *Lítill* 'little' and its antonym *mikill* 'big', with roots *lítil-* (contracted *litl-*), *mikil-*, have strong acc. m. sg. forms *lítinn* and *mikinn* and strong nom./acc. n. sg. *lítit* and *mikit* (i.e. they behave in these cases as though they were *-in*-suffix adjectives, cf., e.g., *opinn* 'open', *tekinn* 'taken' — strong acc. m. sg. *opinn*, *tekinn*, strong nom./acc. n. sg. *opit*, *tekit*; see paradigms 7 and 9). *Mikill* also sometimes has strong dat. n. sg. *myklu*.

(b) The strong nom./acc. n. sg. of *góðr* is *gótt* (cf. point (2) above) or, much more commonly, *gott*, of *margr mart* (also sometimes *margt*) and of *sannr* 'true' *satt*.

(c) The two-syllable adjective *heilagr* 'holy', which drops the *a* of the unstressed syllable on the pattern of those in *-al* etc. (see 3.3.4 and 3.3.8.5 point (1)), regularly undergoes monophthongisation (i.e. the diphthong *ei* changes to a single vowel) in the shortened forms, cf., for example, strong nom./acc. f. pl. *helgar*, weak nom. m. sg. *helgi*.

3.3.8.5 Minor irregularities

The inflexions of Old Norse adjectives exhibit yet other deviations from the basic pattern, but these are less likely to cause the learner problems of recognition.

(1) As already outlined in 3.3.4 (and cf. also 3.1.7.5 point (1)), the unstressed syllables of many disyllabic adjectives lose their vowel when the inflexional ending itself consists of a syllable — except in the strong gen. and dat. f. sg. and strong gen. pl. It remains to be added that not only adjectives with an *-in* or *-al*, *-il*, *-ul* suffix are affected, but the many in *-ig*, *-ug* as well, and that the last, together with *-al*, *-il*, *-ul* types, but unlike those in *-in*, have strong acc. m. sg. forms in *-an* with resulting loss of the preceding syllable (contrast *gamall* 'old' — acc. m. sg. *gamlan*, *auðigr* 'rich' — acc. m. sg. *auðgan* with *heiðinn* 'heathen', *opinn* 'open' — acc. m. sg. *heiðinn*, *opinn*; see paradigms 8, 10). The comparative *-ari* and superlative *-ast* suffixes also commonly trigger loss of the unstressed vowel of disyllabic adjectives (e.g. nom. m. sg., f. sg., etc. comp. *heiðnari* 'more heathen', strong nom. m. sg. sup. *auðgastr* 'richest'; see paradigm 20).

(2) In accordance with the rule stated in 3.3.8.4 point (1), to the effect that consonant + geminate consonant is simplified to consonant + single consonant, adjectives that end in consonant + *t* do not add a further *-t* in the strong nom./acc. n. sg. (e.g. *fluttr* 'conveyed' (pp.) — strong nom./acc. n. sg. *flutt* (< *fluttt); *hvassastr* 'sharpest' (strong nom. m. sg. sup.) — nom./acc. n. sg. *hvassast* (< *hvassastt; see paradigm 12).

(3) Consonants may sometimes be lengthened when immediately following long, stressed vowels. This is the rule with *t* in the strong nom./acc. n. sg., and more or less the rule with *r* in the strong gen. and dat. f. sg. and gen. pl. and in the comparative (e.g. *grár* 'grey' — strong nom./acc. n. sg. *grátt*, strong gen. f. sg. *grár(r)ar*; *hár* 'high' — nom. m.

sg., f. sg., etc. comp. *hær(r)i* (with front mutation); see paradigms 5, 20).

(4) As with nouns (cf. 3.1.7.5 point (2)), the vowels of inflexional endings tend to be dropped when they immediately follow a long vowel of the same or similar quality (e.g. *grár* — strong acc. m. sg. *grán*, strong dat. m. sg., dat. pl. *grám*, strong acc. f. sg., dat. n. sg. and acc. m. pl., all weak forms except nom. m. sg. and dat. pl. *grá*; *trúr* 'faithful' — strong dat. n. sg., weak acc., gen., dat. f. sg. and nom., acc., gen. pl. *trú*; see paradigms 5, 15, 20).

(5) As with nouns (cf. 3.1.7.5 point (4)), *j* is inserted in some adjectives before inflexional endings or suffixes consisting of or beginning in *a* or *u*; in others *v* is inserted before endings or suffixes consisting of or beginning in *a* or *i* (e.g. *nýr* 'new' — strong acc. m. sg. *nýjan*, strong dat. m. sg., dat. pl. *nýjum*, strong acc. f. sg. and acc. m. pl., weak acc., gen., dat. m. sg., nom. f. sg. and n. sg. *nýja*, strong nom. m. sg. sup. *nýjastr*; *døkkr* 'dark' — strong acc. m. sg. *døkkvan*, weak nom. m. sg. *døkkvi*, nom. m. sg., f. sg., etc. comp. *døkkvari*; see paradigms 6, 20).

(6) As a final irregularity, it is worth noting that a few adjectives including the third person possessives are uninflected. These will cause the learner little trouble, since, like adjectives in English, their form remains unchanged whatever their function. Examples are: *einskipa* 'with one ship', *fulltíða* 'full-grown', *andvaka* 'sleepless'. Some of these, e.g. *andvaka*, can also appear in the nom. m. sg. with an *-i* ending: *andvaki*. The possessives are: *hans* 'his', *hennar* 'her', *þess* 'its', *þeir(r)a* 'their', i.e. the genitive forms of the corresponding pronouns which have taken on an additional, adjectival function.

3.3.8.2/3.3.8.3/3.3.8.4/3.3.8.5 Front mutation/Suppletive forms/Deviations from the basic endings/Minor irregularities — Exercise

1. Where in Old Norse adjectival inflexion does front mutation play a role? Give examples.
2. What are the comparative and superlative forms of *góðr*, *lítill*, *mikill*? In what way does the inflexion for degree of these adjectives differ from that of the majority?
3. In what forms of the adjective may inflexional *-r(-)* be assimilated to an immediately preceding *l*, *n* or *s*?
4. Look up the following adjectives in an Old Norse dictionary or in *NION* III and write down the entry forms you find: *breitt, helgustu, trúm, fǫlvir, tekit, færri, mikinn, fǫrlan, miðjum, vaknat*.

3.3.9 Examples of adjective inflexion

Complete paradigms of individual adjectives are now given using the same selection criteria as for nouns (cf. 3.1.8, preamble). While Old Norse grammars in general tend to be over-lavish in their exemplification of nouns, they are sparing in the number of adjective paradigms they include. The current work breaks with this tradition and prints a selection big enough to enable the learner to recognise with the minimum of difficulty the majority of forms likely to be encountered in Old Norse texts. The examples should naturally be studied in conjunction with the guidance given in 3.3.4, 3.3.7 and 3.3.8. Each paradigm is numbered for ease of reference.

Strong inflexion

		(1) Basic pattern: *sjúkr* 'ill'		
		m.	**f.**	**n.**
Sg.	nom.	sjúkr	sjúk	sjúkt
	acc.	sjúkan	sjúka	sjúkt
	gen.	sjúks	sjúkrar	sjúks
	dat.	sjúkum	sjúkri	sjúku
Pl.	nom.	sjúkir	sjúkar	sjúk
	acc.	sjúka	sjúkar	sjúk
	gen.	sjúkra	sjúkra	sjúkra
	dat.	sjúkum	sjúkum	sjúkum

		(2) With root *a* and final *ð*: *harðr* 'hard'		
		m.	**f.**	**n.**
Sg.	nom.	harðr	hǫrð	hart
	acc.	harðan	harða	hart
	gen.	harðs	harðrar	harðs
	dat.	hǫrðum	harðri	hǫrðu
Pl.	nom.	harðir	harðar	hǫrð
	acc.	harða	harðar	hǫrð
	gen.	harðra	harðra	harðra
	dat.	hǫrðum	hǫrðum	hǫrðum

Adjective inflexions and their function

(3) Monosyllable with final *n*: *hreinn* 'pure'			
	m.	**f.**	**n.**
Sg. nom.	hreinn	hrein	hreint
acc.	hreinan	hreina	hreint
gen.	hreins	hreinnar	hreins
dat.	hreinum	hreinni	hreinu
Pl. nom.	hreinir	hreinar	hrein
acc.	hreina	hreinar	hrein
gen.	hreinna	hreinna	hreinna
dat.	hreinum	hreinum	hreinum

(4) Monosyllable with root *a* and final *ss*: *hvass* 'sharp'			
	m.	**f.**	**n.**
Sg. nom.	hvass	hvǫss	hvasst
acc.	hvassan	hvassa	hvasst
gen.	hvass	hvass(r)ar	hvass
dat.	hvǫssum	hvass(r)i	hvǫssu
Pl. nom.	hvassir	hvassar	hvǫss
acc.	hvassa	hvassar	hvǫss
gen.	hvass(r)a	hvass(r)a	hvass(r)a
dat.	hvǫssum	hvǫssum	hvǫssum

(5) With final long vowel: *grár* 'grey'			
	m.	**f.**	**n.**
Sg. nom.	grár	grá	grátt
acc.	grán	grá	grátt
gen.	grás	grár(r)ar	grás
dat.	grám	grár(r)i	grá
Pl. nom.	gráir	grár	grá
acc.	grá	grár	grá
gen.	grár(r)a	grár(r)a	grár(r)a
dat.	grám	grám	grám

(6) With *v* insertion: *fǫlr* 'pale'

		m.	f.	n.
Sg.	nom.	fǫlr	fǫl	fǫlt
	acc.	fǫlvan	fǫlva	fǫlt
	gen.	fǫls	fǫlrar	fǫls
	dat.	fǫlum	fǫlri	fǫlu
Pl.	nom.	fǫlvir	fǫlvar	fǫl
	acc.	fǫlva	fǫlvar	fǫl
	gen.	fǫlra	fǫlra	fǫlra
	dat.	fǫlum	fǫlum	fǫlum

(7) With *-in* suffix: *kominn* 'come' (pp.)

		m.	f.	n.
Sg.	nom.	kominn	komin	komit
	acc.	kominn	komna	komit
	gen.	komins	kominnar	komins
	dat.	komnum	kominni	komnu
Pl.	nom.	komnir	komnar	komin
	acc.	komna	komnar	komin
	gen.	kominna	kominna	kominna
	dat.	komnum	komnum	komnum

(8) With root *a* and *-al* suffix: *gamall* 'old'

		m.	f.	n.
Sg.	nom.	gamall	gǫmul	gamalt
	acc.	gamlan	gamla	gamalt
	gen.	gamals	gamallar	gamals
	dat.	gǫmlum	gamalli	gǫmlu
Pl.	nom.	gamlir	gamlar	gǫmul
	acc.	gamla	gamlar	gǫmul
	gen.	gamalla	gamalla	gamalla
	dat.	gǫmlum	gǫmlum	gǫmlum

(9) With -il and -in suffix: mikill 'big'

		m.	f.	n.
Sg.	nom.	mikill	mikil	mikit
	acc.	mikinn	mikla	mikit
	gen.	mikils	mikillar	mikils
	dat.	miklum	mikilli	miklu
Pl.	nom.	miklir	miklar	mikil
	acc.	mikla	miklar	mikil
	gen.	mikilla	mikilla	mikilla
	dat.	miklum	miklum	miklum

(10) With -ig suffix: auðigr 'wealthy'

		m.	f.	n.
Sg.	nom.	auðigr	auðig	auðigt
	acc.	auðgan	auðga	auðigt
	gen.	auðigs	auðigrar	auðigs
	dat.	auðgum	auðigri	auðgu
Pl.	nom.	auðgir	auðgar	auðig
	acc.	auðga	auðgar	auðig
	gen.	auðigra	auðigra	auðigra
	dat.	auðgum	auðgum	auðgum

(11) With -að suffix: elskaðr 'loved' (pp.)

		m.	f.	n.
Sg.	nom.	elskaðr	elskuð	elskat
	acc.	elskaðan	elskaða	elskat
	gen.	elskaðs	elskaðrar	elskaðs
	dat.	elskuðum	elskaðri	elskuðu
Pl.	nom.	elskaðir	elskaðar	elskuð
	acc.	elskaða	elskaðar	elskuð
	gen.	elskaðra	elskaðra	elskaðra
	dat.	elskuðum	elskuðum	elskuðum

Morphology and syntax

(12) With root *a* and superlative suffix: *harðastr* 'hardest'

		m.	f.	n.
Sg.	nom.	harðastr	hǫrðust	harðast
	acc.	harðastan	harðasta	harðast
	gen.	harðasts	harðastrar	harðasts
	dat.	hǫrðustum	harðastri	hǫrðustu
Pl.	nom.	harðastir	harðastar	hǫrðust
	acc.	harðasta	harðastar	hǫrðust
	gen.	harðastra	harðastra	harðastra
	dat.	hǫrðustum	hǫrðustum	hǫrðustum

Weak inflexion

(13) Basic pattern: *sjúki* 'ill'

		m.	f.	n.
Sg.	nom.	sjúki	sjúka	sjúka
	acc.	sjúka	sjúku	sjúka
	gen.	sjúka	sjúku	sjúka
	dat.	sjúka	sjúku	sjúka
Pl.	nom.	sjúku	sjúku	sjúku
	acc.	sjúku	sjúku	sjúku
	gen.	sjúku	sjúku	sjúku
	dat.	sjúkum	sjúkum	sjúkum

(14) With root *a* and *-al* suffix: *gamli* 'old'

		m.	f.	n.
Sg.	nom.	gamli	gamla	gamla
	acc.	gamla	gǫmlu	gamla
	gen.	gamla	gǫmlu	gamla
	dat.	gamla	gǫmlu	gamla
Pl.	nom.	gǫmlu	gǫmlu	gǫmlu
	acc.	gǫmlu	gǫmlu	gǫmlu
	gen.	gǫmlu	gǫmlu	gǫmlu
	dat.	gǫmlum	gǫmlum	gǫmlum

Adjective inflexions and their function

(15) With final long vowel: *grái* 'grey'

		m.	f.	n.
Sg.	nom.	grái	grá	grá
	acc.	grá	grá	grá
	gen.	grá	grá	grá
	dat.	grá	grá	grá
Pl.	nom.	grá	grá	grá
	acc.	grá	grá	grá
	gen.	grá	grá	grá
	dat.	grám	grám	grám

(16) With *-að* suffix: *elskaði* 'loved'

		m.	f.	n.
Sg.	nom.	elskaði	elskaða	elskaða
	acc.	elskaða	elskuðu	elskaða
	gen.	elskaða	elskuðu	elskaða
	dat.	elskaða	elskuðu	elskaða
Pl.	nom.	elskuðu	elskuðu	elskuðu
	acc.	elskuðu	elskuðu	elskuðu
	gen.	elskuðu	elskuðu	elskuðu
	dat.	elskuðum	elskuðum	elskuðum

(17) With root *a* and superlative suffix: *harðasti* 'hardest'

		m.	f.	n.
Sg.	nom.	harðasti	harðasta	harðasta
	acc.	harðasta	hǫrðustu	harðasta
	gen.	harðasta	hǫrðustu	harðasta
	dat.	harðasta	hǫrðustu	harðasta
Pl.	nom.	hǫrðustu	hǫrðustu	hǫrðustu
	acc.	hǫrðustu	hǫrðustu	hǫrðustu
	gen.	hǫrðustu	hǫrðustu	hǫrðustu
	dat.	hǫrðustum	hǫrðustum	hǫrðustum

Comparative and present participle inflexion

		(18) (With root *a*) *harðari* 'harder'		
		m.	**f.**	**n.**
Sg.	nom.	harðari	harðari	harðara
	acc.	harðara	harðari	harðara
	gen.	harðara	harðari	harðara
	dat.	harðara	harðari	harðara
Pl.	nom.	harðari	harðari	harðari
	acc.	harðari	harðari	harðari
	gen.	harðari	harðari	harðari
	dat.	hǫrðurum	hǫrðurum	hǫrðurum

		(19) *sofandi* 'sleeping'		
		m.	**f.**	**n.**
Sg.	nom.	sofandi	sofandi	sofanda
	acc.	sofanda	sofandi	sofanda
	gen.	sofanda	sofandi	sofanda
	dat.	sofanda	sofandi	sofanda
Pl.	nom.	sofandi	sofandi	sofandi
	acc.	sofandi	sofandi	sofandi
	gen.	sofandi	sofandi	sofandi
	dat.	sofǫndum	sofǫndum	sofǫndum

Degree inflexion

(20) Main types, illustrated by strong and comp. nom. m. sg. forms		
pos.	**comp.**	**sup.**
sjúkr 'ill'	sjúkari	sjúkastr
hreinn 'pure'	hreinni	hreinstr
hvass 'sharp'	hvassari	hvassastr
grár 'grey'	grár(r)i	grástr
fǫlr 'pale'	fǫlvari	fǫlvastr
heiðinn 'heathen'	heiðnari	heiðnastr
auðigr 'wealthy'	auðigri	auðgastr

Irregular comp. and sup. forms involving front mutation and suppletion are dealt with in 3.3.8.2 and 3.3.8.3 above.

Possessive adjective inflexion

		(21) *minn* 'my'		
		m.	**f.**	**n.**
Sg.	nom.	minn	mín	mitt
	acc.	minn	mína	mitt
	gen.	míns	minnar	míns
	dat.	mínum	minni	mínu
Pl.	nom.	mínir	mínar	mín
	acc.	mína	mínar	mín
	gen.	minna	minna	minna
	dat.	mínum	mínum	mínum

		(22) *ykkarr* 'your [dual]'		
		m.	**f.**	**n.**
Sg.	nom.	ykkarr	ykkur	ykkart
	acc.	ykkarn	ykkra	ykkart
	gen.	ykkars	ykkarrar	ykkars
	dat.	ykkrum	ykkarri	ykkru
Pl.	nom.	ykkrir	ykkrar	ykkur
	acc.	ykkra	ykkrar	ykkur
	gen.	ykkarra	ykkarra	ykkarra
	dat.	ykkrum	ykkrum	ykkrum

3.3.9 Examples of adjective inflexion — Exercise

Identify the case, gender, number, type of inflexion (strong, weak, comparative/present participle) and, if comparative or superlative, the degree of the adjectives printed in **bold** in the following sentences. Comment, in addition, on the syntactic function and semantic role of the noun phrases they form part of. Where an adjective exhibits a form other than the strong nominative masculine singular positive — the one used in dictionary entries — give that form as well.

(1) Hann var inn **vaskasti** maðr
 'He was the most-valiant man'
 'He was the most valiant of men'

(2) Hann var **íslenzkr** at kyni, **skyldr** honum
 'He was Icelandic by kin, related to him'

(3) Er þar **mikill** maðr á baki í **blám** klæðum
 'Is there big man on back in dark clothes'
 'There is a big man on horseback there in dark clothes'

(4) Þér hafið **œrnar** bœtr eptir Þorkel, frænda **yðvarn**
 'You have sufficient payments after Þorkel, kinsman your'
 'You have sufficient compensation for Þorkell, your kinsman'

(5) Hann spurði, hverr fyrir skipi því réði enu **vegliga**
 'He asked who over ship that commanded the magnificent'
 'He asked who commanded the magnificent ship'

(6) Þeir áttu **lengri** leið
 'They had longer way'
 'They had a longer route'

(7) Nú má ok þat vera, at **gǫmlum** manni sé eigi **ósárari** sonardauði **sinn**
 'Now may also that be, that to-old man is not unsorer son's-death REFL. POSS.'
 'Now it may also be that to an old man his son's death is not less painful'

(8) Eru honum **sǫgð** tíðindin
 'Are to-him said tidings-the'
 'The news is told to him'

(9) Hann var faðir Eiríks ins **spaka**
 'He was the father of Eiríkr the wise'

(10) Þeir fundu þegar sveininn þar **sofanda** hjá húsi einu
 'They found immediately boy-the there sleeping by house one'
 'They at once found the boy sleeping there beside a certain building'

Adjective inflexions and their function   113

(11)   Hér mun **þinn** þroski **mestr**
       'Here will your advancement greatest'
       'Here is where you will prosper most'

(12)   Hann hélt **ǫll** heit **sín** drengiliga við **sína** menn
       'He kept all promises REFL. POSS. nobly with REFL. POSS. men'
       'He nobly kept all his promises to his men'

(13)   Ek hefi til **fás** hlutazk, síðan ek kom til Íslands
       'I have to few allocated-*sk* since I came to Iceland'
       'I have been active in little since I came to Iceland'

(14)   Þar var brekka **brǫtt** ofan í dalinn
       'There was slope steep down into valley-the'
       'There was a steep slope down into the valley'

(15)   Erlendr vildi ekki, at synir **hans** hefði **lægra** hlut þar í Eyjum
       'Erlendr wanted not that sons his had lower lot there in Islands'
       'Erlendr did not want his sons to have a poorer position there in the Orkneys'

(16)   Gangi sá inn **gamli** maðr fyrir
       'Go that the old man in-front'
       'Let the old man walk in front'

(17)   Hlaut hann þar inn **mesta** heiðr
       'Received he there the greatest honour'
       'There he received the greatest honour'

(18)   Þau váru **allra** skipa **skjótust**
       'They were of-all ships fastest'
       'They were fastest of all ships'

(19)   Þeir ráku fyrir sér sextán **klyfjaða** hesta
       'They drove before them sixteen pack-saddled horses'

(20)   Þar er **svarðlaus** mýrr
       'There is grassless bog'
       'There is a grassless bog there'

(21) Hann lét þar gera steinkastala **góðan**; var þat **ǫruggt** vígi
  'He let there make stone-castle good; was that secure fortress'
  'He had a fine stone castle made there; it was a secure fortress'

(22) Maðrinn var nú miklu **vinsælli** en áðr
  'The man was now much more popular than before'

(23) Hann sótti málit til **fullra** laga
  'He pursued case-the to full laws'
  'He pursued the case to the full extent of the law'

(24) Kona sú in **góða** dýrkaði þann **helga** konung með **mikilli** ást
  'Woman that the good venerated that holy king with great love'
  'The good woman venerated the holy king with great love'

(25) Veita skulum vér **þurfǫndum líkamliga** fœzlu
  'Give shall we to-needing bodily food'
  'We are to give bodily sustenance to the needy'

(26) Fǫstur eru en **hvǫssustu** vápn í gegn djǫfli
  'Fasts are the sharpest weapons against the devil'

(27) Þeir mæltu fund sín á milli í **ákveðnum** stað
  'They arranged meeting self be(-)tween in appointed place'
  'They arranged a meeting between themselves in an appointed place'

(28) Einarr kvað hann mann **gǫfgastan** ok hana fullvel **gipta**
  'Einarr said him man noblest and her full-well married'
  'Einarr said he was a most noble man and she was very well married'

(29) Bakkar **hávir** váru umhverfis
  'Hills high were around'
  'High hills were all around'

(30) Hann bað þann **milda** konung leysa in **seigu** syndabǫnd af sér
  'He bade that gracious king loose the stubborn sin-bonds off self'
  'He prayed to the gracious king to remove the stubborn bonds of sin from him'

3.4 Numerals

Numerals are sometimes regarded as adjectives, and indeed several of the inflexions exhibited by the Old Norse numerals either parallel or are strongly reminiscent of adjectival forms. Numerals may also be found classified as pronouns, and, in more recent grammatical literature, as quantifiers. They are treated here as a separate word class. One of several reasons for separating them from pronouns and adjectives is that three of the Old Norse numerals inflect and function as nouns.

3.4.1 The numerals and their inflexions

As in English, the basic counting system in Old Norse is divided into cardinal numbers (*one*, *two*, *three*, etc.) and ordinal numbers (*first*, *second*, *third*, etc.). The Old Norse numerals (nom. m. sg./pl. where they inflect) are as follows.

	Cardinal	**Ordinal**
1	einn	fyrstr
2	tveir	annarr
3	þrír	þriði
4	fjórir	fjórði
5	fim(m)	fim(m)ti
6	sex	sétti
7	sjau	sjaundi
8	átta	áttandi, átti
9	níu	níundi
10	tíu	tíundi
11	ellifu	ellifti
12	tólf	tólfti
13	þrettán	þrettándi
14	fjórtán, fjǫgurtán	fjórtándi, fjǫgurtándi
15	fim(m)tán	fim(m)tándi
16	sextán	sextándi
17	sjaut(j)án	sjaut(j)ándi
18	át(t)ján	át(t)jándi

19	nítján	nítjándi
20	tuttugu	tuttugundi
21	tuttugu ok einn	tuttugundi ok fyrsti
22	tuttugu ok tveir	tuttugundi ok annarr
30	þrír tigir	þrítugundi
31	þrír tigir ok einn	þrítugundi ok fyrsti
40	fjórir tigir	fertugundi
50	fim(m) tigir	fim(m)tugundi
60	sex tigir	sextugundi
70	sjau tigir	sjautugundi
80	átta tigir	áttatugundi
90	níu tigir	nítugundi

Beyond *nítugundi* the ordinals are not recorded. The cardinals are:

100	tíu tigir, hundrað
110	ellifu tigir, hundrað ok tíu
120	hundrað, hundrað ok tuttugu
1000	þúsund
1200	þúsund

As is apparent from this list, *hundrað* may denote either 100 (*hundrað tírætt* 'a hundred of ten tens' (see below)) or 120 (*hundrað tólfrætt* 'a hundred of twelve tens' 'a "long" hundred'). Correspondingly, *þúsund* = either 1000 or 1200. With figures of this magnitude precision is often unimportant in Old Icelandic literature; where the intention is to express exact numbers or amounts, either the text itself or the edition may make clear what is meant by *hundrað* or *þúsund*.

Many of the above numerals have variant forms (the most common are specified), but none is likely to cause the learner problems of recognition. It is worth noting that the ordinal suffix *-undi* also appears as *-andi* (though *níundi* and *tíundi* are almost universal).

Tigir is nom. pl. of *tigr* (also *tegr*, *tugr*, *tøgr*), a masculine noun meaning 'a group of ten' 'a decade'; *þrír tigir*, for example, thus literally means 'three tens'. *Hundrað* is a neuter noun, and *þúsund* a feminine. All three inflect according to noun paradigms (*tigr* according to paradigm 5 but without the vowel changes associated with root *a*, *hundrað* according to 27 but without the loss of unstressed *a* in dat. sg. and gen./dat. pl., *þúsund* according to 13).

Of the other cardinals, only *einn*, *tveir*, *þrír* and *fjórir* inflect, *einn* for case, gender, number and definiteness (cf., e.g., *þat eina* 'the one'), *tveir*, *þrír* and *fjórir* for case and gender alone. The paradigms are as follows (only the strong forms of *einn* are given).

		einn 'one'		
		m.	**f.**	**n.**
Sg.	nom.	einn	ein	eitt
	acc.	einn	eina	eitt
	gen.	eins	einnar	eins
	dat.	einum	einni	einu
Pl.	nom.	einir	einar	ein
	acc.	eina	einar	ein
	gen.	einna	einna	einna
	dat.	einum	einum	einum

		tveir 'two'		
		m.	**f.**	**n.**
Pl.	nom.	tveir	tvær	tvau
	acc.	tvá	tvær	tvau
	gen.	tveggja	tveggja	tveggja
	dat.	tveim(r)	tveim(r)	tveim(r)

		þrír 'three'		
		m.	**f.**	**n.**
Pl.	nom.	þrír	þrjár	þrjú
	acc.	þrjá	þrjár	þrjú
	gen.	þriggja	þriggja	þriggja
	dat.	þrim(r)	þrim(r)	þrim(r)

		fjórir 'four'		
		m.	**f.**	**n.**
Pl.	nom.	fjórir	fjórar	fjǫgur
	acc.	fjóra	fjórar	fjǫgur
	gen.	fjǫgurra	fjǫgurra	fjǫgurra
	dat.	fjórum	fjórum	fjórum

In the plural, *einn* has the sense 'only' 'just' (e.g. *sagnir einar* 'just tales'), 'some' (*einir heiðnir víkingar* 'some heathen vikings') and 'roughly' 'about' (*einar þrjár* 'about three').

As a numeral (in the sense 'the two') we can include *báðir* 'both'. It has only plural (dual) forms and inflects as follows.

	m.	**f.**	**n.**
nom.	báðir	báðar	bæði
acc.	báða	báðar	bæði
gen.	beggja	beggja	beggja
dat.	báðum	báðum	báðum

It will be seen that *einn* (in its strong form) inflects exactly like the pronoun *hinn* (3.2.2); it is also very similar in its forms to the possessives *minn*, *þinn*, *sinn* and adjectives with the *-in* suffix (3.3.9, paradigms 21 and 7). Certain of the inflexions of *tveir*, *þrír*, *fjórir* and *báðir* are reminiscent of corresponding noun, pronoun and adjective forms. Compare (1) nom. m. *tveir* with nom. m. pl. *þeir* 'they' 'those', and *þrír*, *fjórir*, *báðir* with the common nom. m. pl. ending *-ir*; (2) acc. m. *tvá*, *þrjá* with acc. m. pl. *þá* 'them' 'those', and *fjóra*, *báða* with the common acc. m. pl. ending *-a*; (3) nom./acc. f. *tvær* with nom./acc. f. pl. *þær*, and *þrjár*, *fjórar*, *báðar* with the common nom./acc. f. pl. ending *-ar*; (4) gen. *tveggja*, *þriggja*, *fjǫgurra*, *beggja* with the ubiquitous gen. pl. ending *-a*; (5) dat. *tveim*, *þrim*, *fjórum*, *báðum* with the ubiquitous dat. pl. ending *-(u)m*. Observe also that the nom./acc. n. of all four numerals, like the nom./acc. n. pl. of nouns, pronouns and adjectives, is without a final added *-r*.

The ordinals all inflect as adjectives (3.3.4), but subject to considerable restrictions: *fyrstr* has both strong and weak inflexion (contrast *hann gekk fyrstr* 'he went first' and *hit fyrsta sumar* 'the first summer'), *annarr* only strong, and the remaining ordinals only weak; *þriði* has *j* insertion before *-a* and *-u* (3.3.8.5 point (5)). The paradigm of *annarr* shows a number of irregularities and is therefore given here in full.

		m.	**f.**	**n.**
Sg.	nom.	annarr	ǫnnur	annat
	acc.	annan	aðra	annat
	gen.	annars	annarrar	annars
	dat.	ǫðrum	annarri	ǫðru
Pl.	nom.	aðrir	aðrar	ǫnnur
	acc.	aðra	aðrar	ǫnnur
	gen.	annarra	annarra	annarra
	dat.	ǫðrum	ǫðrum	ǫðrum

In addition to these basic numerals, the learner may encounter *tvinnr/tvennr* 'double' 'twofold' 'consisting of two different things or kinds', *þrennr* 'triple' etc. Both words inflect as strong adjectives. Also adjectival is the suffix *-tøgr*, *-tugr*, which has the sense 'of a number of tens'; it is particularly used of age, e.g. *tvítøgr* (*þrítøgr*, *fertøgr*, *fim(m)tøgr*, etc.) *maðr* 'a man of twenty' ('thirty', 'forty', 'fifty', etc.). For 70 and tens above, the suffix *-rœðr* is more common, e.g. *áttrœðr* 'of eight tens', *tírœðr* 'of ten tens', *tólfrœðr* 'of twelve tens' (cf. above on the 'long' hundred). Uninflected numerals are *tysvar/tvisvar* 'twice', *þrysvar/þrisvar* 'thrice'.

3.4.1 The numerals and their inflexions — Exercise

1. What types of numeral are found in the basic Old Norse counting system?
2. Which of the numerals are nouns?
3. In what way may *hundrað* and *þúsund* be ambiguous?
4. Which of the cardinal numbers inflect, and what points of similarity are there between their paradigms and those of other word classes in Old Norse?
5. Which of the ordinal numbers inflect, and according to which pattern or patterns?

3.4.2 Examples of numeral usage

Inflexions, where they occur, are printed in bold (or the whole word, where the inflected form is identical with the root). Notes explain the relationship between form and function, and usage in general. Compare the inflexions used with those set out or identified above. Observe, too, the differences between Old Norse and English phraseology and sentence formation. Definitions of basic concepts that have already been given are not repeated; if in doubt, the student should in the first instance consult the commentaries that accompany each of the examples of noun usage (3.1.5).

(1) Þat var tíund**a** dag jóla, er Rǫgnvaldr jarl stóð upp
'It was tenth day of-Christmas that Rǫgnvaldr earl got up'
'It was on the tenth day of Christmas that Earl Rǫgnvaldr got up'

Tíunda is an ordinal number in the acc. m. sg., agreeing with *dag*, which is accusative because the phrase of which it is the head is a time adverbial (it answers the question: 'When?'; see 3.1.2). Note that *jól* 'Christmas' is a plural noun.

(2) Sigurðr jarl átti þr**já** sonu a**ðra**; hét ein**n** Sumarliði, annar**r** Brúsi, þrið**i** Einarr rangmunnr
'Sigurðr earl had three sons other; was-called one Sumarliði, second Brúsi, third Einarr rangmunnr'
'Earl Sigurðr had three other sons; one was called Sumarliði, the second Brúsi, the third Einarr wry-mouth'

Þrjá is a cardinal and *aðra* an ordinal number; both are acc. m. (pl.), agreeing with *sonu*, the direct object of the first sentence. *Einn* is a cardinal and *annarr* and *þriði* are ordinal numbers; all three are nom. m. sg., the subjects of their respective sentences (cf. ' . . . the second [was called] . . . the third [was called] . . .'). *Annarr*, unlike almost all other ordinals, has strong inflexion.

(3) Af herfangi því, er vér fám þar, skulum vér fá fátœkum mǫnnum inn fimmtugand**a** penning
'Of booty that which we get there, shall we give to-poor men the fiftieth penny'
'Of the booty which we win there, we will give the fiftieth part to the poor'

Fimmtuganda is an ordinal in the acc. m. sg., agreeing with *penning*, the direct object.

(4) Þar var mikill skáli ok dyrr á báð**um** endum
  'There was big hall and doorway on both ends'
  'There was a big hall there and a doorway at both ends'

Báðum is a plural numerical adjective in the dat., agreeing with *endum*, the noun of the preposition phrase *á báðum endum*. The case of the noun is governed by the preposition *á* (see 3.7, 3.7.4).

(5) Sámr hafði ok fjór**a** tig**u** manna
  'Sámr had also four tens of-men'
  'Sámr also had forty men'

Fjóra is a cardinal in the acc. m., agreeing with the numerical noun *tigu*, the direct object. Together, *fjóra* and *tigu* make up the numeral 'forty'. Numbers which include or consist of the nouns *tigr*, *hundrað* or *þúsund* are followed by a genitive of type, that is, one which expresses the nature of the entity to which the numeral refers (cf. English *hundreds of people*).

(6) Þar var saman tólfræ**tt hundrað** manna
  'There were together duodecimal hundred of men'
  'Altogether there were 120 men there'

Tólfrætt is an adjective in the strong nom. n. sg., agreeing with the numerical noun *hundrað*, the subject. On the genitive *manna*, see (5) above.

(7) Þá er hann var fimtán vetra gamall, reið hann til þings
  'Then when he was fifteen of-winters old, rode he to assembly'
  'When he was fifteen years old, he rode to the assembly'

Fimtán is an uninflected cardinal which together with *vetra* functions as an adverbial of measure. Where a cardinal is thus used in combination with (the appropriate form of) *gamall* 'old', the noun expressing the spans of time by which age is reckoned (here: 'winters') appears in the genitive.

(8) Hann reið á Hǫskuldsstaði við tólft**a** mann
  'He rode to Hǫskuldsstaðir with twelfth man'
  'He rode to Hǫskuldsstaðir with eleven men'

Tólfta is an ordinal in the acc. m. sg., agreeing with *mann*, the noun of the preposition phrase *við tólfta mann*. The case of the noun is governed by the preposition *við* (see 3.7.4). 'With ORDINAL man' is a common way in Old Norse of specifying the total number in a group: the subject (here: 'he') is included in the group and the ordinal gives the total. In this particular example there were twelve altogether: 'he' and eleven others.

(9) Tv**eir** menn ins fimt**a** tig**ar** váru með Eyjólfi
 'Two men of-the fifth ten were with Eyjólfr'
 'Forty-two men were with Eyjólfr'

Tveir is a cardinal in the nom. m., agreeing with *menn*, the subject. *Fimta* is an ordinal in the gen. m. sg., agreeing with *tigar*; *ins fimta tigar* is a partitive genitive, that is, one that expresses the whole of which the number or numbers singled out for mention (here: 'two men') are a part (see 3.2.6, sentence 20). Note how the number is expressed: the fourth 'ten' ends at 40 and the fifth at 50, thus two of the fifth ten, i.e. two on the way from 40 towards 50, is 42.

(10) En frá Snæfellsnesi er fj**ǫgurra** dœgra haf í vestr til Grœnlands
 'But from Snæfellsnes is four days' sea in west to Greenland'
 'But from Snæfellsnes it is four days' sailing to the west to Greenland'

Fjǫgurra is a cardinal in the gen., agreeing with *dœgra*; *fjǫgurra dœgra* is a descriptive genitive, that is, one which modifies a noun (here: 'sea') by expressing a quality or characteristic associated with it.

(11) Rǫgnvaldr jarl gaf Haraldi jarli anna**t** skipit; þat hét Fífa, en anna**t** hét Hjálp
 'Rǫgnvaldr earl gave to-Haraldr earl the-one ship-the; it was-called Fífa, and the-other was-called Hjálp'
 'Earl Rǫgnvaldr gave Earl Haraldr the one ship; it was called Arrow and the other was called Help'

Annat is an ordinal. In the first sentence it appears in the acc. n. sg., agreeing with *skipit*, the direct object. In the third sentence it is nom. n. sg. and is the subject. Note that *annarr* not only means 'second', 'other', but 'the one' and 'the other' of two entities. Observe further that *skipit* is definite (i.e. it is accompanied by the (suffixed) definite article); this gives the construction partitive sense (cf. (9) above), i.e. it means literally 'the one of the [two] ships'.

(12) Kómu sendimenn til jarls **þrimr** nóttum síðarr
 'Came messengers to earl three nights later'
 'The messengers came to the earl three nights later'

Þrimr is a cardinal in the dat., agreeing with *nóttum*. *Þrimr nóttum* is an adverbial of degree, used together with comparatives to express by how much one entity is more than another; *þrimr nóttum síðarr* thus means literally 'later by three nights'.

3.4.2 Examples of numeral usage — Exercise

1. In what different ways may *annarr* be used?
2. How might one say in Old Norse: 'with six other men'?
3. What types of genitive construction are used in conjunction with numerals?
4. How might one say 'fifty-six' in Old Norse?
5. Give the case, gender and number (as appropriate) of the numerals (printed in bold) in the following sentences, and explain their syntactic function and semantic role:

    (a) Hann hafði **fjǫgur** skip ok **tíu tigu** manna
     'He had four ships and a hundred men'
    (b) Þeir gengu þaðan inn **þrettánda** dag jóla
     'They went from there on the thirteenth day of Christmas'
    (c) Haraldr jarl var þá nær **tvítøgum** manni
     'Earl Haraldr was then a man of nearly twenty'
    (d) Þeir sátu í skemmu **einni** skammt frá sænum
     'They sat in a certain building a short distance from the sea'
    (e) Eptir fall Rǫgnvalds jarls var Haraldr jarl í Orkneyjum **átta** vetr ins **fimmta tigar**
     'After the fall of Earl Rǫgnvaldr, Haraldr was earl in the Orkneys for forty-eight years'
    (f) Hét **annarr** Sǫrli ok **annarr** Þorkell
     'The one was called Sǫrli and the other Þorkell'

3.5 Adverbs

Adverbs are sometimes defined as words that modify the verb or specify its action (e.g. English *quickly* in *he ran quickly*, which denotes the manner of the running). In fact, the function of many words that are traditionally classed as adverbs does not fit this definition. Indeed the adverb word class serves as a kind of dustbin into which items that do not obviously belong to any other category can be put. In the English sentence: *unfortunately, they could not come*, for example, *unfortunately* is classed as an adverb, yet it says nothing about the 'coming', but means rather: 'I/we think it is unfortunate they could not come'.

As in English, adverbs in Old Norse are a heterogeneous group. One feature they all share, however, is that they do not inflect for number, person, case or gender. Most, like adjectives, inflect for degree (see below), but that is all. The learner therefore needs to master nothing more than the meanings of adverbs and to be able to recognise their comparative and superlative forms.

3.5.1 Adverb formation

Although a number of Old Norse adverbs appear to be primary (not transparently derived from other words, e.g. *mjǫk* 'very', *svá* 'thus' 'so', *þá* 'then', *vel* 'well'), the majority are derivatives. Many are based on adjectives. A particularly common way of forming adverbs from adjectives is by adding an *-a* suffix (e.g. *illa* 'badly' from *illr* 'bad'); equally common is the use of the strong nom./acc. n. sg. form of the adjective with adverbial function (e.g. *skjótt* 'quickly' from *skjótr* 'quick'). Adverbs derived from adjectives with the commonly occurring *-ligr* suffix are formed in the same way as *illa* (e.g. *makligr* 'fitting', *makliga* 'fittingly'); sometimes *-liga* is added to the root of other adjectives (e.g. *glǫggr* 'clear', *glǫggliga* 'clearly'), and thus itself becomes an adverb suffix. A number of adverbs are fossilised case-forms of adjectives or nouns (e.g. *jafnan* 'always' 'constantly' from *jafn* 'equal' 'even', *alls* 'altogether' 'at all' from *allr* 'all', *miklu* 'much' (emphasising comparatives as in *miklu meiri* 'much greater') from *mikill* 'big', *loks* 'finally' from *lok* n. 'end', *stundum* 'sometimes' from *stund* f. 'while' 'time').

Many adverbs indicating movement towards a place have counterparts formed with an *-i* suffix that denote rest in a place and others with an *-an* suffix meaning movement from a place (e.g. *inn* 'in', *inni* 'inside', *innan* 'from within'). Some have only two of the forms (e.g. *norðr* 'northwards' 'in the north', *norðan* 'from the north' (with root *norð-*); thus also the other compass-point adverbs — on *suðr* 'southwards', *sunnan* 'from the south', see p. 126). Certain of these locational adverbs can have special meanings (e.g. *útan* 'from without' and thus 'from Iceland', seen from the perspective of Norway). The threefold distinction: 'to a place', 'in a place' and 'from a place' is also found in the commonly occurring *hingat* — *hér* — *heðan* 'hither — here — hence', *þangat* — *þar* — *þaðan* 'thither — there — thence', *hvert* — *hvar* — *hvaðan* 'where (to) — where — whence' (it should be noted that none of these words has the slightly archaic ring of some of the English equivalents). Adverbs with the *-an* suffix combine with a preceding *fyrir* (cf. 3.7.1, 3.7.4) to form prepositional phrases indicating position relative to another (fixed) position (e.g. *fyrir norðan heiðina* 'north of the heath', *fyrir ofan húsin* 'above the buildings'; note the idiomatic *fyrir norðan/sunnan land* 'in the north/south of Iceland').

3.5.2 Inflexion for degree

The suffixes used to form the comparative and superlative of adverbs are the same as those found in adjectival comparison, namely *-(a)r*, *-(a)st*. As examples we may cite *opt* 'often' and *lengi* 'long' 'for a long time'.

positive	**comparative**	**superlative**
opt	optar	optast
lengi	lengr	lengst

Adverbs like *skjótt* that consist of the strong nom./acc. n. sg. adjective mostly have the corresponding adjective form in the comparative as well (e.g. *skjótara* 'more quickly', with an *-ara* suffix, *lengra* 'farther', from *langt*). In the superlative of such adverbs the strong nom./acc. n. sg. form is always used (e.g. *skjótast* 'most quickly', *lengst* 'farthest' with the *-(a)st* suffix (cf. 3.3.8.5 point (2)), added to the roots *skjót-*, *leng-* rather than to the positive adverb forms *skjótt*, *langt*). Occasionally the *-(a)ra* comparative ending can be found in adverbs other than those of the *skjótt* type.

Other minor deviations from the above pattern include the addition of an extra *r* to many comparatives in *-ar* (e.g. *optar(r)* 'more often', *framar(r)* 'farther forward' 'farther on' from *fram* 'forward') and the spread of comparative *r* into many superlatives (e.g. *frama(r)st* 'farthest forward' 'farthest on', *inna(r)st* 'farthest in'). As the brackets in the examples indicate, regular forms may also be found.

Like adjectives, adverbs that form the comparative with the *-r* and the superlative with the *-st* suffix undergo front mutation of back root vowels (see 3.1.7.2 and 3.3.8.2). Few adverbs are in fact affected. Common ones are *lengra* 'farther', *lengst* 'farthest' (see above), *fremr* 'farther forward', *fremst* 'farthest forward' (alternative comparative and superlative forms to *framar(r)*, *frama(r)st*, see above), and the irregular *fjarri* 'far off' — *firr* 'farther off' — *first* 'farthest off' and *gǫrva* 'thoroughly', 'precisely' — *gørr* 'more thoroughly' — *gørst* 'most thoroughly'.

Also in common with adjectives, a small group of adverbs have suppletive forms in the comparative and superlative (see 3.3.8.3). The ones likely to be encountered regularly by the learner are:

gjarna —— *heldr* —— *helzt*		'willingly', 'rather', 'most of all'
illa —— *verr* —— *verst*		'badly', 'worse', 'worst'
lítt ——*minnr* —— *minst*		'little', 'less', 'least'
mjǫk —— *meir(r)* —— *mest*		'much', 'more', 'most'
vel —— *betr* —— *bezt*		'well', 'better', 'best'

One or two of the deviations and minor irregularities affecting adjectives (3.3.8.4, 3.3.8.5) can be found in the comparative and/or superlative forms of adverbs also. Attention has already been drawn to the loss of neuter *-t* in superlatives of the *skjótast* type (3.3.8.5 point (2)). Further to be noted are consonantal assimilations (3.3.8.4 point (1), cf., e.g., *seinna* 'more slowly' 'later' < **seinra*) and loss of unstressed syllables in disyllabic adverbs when a further syllable is added (3.3.8.5 point (1), cf., e.g., *sjaldan* 'seldom' — *sjaldnar* 'more seldom' —*sjaldnast* 'most seldom').

Occasionally the alternation *ðr* — *nn* seen in nouns like *muðr* 'mouth', acc. *munn*, gen. *munns* etc. (cf. 3.1.7.4 point (5)) also distinguishes different forms of adverbs. We have already noted that the *-an* form of *suðr* is *sunnan*; its comparative and superlative manifestations are *sunnar(r)*, *sunna(r)st* respectively.

3.5.3 Examples of adverb usage

On the pattern of exemplification, see the preambles to 3.1.5, 3.2.6, 3.3.6 and 3.4.2. Adverbs are given in bold type.

(1) Þeir kurruðu **illa** um brottvist sína
'They grumbled badly about absence REFL. POSS.'
'They grumbled a lot about their having to be away'

Illa is an adverb of manner; it describes the way in which 'they' grumbled.

(2) **Þar** eru **jafnan** dregin skip **yfir**
'There are regularly dragged ships across'
'Ships are regularly dragged across there'

Þar is an adverb of place; it is the 'rest' counterpart to *þangat* 'thither' and *þaðan* 'thence' (cf. (5) below), denoting neither movement to nor from a place. *Jafnan* may loosely be described as an adverb of time; it denotes the regularity with which the event described takes place. *Yfir* is a preposition used here as an adverb of place; it denotes movement within a specified area.

(3) Tóku menn **þá** róðr mikinn ok fóru **ákafliga**
'Began men then rowing big and went furiously'
'Then men began to row hard and they travelled at a furious pace'

Þá is an adverb of time; it denotes the point in time at which men started to row. *Ákafliga* is an adverb of manner; it describes the way in which the vessels moved.

(4) Þessu var **skjótt** neitat
'This was quickly refused'

Skjótt is an adverb of manner derived from the nom./acc. n. sg. of the adjective *skjótr* 'quick'; it describes the speed with which the refusal was made.

(5) Magnús konungr helt **þaðan** í Suðreyjar
'Magnús king continued thence to Hebrides'
'King Magnús went on from there to the Hebrides'

Þaðan is an adverb of place; the *-an* suffix imparts to it the sense of movement from a place.

(6) Magnús konungr helt **sunnan** með Skotlandi
'Magnús king continued from-south along Scotland'
'King Magnús continued northwards along the coast of Scotland'

Sunnan is an adverb of place; the *-an* suffix imparts to it the sense of movement from a place. Note, however, that here it seems more natural in English to render the movement as motion towards, i.e. 'northwards' (cf. further: *ofan* 'from above' 'down', *neðan* 'from underneath' 'up').

(7) Hann eignar sér **svá** allar eyjar fyrir vestan Skotland
'He assigns to-self thus all islands west of Scotland'
'He thus takes possession of all the islands west of Scotland'

Svá is an adverb of manner; it refers to the way in which 'he' takes possession of the islands. Note the compound preposition *fyrir vestan* incorporating the adverb of place *vestan* (see 3.5.1).

(8) Hann fór **þegar austr** til Nóregs
'He went immediately east to Norway'

Þegar is an adverb of time; it denotes the lack of any interval before 'he' left for Norway. *Austr* is an adverb of place, here denoting movement towards the place.

(9) Eysteinn konungr tók við honum **forkunnar vel**
'King Eysteinn received him exceedingly well'

Forkunnar is an adverb of degree; it describes how well 'he' was received (as the *-ar* ending suggests, this is in origin the gen. sg. form of a noun, *forkuðr* f. 'strong desire', see 3.1.7.4 point (5)). *Vel* is an adverb of manner; it describes the way in which Eysteinn received 'him'.

(10) Þá rœddi Kali um, at þeir myndi eigi fara **lengra**
'Then spoke Kali about that they would not go farther'
'Then Kali said that they would not go any farther'

For *þá*, see (3) above. *Lengra* is an adverb of place in the comparative; it denotes movement additional to that already made towards a place.

(11) **Litlu síðarr** gekk maðrinn **út**
'A little later the man went out'

Síðarr is an adverb of time in the comparative; it compares the time the man went out with an earlier event. *Út* is an adverb of place; it denotes movement towards the outside. Although *litlu* is in form the strong dat. n. sg. of the adjective *lítill* (cf. 3.3.8.4 point (3)), it functions here as an adverb of degree, expressing how much later the event described took place.

(12) Þórðr vann **þá allra sýsligast**
'Þórðr worked then of-all most-briskly'
'Then Þórðr worked more briskly than ever'

For *þá*, see (3) above. *Sýsligast* is an adverb of manner in the superlative; it describes the way in which Þórðr worked and defines it as the highest degree of that manner of working. Although *allra* is in form the gen. pl. of the adjective *allr*, it functions here as an intensifying adverb: Þórðr did not just work most briskly, but most briskly of all (things).

3.5.1/3.5.2/3.5.3 Adverb formation/Inflexion for degree/Examples of adverb usage — Exercise

1. In what ways do adverbs inflect in Old Norse?
2. Give examples of three common ways of deriving adverbs in Old Norse.
3. What is the basic meaning of (a) the *-i* and (b) the *-an* adverb suffix?
4. How are the comparatives and superlatives of adverbs formed?
5. Give the positive and superlative forms of the following adverbs: *minnr*, *lengra*, *betr*, *fljótara*, *síðarr*.
6. Explain the form (where appropriate) and the function of the adverbs (printed in bold) in the following sentences.

    (a) Heldu þeir **þá þegar suðr** í Eyjar
    'They then at once went south to the Orkneys'
    (b) Þeir vǫrðusk **drengiliga**
    'They defended themselves manfully'
    (c) Hundrinn hljóp **ofan** til skipa
    'The dog ran down to the ships'
    (d) Þeir kómu **heldr síð**
    'They came rather late'
    (e) Skip Sveins gekk **meira**
    'Sveinn's ship went faster'
    (f) Sveinn varð **seinst** búinn
    'Sveinn was ready last'

3.5.4 Adverbs and adverbials

In the above we have dealt almost exclusively with adverbs, that is, single words whose basic function is adverbial and which are therefore assigned to the adverb word class. However, as *litlu* and *allra* in example sentences (11) and (12) above indicate, non-adverbs can sometimes be used in such a way that they assume adverbial function. This applies not only to single words, but to whole phrases. Many preposition phrases, for example, are reducible to adverbs. Thus *í* + a placename is in a sense the equivalent of *þar* 'there' or *hér* 'here' in that it answers the question 'where' (e.g. *í Nóregi* 'in Norway'), and *í* + a noun denoting a point in time or a period of time is the equivalent of *þá*, answering the question 'when' (e.g. *í þeim tíma* 'at that time'). Noun phrases, too, may have adverbial function (e.g. *þat var einn dag* 'that happened one day' where *einn dag* is accusative and expresses a point in time; cf. 3.1.2 and 3.1.5, sentence 10). Even complete dependent sentences may be reducible to a single adverb and thus be shown to have adverbial function (e.g., *meðan hann lifði* 'while he lived' refers to a period of time and can be replaced by *þá* 'then').

Phrases or clauses that have adverbial function are known as adverbials. But since adverbs by definition also have adverbial function, they are clearly adverbials too. The difference between the two is a matter of perspective. Adverbs are a word class on a par with nouns, adjectives, verbs, etc., while adverbials are functional elements in the sentence, comparable to subjects, objects, etc. Although this *Grammar* attempts as far as practicable to integrate morphology and syntax, its different sections are rooted firmly in the word class. Adverbials will therefore not be further discussed. In fact, Old Norse and English do not differ greatly with respect to adverbial formation and use, so it is unlikely the student will encounter much difficulty in recognising Old Norse adverbials for what they are.

3.6 Verb inflexions and their function

Traditionally the verb has been defined as a 'doing' or 'action' word. This definition, based on meaning, is not wholly satisfactory, since it can be shown that many words classed as verbs do not denote actions (e.g. English *seem*, *need*, *must*). Verbs can also be defined by their morphology, i.e. as words which (may) have different forms to distinguish, *inter alia*, person, number, tense, mood, and voice. In terms of function, verbs are the non-reducible part of the predicate. On the one hand we have the subject — 'what the sentence is about' (cf. 3.1.5, sentence 1), on the other the predicate — what is said of the subject. Every predicate must contain a verb; it will usually contain more than this, but some predicates consist of a verb alone (e.g. English *John* (noun/subject) *arrived* (verb/predicate)).

The verb in Old Norse is most easily recognised by its morphological features. It inflects for person, number, tense, mood, and, to a limited extent, voice (see further below). Analysis will also show it to be the non-reducible part of the predicate, but such analysis may often be difficult for the learner. In any case, what s/he needs first and foremost to acquire is knowledge of the different verbal forms and an understanding of their meaning. We begin, therefore, with a brief introduction to person, number, tense, mood and voice and a schematic account of how these categories are expressed in Old Norse.

3.6.1 Person and number

As explained in the case of the pronouns (cf. 3.2, 3.2.1), person in linguistic description refers to the perspective from which the participants in a situation are viewed. We saw that in Old Norse, as in English, there were three persons, represented by the pronouns *ek* 'I', *vit* 'we two', *vér* 'we [pl.]' (1st person), *þú* 'you', *(þ)it* 'you two', *(þ)ér* 'you [pl.]' (2nd person), *hann* 'he', *hon* 'she', *þat* 'it', *þeir* 'they [m.]', *þær* 'they [f.]', *þau* 'they [n.]', *sik* 'self' 'selves' (3rd person).

In English, the form of the verb may occasionally change depending on which person (in the grammatical sense) is used as subject (e.g. *I/you/we/they sing*, but *he sings*). In older English, and still today with the verb *to be*, there are further changes (e.g. *I/we/ye/they sing*, *thou singest, he singeth*; *I am, you/we/they are, he is*). In Old Norse each person, singular and dual/plural, by and large has its own distinctive verbal inflexion. Thus if we wish to render 'I judged' in Old Norse, we must say *ek dæmða*, but 'you [sg.] judged' is *þú dæmðir*, 'he judged' *hann dæmði*, 'we [pl.] judged' *vér dæmðum*, 'you [pl.] judged' *(þ)ér dæmðuð*, 'they [m.] judged' *þeir dæmðu*. Note that it is the person and number of the **subject** that determines the form of the verb. Further that it is only **person** in conjunction with the **singular : plural distinction** that triggers this verbal agreement (on the concept of agreement, see 3.3.1); the gender of 3rd person subjects never affects the form of the verb, nor does the dual : plural distinction ('she judged' is thus *hon dæmði*, 'we two judged' *vit dæmðum*, 'you two judged' *(þ)it dæmðuð*, 'they [f.] judged' *þær dæmðu*, etc.)

3.6.2 Tense

Tense is a difficult concept to define. In the broadest sense it refers to the way in which a verb marks the time at which whatever it denotes takes place. The relationship between tense and time is, however, anything but clear-cut. Thus, what is generally agreed to be the past tense in English (alternatively known as the preterite or imperfect) may express a counter-factual rather than a temporal sense (e.g. *if I **knew** — but I don't*), and what is accepted as the present may refer to the future (e.g. *Helen **performs** there tomorrow*), the past (e.g. *I **hear** that you plan to move*) or a regular occurrence (e.g. *the sun **rises** in the east*). Nor do the problems end there. While we may express past time in English with the past tense (e.g. *David came yesterday*), and present time with the present (e.g. *I am bored*), there is no corresponding verb-form with which to express the future. Indeed, English has no other **morphological** tenses than the present and the past. Some argue that verb phrases like *shall come* and *will come* represent the English future tense, and further that *have come* represents the 'perfect' and *had come* the 'pluperfect'. Others go further and claim that *would come* and *should come* are 'conditional', but this is all rather far removed from English morphology. To be sure, *have come* and *had come* express something different from *came* and from each other (chiefly differences of time orientation), and *would come* does not mean the same as *will come*, but if tense is to be related solely or chiefly to meaning, the need for clarity requires the creation of a separate term to denote **tense-forms**, that is, variations in the morphology of the verb whose primary function is to signal temporal meanings.

The difficulty is, no such term obviously suggests itself. 'Tense' in the sense 'tense-forms', is well established, traditional usage. Since the lack of clarity arises from the application of the term to a variety of periphrastic (i.e. separate-word) constructions that express meanings similar or identical to those expressed by tense-forms, it seems better to choose different terms for the periphrastic constructions. Verb phrases with temporal and related meanings that are not simple tense-forms will accordingly be described as 'phrases' or 'constructions', and, where necessary, terms like 'perfect construction', 'future construction', etc. will be used.

All Germanic languages share with English the minimal tense system outlined above — using 'tense' in the sense just defined. Old Norse thus exhibits a contrast between present and past tense inflexions, but has no set of endings whose primary purpose is to mark the future, in contrast to French or Latin, for example. Nor does it have individual inflexions for the perfect, the pluperfect or any other of the wide range of tenses that may be found in some other languages. In place of such tenses, much as English, it employs periphrastic constructions involving what are called auxiliary verbs (i.e. ones subordinate to the main verb, which express mood, voice, time orientation etc.). English *I have* (aux.) *killed* (main) *the vikings* thus has its Old Norse counterpart in *ek **hefi drepit** víkingana*, and *I will* (aux.) *kill* (main) *the vikings* in *ek **mun drepa** víkingana* (see further 3.6.7, 3.9.7.1).

The past is distinguished from the present in Old Norse in much the same way as in English: either by root vowel change (e.g. Old Norse *ek tek* — *ek tók*, English *I take* — *I took*) or the suffixation of *-ð*, *-d* or *-t* (e.g. Old Norse *ek fylgi* — *ek fylgða*, English *I follow* — *I followed*; note, regarding the varying form of the suffix in Old Norse, that what is written 'ed' in English is not always pronounced as a simple *d*, cf. *voted*, *walked*). Traditionally these two types of past tense formation are known as **strong** and **weak**. As in the case of noun and adjective inflexion, the terms themselves have no special significance, and one could as easily speak of 'type A' and 'type B'.

A further difference between present and past, as *fylg**i*** versus *fylgð**a*** indicates, lies in some of the personal inflexions, but this is of secondary importance compared with the root vowel alternation or the presence or absence of the *-ð/-d/-t* suffix. The vowel alternation and the occurrence or otherwise of the suffix affect all forms of the tense concerned and are more immediately obvious. Some of the personal inflexions, on the other hand, are identical in both tenses (e.g. *þú fylg**ir*** 'you follow' — *þú fylgð**ir*** 'you followed', and cf. *tek* — *tók* above with zero ending).

3.6.3 Mood

Mood is sometimes known as 'modality', and refers in its broadest sense to the attitude of a speaker or writer to what s/he is saying. Mood is thus concerned with matters like certainty, vagueness, possibility, will, obligation, etc. and the ways in which they may be expressed. In English, modal auxiliaries (subordinate verbs expressing mood, cf. 3.6.2) like *ought*, *shall*, *may*, etc. are widely used to convey such attitudes, and that is also the case in Old Norse. To a limited extent, English may also employ inflexion, i.e. in addition to indicating person, number and present or past tense, forms of the verb may suggest something about the speaker's or writer's attitude to what is being said. In the sentence:

>He **goes** every day

the 'going' is presented as factual — as taking place — whereas in:

>I suggest that he **go**

the 'going' is merely something that is envisaged. Similarly, in:

>I **was** single then

the speaker or writer presents his/her unmarried status at a time in the past as fact. In:

>If I **were** single . . .

on the other hand, the presupposition is that the speaker/writer is married, and the counter-factual sense of the hypothesis is (in part) conveyed by the form of the verb. Both *was* and *were* are 1st person singular past tense forms of *to be* in English, but they indicate different attitudes to the truth value of what is said on the part of speaker or writer. *Was*, as also *goes* in the previous pair of examples, represents what is known as the **indicative** mood, *were*, together with *go* in the previous pair, the **subjunctive**.

Beyond these cases (3rd person singular present of most verbs and 1st (and 3rd) singular past of *to be*), there is little of mood inflexion in English. In Old Norse, in contrast, each verb has two full sets of endings. As in English, indicative endings are used by and large in sentences where the predicate denotes something regarded by the speaker/writer as factual or certain. Subjunctive endings are found chiefly in sentences where the predicate denotes something regarded by the speaker/writer as hypothetical: a wish, request, instruction, supposition, possibility, etc. In addition, Old Norse has an **imperative** mood (used for commands — see below), but this only manifests itself in the 2nd person singular (some have reckoned with 1st and 2nd pl. imperatives, but these are distinctive usages, not forms). Contrastive examples, illustrating differences between indicative, subjunctive and imperative forms in the present tense and indicative and subjunctive forms in the past (there is no past imperative) are: *þú kastar* 'you throw' (indic.) — *nema þú kastir* 'unless you throw' (subj.) — *kasta (þú)* (or: *kastaðu*, cf. 3.2.1) 'throw!' (imp.); *þeir dæmðu* 'they judged' (indic.) — *þó þeir dæmði* 'though they judged' (subj.).

3.6.4 Voice

Voice is a term used to denote the way in which the relationship between the subject and the object of a verb is expressed. The main distinction in many languages, and the only one it is useful to make in Old Norse, is between **active** and **passive**. If in English we say *John hit him*, the subject is also the agent (i.e. John is the one who does the hitting, cf. 3.1.5, sentence 1). But we may turn the sentence round, as it were, and say *he was hit* (*by John*), where the subject, 'he', is the goal of the action, or the 'patient', and the agent appears (optionally) in a preposition phrase (cf. 3.7). The first type of construction is known as active and the second as passive.

Old Norse forms passive verb phrases in much the same way as English (e.g. *þeir halda hátíð mikla* 'they hold a great festival' (act.) — *hátíð mikil er haldin* 'a great festival is held' (pass.); *þeir nefndu hann Óláf* 'they named him Óláfr' (act.) — *hann var nefndr Óláfr* 'he was named Óláfr' (pass.)). Morphologically, such passives are periphrastic: the main verb does not itself inflect for voice, rather we have the appropriate form of the present or past tense of the verb *vera* '[to] be' used as an auxiliary in combination with the past participle of the main verb, which inflects as an adjective (*haldin*, nom. f. sg., agrees with *hátíð*, *nefndr*, nom. m. sg., agrees with *hann*, cf. 3.3.1). (See further 3.9.7.2.)

Old Norse does, however, possess an inflexion that sometimes has passive function. This is the *-sk* form of the verb (so-called because in most manifestations it consists of an *-sk* added to the appropriate verbal ending). It would be misleading, however, to consider the *-sk* a passive form since it more commonly appears with other functions (see 3.6.5.3). Examples of passive usage are: *hann fyrirdœmisk af illum mǫnnum* 'he is condemned by wicked men', *á hans dǫgum byggðisk Ísland* 'in his days Iceland was settled', *hann fannsk eigi* 'he was not found' 'he could not be found'. *Fyrirdœmi**sk*** 'is condemned' contrasts with *fyrirdœmir* 'condemns', *byggði**sk*** 'was settled' with *byggði* 'settled' and *fann**sk*** 'was found' with *fann* 'found'.

3.6.1/3.6.2/3.6.3/3.6.4 Person and number/Tense/Mood/Voice — Exercise

1. In what ways do person and number affect the form of the verb in Old Norse?
2. How many tenses may the Old Norse verb be said to have, and why?
3. How is the past tense distinguished from the present in Old Norse?
4. How is the subjunctive mood marked in Old Norse, and what are its chief functions?
5. To what extent can the passive voice be expressed by inflexions in Old Norse?

3.6.5 Basic verb inflexions

Having introduced the main categories of the Old Norse verb, we will now present the basic inflexions by which these categories are expressed. The emphasis is on 'basic'. As in the case of nouns, pronouns and adjectives, it is important for the learner not to lose sight of the wood for the trees. Deviations from the basic patterns are not infrequent, but there is little point in trying to learn those until the essentials have been mastered. In any case, it will often be possible to recognise an irregular form for what it is once one has become familiar with the underlying system. (For students keen to see the full range of inflexions, the grammars cited in the preamble to 3.1.4 are recommended.)

3.6.5.1 Endings

This section sets out the inflexions that are attached to the verbal root, i.e. the personal endings and the past tense suffix of weak verbs (see 3.6.2). Because strong verbs lack a past tense suffix and some of their personal forms are different from those of the weak verbs, it is clearest to provide separate tables for the two types. The student should observe, however, that the majority of personal endings are common to both strong and weak verbs. With either type, each tense potentially has six different endings for the indicative and six for the subjunctive (three persons, 1st, 2nd and 3rd, times two numbers, singular and plural), and also the 2nd sg. present imperative. In reality the number is smaller because the same form can occur in more than one position. The endings are as follows (~ = zero, i.e. there is no ending, the form consisting of root alone (e.g. *ek* **tek** 'I take', *hon* **tók** 'she took'); actual paradigms are given in 3.6.10).

	Strong verbs	
	Indicative	**Subjunctive**
1st sg. pres.	~	-a
2nd sg. pres.	-r	-ir
3rd sg. pres.	-r	-i
1st pl. pres.	-um	-im
2nd pl. pres.	-ið	-ið
3rd pl. pres.	-a	-i
1st sg. past	~	-a
2nd sg. past	-t	-ir
3rd sg. past	~	-i
1st pl. past	-um	-im
2nd pl. past	-uð	-ið
3rd pl. past	-u	-i

Imperative (2nd sg. pres.)   ~

	Weak verbs	
	Indicative	**Subjunctive**
1st sg. pres.	~/-a/-i	-a
2nd sg. pres.	-r/-ar/-ir	-ir
3rd sg. pres.	-r/-ar/-ir	-i
1st pl. pres.	-um	-im
2nd pl. pres.	-ið	-ið
3rd pl. pres.	-a	-i
1st sg. past	-ða/-da/-ta	-ða/-da/-ta
2nd sg. past	-ðir/-dir/-tir	-ðir/-dir/-tir
3rd sg. past	-ði/-di/-ti	-ði/-di/-ti
1st pl. past	-ðum/-dum/-tum	-ðim/-dim/-tim
2nd pl. past	-ðuð/-duð/-tuð	-ðið/-dið/-tið
3rd pl. past	-ðu/-du/-tu	-ði/-di/-ti

Imperative (2nd sg. pres.)   ~/-a

Verb inflexions and their function

Certain regularities and patterns will be observed in these paradigms.

(1) The 2nd and 3rd person sg. present indic. always end in -*r*; this is what distinguishes them from the 1st person, which either has no ending or a vowel (the same vowel, minus the following *r*, as is found in the 2nd and 3rd person).

(2) The 1st person pl. always ends in -*m*: -*um* in the indicative, -*im* in the subjunctive.

(3) The 2nd person pl. always ends in -*ð*: -*ið* in the present indicative and the subjunctive, -*uð* in the past indicative.

(4) The 3rd person pl. always ends in a vowel: -*a* in the present indicative, -*u* in the past indicative, -*i* in the subjunctive.

(5) The 1st person sg. ends in -*a* in most cases, the exceptions being the present indicative of many verbs, and the past indicative of strong verbs.

(6) The 2nd person sg. ends in -*ir* in most cases, the exceptions being the same as those noted in (5).

(7) The 3rd person sg. ends in -*i* in the past indicative of weak verbs and in the present and past subjunctive.

(8) The 1st person sg. present and past indicative of strong verbs has no ending.

(9) The subjunctive endings of the present and past tense are the same, except that in weak verbs they are preceded by an -*ð*, -*d* or -*t* suffix.

These are the essential verb endings of Old Norse. Certain variations on this pattern can be found, but if the student has mastered the above table s/he should be able to recognise the overwhelming majority of endings encountered.

3.6.5.1 Endings — Exercise

1. In what way does the ending of the 2nd and 3rd person sg. present indic. differ from that of the 1st?
2. Which verb-form ends in -*t*?
3. What endings does the 3rd person pl. exhibit, and in what forms are the different endings to be found?
4. What characterises all 1st person pl. endings?
5. Which verb-forms have zero ending?
6. In what ways do the indicative endings of strong and weak verbs differ?
7. What endings does the 2nd person pl. exhibit, and in what forms are the different endings to be found?
8. What characterises the subjunctive endings?

3.6.5.2 Vowel alternations

In order to grasp the grammatical function of individual verb-forms, and thus their sense, it is not sufficient simply to be familiar with the various endings. It is also necessary to know the fundamentals of the vowel alternations that occur in the root syllables of the majority of verbs. These are of different kinds. Some are readily predictable, others less so, and some are not predictable at all.

Wholly predictable is the change *a* > *ǫ* caused by labial mutation. It will have been seen that a number of verb endings contain or consist of *u*. As explained in relation to nouns and adjectives (3.1.7.1, 3.3.8.1), it is a rule of Old Norse that *a* cannot appear before *u* or *v*, but alters instead to *ǫ* in stressed syllables and to *u* in unstressed. Thus it is no surprise to find that although *kasta* '[to] throw', for example, has root *a*, the 1st pl. present indic. is (*vit/vér*) *kǫstum*, the 1st pl. past indic. (*vit/vér*) *kǫstuðum*, 2nd pl. past indic. (*þit/þér*) *kǫstuðuð*, 3rd pl. past indic. (*þeir*) *kǫstuðu*.

Front mutation (cf. 3.1.7.2, 3.3.8.2) also causes root vowel alternations in verbs. This too is predictable, but not directly from the verb-forms themselves since the conditioning factor has in many cases disappeared. All the student needs to know, however, is in which forms of which verbs to expect front mutation, and to be aware of the back : front correspondences arising from it.

The three parts of the verbal paradigm affected by front mutation are the entire present indicative and subjunctive of one class of weak verb, the singular present indicative of strong verbs, and the past subjunctive of all verbs with the exception of one weak class.

Weak verbs with a short root syllable (cf. 2.1.4) and a -*ja* infinitive (infinitive = the dictionary entry form, corresponding to the English 'to' form as in *to go*, *to hear*; see 3.6.6) have front mutation throughout the present tense (and also in the infinitive), but mostly revert to the original root vowel in the past indicative. Virtually all verbs of this type have either *a* or *u* in the past indicative, which mutates to *e*, *y* respectively in all other tensed forms (e.g. *hann velr* 'he chooses'— *hann valði* 'he chose', *ek spyr* 'I ask' — *ek spurða* 'I asked').

All strong verbs that are susceptible (i.e. those with original back root vowels) exhibit front mutation in the singular present indicative. The back : front correspondences that arise (contrasting 3rd pl. with 3rd sg.) are as follows:

a — e	(fara — ferr)	'go', 'goes'
á — æ	(gráta — grætr)	'weep', 'weeps'
o — ø	(sofa — søfr (> sefr))	'sleep', 'sleeps'
ó — œ	(blóta — blœtr)	'sacrifice', 'sacrifices'
ú — ý	(lúka — lýkr)	'end', 'ends'
ǫ — ø	(hǫggva — høggr)	'strike', 'strikes'
au — ey	(hlaupa — hleypr)	'leap', 'leaps'
jó — ý	(skjóta — skýtr)	'shoot', 'shoots'
jú — ý	(fljúga — flýgr)	'fly', 'flies'

The last two examples illustrate a more complex process than straightforward front mutation: ?*jó > *jœ > *jý > ý and *jú > *jý > ý.

All disyllabic past subjunctive forms with original back root vowels exhibit front mutation. The back : front correspondences that arise (contrasting 3rd pl. indic. with 3rd pl. subj. unless otherwise stated) are as follows:

a — e	(valði (3rd sg.) — velði 'chose')	
á — æ	(báru — bæri 'carried')	
ó — œ	(fóru — fœri 'went')	
u — y	(brunnu — brynni 'burnt')	
jo — y	(bjoggu — byggi 'lived')	
jó — ý	(hljópu — hlýpi 'leapt')	

On the correspondences *jo — y* and *jó — ý*, see above.

Breaking (cf. 3.1.7.3) may also cause root vowel alternation in verbs. The plural present indicative and the present subjunctive of a small number of common strong verbs have the diphthong *ja*, while the singular present indicative has the original *e* (e.g. *þeir gjalda* 'they pay' — *hann geldr* 'he pays'). As with the workings of front mutation, the dichotomy is thus between the singular present indicative on the one hand and the rest of the present on the other, though here it is the latter that has undergone the change.

Strong verbs, as already noted, form their past tense by root vowel change. The alternations concerned, known as 'vowel gradation' or by the German term *Ablaut*, have nothing to do with mutation or breaking, but are a feature inherited from a pre-Germanic stage of language development. With its origin rooted so far back in linguistic history, the factors that shaped vowel gradation have long since disappeared, and there is therefore nothing like the *u* of labial mutation or even the historical *i* of front mutation to warn us what vowels to expect and when to expect them. The alternations concerned are not arbitrary, however, but conform to regular patterns, so as soon as one particular form of a strong verb is encountered, it is often possible to predict what the root vowels of all the other forms will be.

Here we are concerned with the present and past tenses. In these a maximum of three different gradation vowels are found, one throughout the present (subject to front mutation in the singular indicative and to breaking in the plural indicative and subjunctive), another in the singular past indicative, a third in the plural past indicative and the past subjunctive (the latter also subject to front mutation). In all, there are six regular gradation series, that is, ways in which root vowels may alternate, and a few minor patterns found only in a small number of verbs, albeit some quite common ones. One series, for example, has *í* in the present tense, *ei* in the sg. past indic., and *i* in the remaining past tense forms. If therefore we come across the sentence *hann greip sverð sitt* 'he grasped his sword', we may deduce (a) that *greip* is a singular past tense form (in the absence of the *-r* 3rd sg. present ending or the *-i* of the subjunctive, and noting that there is in any case no verb *greipa), and (b) that the root of the present tense will be *gríp-* and of the past plural and past subjunctive *grip-*. Another series has *a* in the present, *ó* throughout the past. An unfamiliar verb-form *fór* (there being no *fóra) may therefore be taken as singular past and its present root confidently assumed to be *far-*, but with front mutation in the singular present indicative (cf. *hon ferr* 'she goes', *þér farið* 'you [pl.] go', *hon fór* 'she went'). The six basic vowel gradation series have the following alternations in the present, past sg. indic., and past pl. indic./past subj. (front mutation forms are given in brackets):

(1) *í* —— *ei* —— *i*
(2) *jó/jú* (*ý*) —— *au* —— *u* (*y*)
(3) *e* —— *a* —— *u* (*y*)
(4) *e* —— *a* —— *á* (*æ*)
(5) *e* —— *a* —— *á* (*æ*)
(6) *a* (*e*) —— *ó* —— *ó* (*æ*)

It will be observed that (4) and (5) are identical. This is because a complete series also takes in the past participle (see 3.6.6), and there the root vowel of (4) and (5) does vary. As noted above, certain verbs which form their past tense by vowel change follow patterns other than the six just described. We find *a — e —e, á — é — é, au — jó — jó, ei — é — é* and variations on each. Most of the few verbs involved are very common, and it is probably sensible for the student to learn them individually as they are encountered.

In order to flesh out this rather abstract account, a verb illustrating each of the six series and the minor patterns is now provided; the forms are cited in the following order (the pl. past subj. has the same root vowel as the sg., and indeed the 3rd pl. has exactly the same form as the 3rd sg.; only the basic meaning(s) of the verb are given):

3rd sg., pl. present indic., 3rd sg., pl. past indic., 3rd sg./pl. past subj.

ríðr —— ríða —— reið —— riðu —— riði 'ride'
brýtr —— brjóta —— braut —— brutu —— bryti 'break'
dettr —— detta —— datt —— duttu —— dytti 'fall'
stelr —— stela —— stal —— stálu —— stæli 'steal'
drepr —— drepa —— drap —— drápu —— dræpi 'kill'
grefr —— grafa —— gróf —— grófu —— græfi 'dig'
fellr —— falla —— fell —— fellu —— felli 'fall'
ræðr —— ráða —— réð —— réðu —— réði 'advise' 'rule'
hleypr —— hlaupa —— hljóp —— hljópu —— hlýpi 'leap' 'run'
leikr —— leika —— lék —— léku —— léki 'play'

3.6.5.2 Vowel alternations — Exercise

1. Enumerate the different factors that cause root vowel alternation in the Old Norse verb.
2. Why does *kastar* have root vowel *a* and *kǫstum* root vowel *ǫ*?
3. Which three parts of the verbal paradigm are affected by front mutation?
4. Account for the difference in root vowel between *ráða* and *ræðr*, *brjóta* and *brýtr*, *taka* and *tekr* and *gjalda* and *geldr*.
5. Account for the difference in root vowel between *tóku* and *tæki*, *brutu* and *bryti* and *krǫfðu* and *krefði*.
6. What is meant by vowel gradation? What part does it play in the inflexion of strong verbs?

3.6.5.3 The -sk *form*

As indicated above (3.6.4), the *-sk* form of the verb consists for the most part of an *-sk* suffix added to existing endings. Where the final sound in an ending is *-r*, this is assimilated to the *s* and the resulting *ss* is then simplified (e.g. *finnsk* 'is found', 3rd sg. present indic., < **finnssk* < **finnrsk*). Where the final sound of an ending is *-ð* or *-t*, the juxtaposition with *s* is rendered *z* (e.g. *fæðizk* 'are brought up', 2nd pl. present indic., < **fæðiðsk*; cf. 2.1.3). This applies even where *ð* or *t* is juxtaposed to *s* after the assimilation of *r* as just outlined (e.g. *gezk* 'is begotten', 3rd sg. present indic., < *getsk* < **getssk* < **getrsk*).

In older texts the 1st person singular forms deviate from this pattern: they appear with an *-umk* ending attached to the plural root of the relevant tense and mood (e.g. *ek kǫllumk* 'I am called', with labially mutated root *kall-*, *ek ráðumk frá* 'I refrain from', with root *ráð-*, contrast *ek ræð* 'I advise'). 1st person *-sk* verbs are not very common at all, however, especially 1st person singular (and very rarely do they have passive sense either in the singular or plural, cf. *ráðumk* above).

In younger texts not only is the 1st person sg. *-umk* replaced by the 2nd/3rd person sg. form, but a bewildering variety of suffixes is found as well as or in place of *-sk*, *-umk*. The more common are *-zk* (which spreads from its original domain, cf. above), *-s*, *-z*, *-st* and *-zt*; hybrids such as 1st sg. *-umsk*, *-ums* also occur. Ultimately, the *-st* form replaces all the others, and is the one used in modern Icelandic, Faroese and Norwegian *nynorsk*.

Most normalised texts will use the forms set out in the table below, but even where that is not the case, or the student is confronted with an unnormalised text, there should be few problems of recognition. What needs to be remembered is, first: that *-umk*, *-sk*, *-zk*, *-s*, *-z*, *-st*, *-zt*, etc. are variant realisations of a single underlying form and choice of any particular one does not change the meaning; second: that in most cases the suffix — whichever is employed — will simply be attached to the verbal ending (e.g. *nefndisk* 'named him/herself' 'was named' consists of *nefn-di-sk*: root + 3rd sg. past ending + *-sk*); the exceptions to this rule have been described above.

With these reservations, the *-sk* form of the verb may be set out as follows. (Both personal and *-sk* endings are given; actual paradigms will be found in 3.6.10.)

Strong verbs

	Indicative	Subjunctive
1st sg. pres.	-umk	-umk
2nd sg. pres.	-sk	-isk
3rd sg. pres.	-sk	-isk
1st pl. pres.	-umsk	-imsk
2nd pl. pres.	-izk	-izk
3rd pl. pres.	-ask	-isk
1st sg. past	-umk	-umk
2nd sg. past	-zk	-isk
3rd sg. past	-sk	-isk
1st pl. past	-umsk	-imsk
2nd pl. past	-uzk	-izk
3rd pl. past	-usk	-isk

Imperative (2nd sg. pres.)   -sk

Weak verbs

	Indicative	Subjunctive
1st sg. pres.	-umk	-umk
2nd sg. pres.	-sk/-ask/-isk	-isk
3rd sg. pres.	-sk/-ask/-isk	-isk
1st pl. pres.	-umsk	-imsk
2nd pl. pres.	-izk	-izk
3rd pl. pres.	-ask	-isk
1st sg. past	-ðumk/-dumk/-tumk	-ðumk/-dumk/-tumk
2nd sg. past	-ðisk/-disk/-tisk	-ðisk/-disk/-tisk
3rd sg. past	-ðisk/-disk/-tisk	-ðisk/-disk/-tisk
1st pl. past	-ðumsk/-dumsk/-tumsk	-ðimsk/-dimsk/-timsk
2nd pl. past	-ðuzk/-duzk/-tuzk	-ðizk/-dizk/-tizk
3rd pl. past	-ðusk/-dusk/-tusk	-ðisk/-disk/-tisk

Imperative (2nd sg. pres.)   -sk/-ask

Although we are concerned in this section with form rather than function, a few lines on the use of the -*sk* form will not be amiss.

The Old Norse -*sk* verb is often termed the 'middle voice'. This is unhelpful because we are dealing here not with a voice in the sense of the active or passive (cf. 3.6.4), but with a verbal inflexion that has a variety of functions. One such is reflexive: the -*sk* suffix can often be the equivalent of the reflexive pronoun *sik* (e.g. *hann nefndi sik/nefndisk* 'he named himself'). It will be seen, however, that 'he named himself' or 'he called himself' overlaps semantically with 'he was named' 'he was called', and it is probably in constructions of this kind that -*sk* first came to take on a passive function. The -*sk* suffix can also have reciprocal function (e.g. *bítask* 'bite each other', *gefask* 'give each other'). In the case of many verbs, the addition of -*sk* simply imparts, or may impart, a different meaning from that of the simple form (e.g. *gera* '[to] do' — *gerask* '[to] become', *minna* '[to] remind' — *minnask* '[to] remember'). Some verbs only exist in an -*sk* guise (e.g. *óttask* '[to] fear'). For the learner the best procedure is probably to treat -*sk* verbs as separate words from their non-*sk* counterparts, until s/he has developed some feel for Old Norse. (See further 3.9.8.3.)

3.6.5.3 The -sk *form — Exercise*

1. Of what elements are the majority of -*sk* verb-forms composed?
2. What happens when the -*sk* suffix is added to a verbal ending in -*ð* or -*t*?
3. Why do we find the 3rd sg. present indic. -*sk* forms *kallask*, *teksk*, *nefnisk* and not *kallarsk, *tekrsk, *nefnirsk?
4. Where is the suffix -*umk* found, and what form of the verbal root is it attached to?
5. In what guises other than -*sk* and -*umk* does the -*sk* form of the verb appear?
6. Enumerate the principal functions of the -*sk* verb-form.

3.6.6 Finite and non-finite forms; principal parts

So far we have discussed only present and past tense forms of the verb. The reason for treating these separately, and first, is that they are central to every sentence. It was pointed out in 3.6 that the verb is the 'non-reducible part of the predicate', but it would be more precise to say that it is the **tensed** verb that is the essential element — and in Germanic languages that means a verb in the present or past tense. Thus we may attest in English: *he sings* and *he sang*, but not: *he sing, *he sung or *he singing. Nevertheless, *sing*, *sung* and *singing* are considered to belong to the same lexical item (dictionary word) as *sings* and *sang*, and to that extent to represent the same word class. In terms of function, however, *sing*, as in *to sing*, behaves more like a noun (compare *I want to sing* and *I want beer*, in which *to sing* and the noun *beer* occupy the same slot in the sentence), and *sung* and *singing* more like adjectives (compare *a sung chorus*, *the singing detective* and *a noisy chorus*, *the smart detective*, in which *sung*, *singing* occupy the same slots as the adjectives *noisy*, *smart*; note that *singing* may also be a pure noun as in *I like singing*, but then it is not considered part of the verb at all).

There is thus every reason to make a distinction between *to sing*, *sung* and *singing* on the one hand and *sings* and *sang* on the other. In grammatical description the former are commonly said to represent the non-finite parts of the verb, the latter the finite. This terminology is based on the observation that *sings* and *sang* make a contrast of tense; they are in one way or another bound by time. The same is not true of *to sing*, *sung* and *singing*, which are independent of time. That is perhaps not immediately obvious in the case of *sung* or *singing*. *Sung* appears to refer to the past (*I have sung mass*), and is even called a 'past participle'. Consider, however, *the hymn was/is/will be sung in unison*, where the time distinctions are not applicable to *sung*, but are in the finite verbs, *was/is/will*. *Singing* is even harder to connect with past, present or future. It is known as a 'present participle', but is in fact timeless (cf. *the singing detective*); in verb phrases of the type *was/is/will be singing*, it is again the finite verbs that provide the time reference.

Old Norse has the same non-finite forms as English, to wit: the infinitive — *at syngja* 'to sing', the past participle — *sunginn* 'sung', and the present participle — *syngjandi* 'singing'. Mention is occasionally made of a 'past infinitive', but the form concerned is in origin the 3rd pl. past indic. and its use as an 'infinitive' seems to have arisen through the recasting of certain finite clauses on analogy with common constructions that employ the standard infinitive. Very few 'past infinitive' forms are attested, in Old Norse prose only three regularly. The usage is illustrated in 3.9.4.

Being non-finite forms, the infinitive and the participles do not have verbal inflexion. The Old Norse infinitive is not inflected at all. It regularly ends in -*a*, to which the -*sk* form may be suffixed as appropriate (e.g., *berja* 'beat', *berjask* 'fight [literally: beat each other]'). The participles, as we have seen (3.3.9, paradigms 7, 11, 16, 19; also 3.3.6, sentences 1, 4, 7, 22), inflect as adjectives. The past participle of strong verbs has the adjectival -*in* suffix, that of weak the same -*ð*, -*d*, -*t* suffix as the past tense (e.g. *farinn*, *farit* 'gone', from *fara*, *krafðr*, *kraft* 'demanded', from *krefja*, strong nom. m. and nom./acc. n. sg. in both cases). The -*sk* inflexion is added to the nom./acc. n. sg. form in various periphrastic constructions (e.g. *hafa farizk* 'have perished' (*farit* + *sk*, with *ts* written *z*), *var sætzk* 'was come to terms [i.e. terms were agreed]' (*sætt* + *sk*)). The present participle is formed with an -*and* suffix, as shown in 3.3.9, paradigm 19. It does not normally take the -*sk* inflexion.

Although the non-finite verb-forms in terms both of inflexion and function are largely non-verbal, they are nevertheless, as noted above, considered to belong to the same word class as the finite. This is because it is counter-intuitive to view the present and past tense of any given verb as a separate word from the infinitive and the participles. The non-finite forms thus have their place in the verbal paradigm. Indeed, the infinitive is usually taken as the basic form — as the word itself, of which all the other manifestations are inflected parts. That is why the infinitive regularly appears as the dictionary entry form.

As we have seen, the endings of verbs in Old Norse and the root vowel alternations caused by labial and front mutation and breaking are predictable. This means that it is only necessary to cite a minimal number of basic forms for the student to be able to identify a particular verb-form s/he has encountered, i.e. to determine what verb it is part of and its person, number, tense and mood. These basic forms, known as 'principal parts', include the infinitive and the past participle. From the infinitive it is possible to deduce all the present tense forms (provided the person and number endings and the workings of labial and front mutation and breaking are known). From the 3rd sg. past indicative (or alternatively the 1st or 2nd person) all the past tense forms of weak verbs can be readily predicted. This is less true of strong verbs: many undergo vowel change between the singular and plural past indicative, so they need to be cited in both a singular and plural form; the past subjunctive of strong verbs, on the other hand, can be deduced from the plural indicative (once again, provided the inflexional basics are known). Finally, the past participle needs to be given since those of strong verbs usually exhibit further root vowel change; a few weak verbs, too, show irregular forms, but for the most part their participles are deducible from the past tense. We thus have a minimum of three principal parts for weak verbs and four for strong. Front-mutated present singular indicatives and past subjunctives may be included as optional extras, but these are non-essential. The decision whether or not to cite them will depend on how much help one thinks the learner needs.

This is how the system works. A strong verb like *rjúfa* 'break' 'violate' will be listed in a grammar or dictionary with its infinitive, *rjúfa*, the 3rd (or 1st) sg. past indic. *rauf*, 3rd (or 1st) pl. past indic. *rufu* (*rufum*), and pp. *rofinn* or *rofit* (the choice in the case of the pp. being between the strong nom. m. or nom./acc. n. sg. forms). From the infinitive, the present sg. indic. forms *rýf*, *rýfr* can be deduced by applying the appropriate endings and the rule: 'in the present sg. indic. strong verbs with back root vowels undergo front mutation'. All the other present tense forms will have root *rjúf-*. The 1st, 2nd and 3rd sg. past indic. have root *rauf-* with the *-t* ending added in the 2nd person. The 1st, 2nd and 3rd pl. past indic. have root *ruf-* plus the appropriate endings, and from this the subjunctive root *ryf-* can be deduced, to which the appropriate subjunctive endings are added. The participial root is *rof-*, which remains unchanged whatever the adjective ending.

A weak verb like *krefja* 'demand' will be listed with infinitive *krefja*, 3rd (or 1st) sg. past indic. *krafði* (*krafða*), and pp. *krafðr* or *kraft*. From the infinitive all the present tense forms can be deduced simply by adding the appropriate endings. (One will need to recognise the type of weak verb involved (see below) to know whether the indicative sg. endings are ~, *-a* or *-i* (1st), *-r*, *-ar* or *-ir* (2nd/3rd), but this variation is unlikely to cause problems of understanding to the reader of Old Norse.) From the 3rd or 1st sg. past indic. all the past tense forms can be deduced by applying the appropriate endings, the labial mutation rule, and the rule: 'all disyllabic past subjunctive forms with original back root vowels exhibit front mutation'. Thus, the pl. indic. root + *-ð* suffix of *krefja* will be *krǫfð-*, because all three plural endings begin with *u*;

the subjunctive root + -*ð* suffix will be *krefð-*, because *a* is a back vowel and thus susceptible to front mutation. The pp. root + suffix, *krafð-*, will undergo labial mutation like any other adjective (cf. 3.3.8.1), so we find that the strong dat. m. and nom. f. sg. forms, for example, are *krǫfðum* and *krǫfð* respectively.

In the case of the majority of weak verbs, which, unlike *krefja*, have the same root vowel in the past indic. as in the present, often only the past suffix (with 'connecting vowel' where appropriate; see below) is given in addition to the infinitive (e.g. *kalla* (*að*) 'call', *hefna* (*d*) 'avenge', *œpa* (*t*) 'shout'). From this minimal information all forms of the verb concerned are deducible. *Kalla* undergoes only labial mutation of the root vowel since it is trisyllabic (a three-syllable word) in the past tense; *hefna* and *œpa* already have a front-mutated root vowel and this cannot undergo further mutation.

Having now established what the principal parts of strong and weak verbs are, and how any form of a given verb may be deduced from these, we conclude this section by listing the principal parts of a strong and weak verb of each major type, and then explaining more fully what is meant by 'type' of weak verb. The principal parts of each verb are listed in the following order (those in brackets are optional, see above; the pp. is given in the strong nom. m. sg. form):

inf., indic. (3rd sg. pres.), 3rd sg. past, 3rd pl. past, (subj. 3rd sg./pl. past), pp.

Strong verb type 1: *bíta* 'bite'
bíta —— bítr —— beit —— bitu —— biti —— bitinn

Strong verb type 2: *skjóta* 'shoot'
skjóta —— skýtr —— skaut —— skutu —— skyti —— skotinn

Strong verb type 3: *bresta* 'burst'
bresta —— brestr —— brast —— brustu —— brysti —— brostinn

Strong verb type 4: *bera* 'bear'
bera —— berr —— bar —— báru —— bæri —— borinn

Strong verb type 5: *reka* 'drive'
reka —— rekr —— rak —— ráku —— ræki —— rekinn

Strong verb type 6: *fara* 'go'

fara —— ferr —— fór —— fóru —— færi —— farinn

Minor strong verb types:
falla 'fall', *gráta* 'cry', *hlaupa* 'leap' 'run', *leika* 'play'

falla —— fellr —— fell —— fellu —— felli —— fallinn
gráta —— grætr —— grét —— grétu —— gréti —— grátinn
hlaupa —— hleypr —— hljóp —— hljópu —— hlýpi —— hlaupinn
leika —— leikr —— lék —— léku —— léki —— leikinn

Weak verb type 1: *krefja* 'demand'

krefja —— krefr —— krafði —— krǫfðu —— krefði —— krafðr

Weak verb type 2: *kalla* 'call'

kalla —— kallar —— kallaði —— kǫlluðu —— kallaði —— kallaðr

Weak verb type 3: *heyra* 'hear'

heyra —— heyrir —— heyrði —— heyrðu —— heyrði —— heyrðr

The three types of weak verb differ in a number of ways. For the learner what will be most noticeable is: type 1 has root vowel change between the present and past indic. (*krefja — kr**a**fði*) and no vowel in the sg. present indic. endings (*hann krefr*); type 2 has a 'connecting vowel' *a* in the past tense (*kall**a**ði*) and *a* in the sg. present indic. endings (*hann kall**a**r*); type 3 has the same root vowel throughout, no connecting vowel in the past tense and *i* in the sg. present indic. endings (*hann heyr**i**r*). The three distinct past tense suffixes, *-ð*, *-d* and *-t*, are distributed not according to type of verb, but phonetic environment, so that *ð* occurs after vowels and most voiced consonants (*kallaði*, *fáði* 'coloured', *krafði*, *heyrði*), *d* chiefly after *n* (*hefndi* 'avenged'), and *t* after unvoiced consonants (*vakti* 'wakened', *æpti* 'shouted'). In the earliest texts *þ* is found after unvoiced consonants, and from the late thirteenth century onwards *d* replaces *ð* after certain voiced consonants, particularly *l* and *m* (*valði/valdi* 'chose', *dæmði/dæmdi* 'judged').

3.6.6 Finite and non-finite forms; principal parts — Exercise

1. What essential differences are there between finite and non-finite verb-forms?
2. What non-finite verb-forms are found in Old Norse?
3. What is meant by the 'principal parts' of an Old Norse verb, and why are these important?
4. Look up the verb *hljóta* in an Old Norse dictionary or in the Glossary in *NION* III. Give the four basic principal parts and thereafter the 1st person sg. present indic., the 3rd pl. present indic. and subj., the 2nd pl. past indic., and 3rd pl. past subj.
5. Look up the verb *verja* '[to] defend'. Perform the same operation as for *hljóta* in question 4.
6. How many types of strong and weak verb are there in Old Norse?
7. What distinguishes the different types of weak verb?
8. What determines the form of the past tense suffix of weak verbs?

3.6.7 Preterite presents and other irregular verbs

The preterite present verbs of Old Norse form a small but important class — important because virtually all its members are extremely common. The majority are modal auxiliaries (verbs subordinate to the main verb, which express mood, e.g. English *I* **would** *come*, *she* **might** *go*; cf. 3.6.3). The term 'preterite present' reflects the fact that verbs of this type have strong past tense forms in the present; in the past they inflect for the most part like weak verbs, though not all of them have the dental suffix associated with weak inflexion. The reason for the preterite present aberration lies in linguistic pre-history. Put at its most simple, the Germanic past tense is a development of an earlier perfect, which expressed completed action or the state obtaining after the action. While the perfects of most verbs happily made the transition to past, those of what became the preterite presents seem so firmly to have expressed present state that they were ultimately absorbed into the present tense by the creation of new (weak) past tense forms. Thus, ON *vita* 'know' is related to Latin *vidēre* 'see' 'perceive', and *hon veit* 'she knows' (cf. past tense *beit* 'bit', *leit* 'looked', etc.) must derive from a form that originally meant something like 'she has perceived'.

The principal parts of the preterite presents are listed in the following order (the pp. is given in the strong nom./acc. n. sg. form, for some verbs the only one used; note the infinitives *munu* and *skulu*, modelled on the 3rd pl. present indic., which in virtually all verbs has the same form as the infinitive):

inf., 3rd sg., pl. pres. indic., 3rd sg. pres. subj., 3rd sg. past indic., subj., pp.

eiga 'own'
eiga — á — eigu — eigi — átti — ætti — átt

kunna 'know' 'understand'
kunna — kann — kunnu — kunni — kunni — kynni — kunnat

mega 'be able to'
mega — má — megu — megi — mátti — mætti — mátt/megat

muna 'remember'
muna — man — munu — muni — mundi — myndi — munat

munu 'will' 'shall' (denoting future time or uncertainty)
munu — mun — munu — muni/myni — mundi — myndi — (lacking)

skulu 'shall' (denoting obligation or intention)
skulu — skal — skulu — skuli/skyli — skyldi — skyldi — (lacking)

unna 'love'
unna — ann — unnu — unni — unni — ynni — unnt/unnat

vita 'know'
vita — veit — vitu — viti — vissi — vissi — vitat

þurfa 'need'
þurfa — þarf — þurfu — þurfi — þurfti — þyrfti — þurft/þurfat

Two verbs not historically preterite presents have something in common with the above. They are *vilja* 'wish' 'want', a weak modal auxiliary with (in later texts) 2nd sg. present indic. in *-t* like the other preterite presents, and *vera* 'be', a highly irregular strong verb basically of type 5 but with preterite-type forms in the present indic. (2nd sg. *ert*, 2nd, 3rd pl. *eruð, eru*; note also 1st sg. *em*). Of *vilja* the same principal parts are given as for the preterite presents above; of *vera* the same plus the 3rd pl. past indic. (cf. the principal parts of strong verbs in 3.6.6 above):

vilja — vill — vilja — vili — vildi — vildi — viljat
vera — er — eru — sé — var — váru — væri — verit

In addition to the above, there is a small group of common verbs that have regular strong present tense forms, but a past whose root undergoes radical change, metamorphosing to initial consonant(s) + *er* or *ør*, to which weak endings are attached. The pp. has the same root as the infinitive and the *-in* participial suffix of a strong verb. The verbs concerned are *gnúa* 'rub', *gróa* 'grow', *róa* 'row', *sá* 'sow', *snúa* 'turn'. Two examples will suffice (citing the same principal parts as for the preterite presents above).

róa — rær — róa — rói — reri/røri — reri/røri — róit
snúa — snýr — snúa — snúi — sneri/snøri — sneri/snøri — snúit

Finally, the principal parts of *valda* 'cause', *gøra/gera* 'do' 'make', *hafa* 'have' and *verða* 'become' are given, the first because it is highly irregular (with strong forms in the present, a radically altered root and weak endings in the past), the latter three because they are extensively used in a variety of constructions (*hafa* and *verða* often as auxiliaries) and exhibit certain forms that may not be wholly transparent. For *valda*, *gøra/gera* and *hafa*, with weak pasts, it is enough to cite inf., 3rd sg. pres. indic., 3rd sg. past indic. and subj., and pp. (for *gøra/gera* with root vowel change only in the pp. fewer forms would in fact do); for *verða*, the full complement of strong verb principal parts is given (cf. 3.6.6). The pp. is in each case in the strong nom./acc. n. sg. form.

valda —— veldr —— olli —— ylli —— valdit
gera —— gerir —— gerði —— gerði —— gǫrt
hafa —— hefr/hefir —— hafði —— hefði —— haft
verða —— verðr —— varð —— urðu —— yrði —— orðit

3.6.7 Preterite presents and other irregular verbs — Exercise

1. What is the meaning of the term 'preterite present'?
2. What inflexional features characterise preterite present verbs?
3. What function do many preterite present verbs have?
4. Study the principal parts of *kunna* (above), and then give the following forms: 2nd person sg. and pl. present indic., 1st pl. present subj., 3rd pl. past indic. and subj.
5. What forms do *vilja* and *vera* have in common with preterite present verbs?
6. What is unusual about the inflexion of (a) *gróa*, (b) *valda*, (c) *hafa*?

3.6.8 Examples of verb usage

Following the same procedure as for other word classes, examples are now given of verbs in function. With the vast range of verbal forms and functions that exists, only a selection can be illustrated, with the emphasis on the most common types. Equally, because so many different features are involved — person and number, tense, mood, voice, *-sk* forms, periphrastic constructions — and several features combine in the one verb phrase, it has proved difficult to order the examples in any meaningful way. Note that the verbal inflexions being illustrated (or the whole word where there is no difference from the root of the infinitive or an inflexion cannot easily be discerned) are printed in bold type. To underline the grammatical relations involved, bold is also used for the subject, which triggers the person and number form in the verb. Compare the inflexions used below with those set out and discussed in 3.6.5, 3.6.6 and 3.6.7.

(1) **Hann** b**ýr** ferð sína ok f**ór** til Nóregs
'He prepares journey REFL. POSS. and went to Norway'
'He gets ready to depart and went to Norway'

Býr is 3rd sg. present indic. of the strong verb *búa* (minor type). *Fór* is 3rd sg. past indic. of the strong verb *fara* (type 6). Indicative is used because factual statements are being made about what happened. The abrupt change from present to past tense is characteristic of Old Norse prose style.

(2) **Jarl** svar**ar** ok b**að** konung gef**a** sér frest at hugs**a** þetta mál
'Earl answers and bade king give self respite to consider this matter'
'The earl answers and asked the king to give him time to consider this matter'

Svarar is 3rd sg. present indic. of the weak verb *svara* (type 2). *Bað* is 3rd sg. past indic. of the strong verb *biðja* (type 5, but with root *i* in the inf. and present tense, see 3.6.9.1 point (5)). Indicative is used in both cases because factual statements are being made about what happened. *Gefa* is an infinitive, a complement of *bað*; it has no overt subject, but *konung*, the object of *bað*, functions as covert (understood) subject (i.e. it is the king who is to do the giving; see further (24) below and 3.9.4). *Hugsa* is likewise an infinitive, a complement of *frest*; again there is only a covert subject: the earl (i.e. it is he who is to do the considering).

(3) **Þorfinnr** vi**ssi** eigi, at **Brúsi** hafð**i** upp gef**it** ríki sitt
'Þorfinnr knew not that Brúsi had up given realm REFL. POSS.'
'Þorfinnr did not know that Brúsi had surrendered his realm'

Vissi is 3rd sg. past indic. of preterite present *vita*. *Hafði* is 3rd sg. past indic. of weak *hafa* (type 3, but irregular, see 3.6.7); together with the pp. *gefit*, from *gefa* (strong type 5), it forms a so-called 'past perfect' construction, the equivalent of English 'had given' (the strong nom./acc. n. sg. form of the pp., when used in perfect and past perfect constructions, is known as the supine, see 3.9.7.1). On the use of the indicative mood, see (1) and (2) above.

(4) Skil**ðusk þeir** með kærleikum
'They parted with friendship'

Skilðusk is 3rd pl. past indic. of weak *skilja* (type 1) with the *-sk* suffix (*skilðu + sk*). On the use of the indicative, see (1) and (2) above. *Skilja* means 'separate' 'divide'; the *-sk* form imparts a reciprocal sense: 'they separated (from) each other'.

(5) Eptir þat sef**ask Rǫgnvaldr**
'After that Rǫgnvaldr calms down'

Sefask is 3rd sg. present indic. of weak *sefa* (type 2) with the *-sk* suffix (*sefar + sk* with assimilation *rs > ss* and simplification *ss > s* in unstressed position (see 3.6.5.3)). On the use of the indicative, see (1) and (2). *Sefa* means 'soothe' 'calm'; the *-sk* form is probably in origin a reflexive ('calms himself'), but it can also be conceived as passive ('is soothed'), and thus illustrates how the function of the *-sk* form could develop from reflexive to passive.

(6) **Sumir menn** segja, at **hann** hafi fallit
'Some men say that he has fallen'

Segja is 3rd pl. present indic. of weak *segja* (type 3, but with vowel change in the past tense, see 3.6.9.2 point (5)). *Hafi* is 3rd sg. present subj. of weak *hafa* (see (3)); together with supine *fallit*, from *falla* (strong minor type), it forms a perfect construction (see (3)). Observe the difference between the use of the indicative and subjunctive: that 'men say' is what the writer reports as fact; that 'he has fallen' is not what the writer says, but what he claims other people say, and thus from the writer's point of view no longer a statement of fact.

(7) Ef þú vill eigi ger**ask** minn maðr, þá **er sá annarr kostr**, at **ek** setja þann mann yfir Orkneyjar, er **ek vil**.
'If you will not make-*sk* my man, then is that other choice, that I put that man over Orkneys whom I want'
'If you are not willing to become my man, then the alternative is that I put whatever man I want in charge of the Orkneys'

Vill is 2nd sg. present indic. of weak *vilja* (type 1, but irregular, see 3.6.7 and 3.6.9.1 point (11)); together with inf. *gerask*, *-sk* form of weak *gera* 'do' 'make' (type 3, but irregular, see 3.6.7), it forms a modal construction (see 3.6.3). *Gerask* has a different meaning from *gera*, though the origin of the sense 'become' can probably be sought in the reflexive 'make oneself'. *Er* is 3rd sg. present indic. of irregular *vera* (3.6.7). *Setja* is 1st sg. present subj. of weak *setja* (type 1, but with no vowel alternation between present and past, see 3.6.9.3). *Vil* is 1st sg. present indic. of *vilja* (see above); here, too, it functions as a modal, although not accompanied by an overt infinitive (the sense, however, is 'whom I want to put'). Observe the difference between the use of the indicative and subjunctive. In present tense conditional sentences beginning with *ef* 'if' (see 3.8.2.4) the indicative is normally used even though no statement of fact is being made, hence *vill*. In the independent sentence which follows there is hardly a recording of fact either, rather a statement of the situation that will obtain if the condition is not fulfilled, but such sentences, too, have the indicative. *Setja*, however, denotes a wholly hypothetical action, and is accordingly subjunctive. With *vil* we are once again back with the indicative: the speaker's will is presented as real and immediate.

158   *Morphology and syntax*

(8)   **Hann** tó**k** til orða ok gn**eri** nefit
       'He took to words and rubbed nose-the'
       'He started to speak and rubbed his nose'

Tók is 3rd sg. past indic. of strong *taka* (type 6, but with root *e* in the pp., see 3.6.9.1 point (4)). *Gneri* is 3rd sg. past indic. of irregular *gnúa* (3.6.7). Both statements are factual and the indicative is therefore used.

(9)   Vár**u sumir** drep**nir**, **sumir** á braut rek**nir**
       'Some were killed, some driven away'

Váru is 3rd pl. past indic. of irregular *vera* (3.6.7); together with the pp.s *drepnir* and *reknir*, from *drepa* and *reka* (both strong type 5), it forms passive constructions, the equivalent of English 'were killed', '(were) driven' (in such constructions the pp. inflects as a strong adj. (see 3.6.4), here nom. m. pl., agreeing with the subjects *sumir . . . sumir*). For the use of the indicative, see (1) and (2).

(10)   Hef**ir þú** eigi heyr**t** þat, at **ek em** ekki vanr at bœt**a** þá menn fé, er **ek** læ**t** drep**a**
       'Have you not heard that, that I am not accustomed to compensate those men with-money whom I let kill'
       'Have you not heard that I am not accustomed to paying compensation for the men I cause to be put to death'

Hefir is 2nd sg. present indic. of weak *hafa* (type 3, but irregular, see 3.6.7); together with the supine *heyrt*, from *heyra* (weak type 3), it forms a perfect construction (see (3)). *Em* is 1st sg. present indic. of irregular *vera* (3.6.7). *Bœta* is an infinitive, a complement of *vera vanr* 'be accustomed'; its covert subject is the *ek* of the finite sentence: *ek em ekki vanr* (see (2)). *Læt* is 1st sg. present indic. of strong *láta* (minor type); it acts here as an auxiliary, and together with the infinitive (*drepa*, strong type 5) forms a construction with the sense 'cause to be killed' 'have killed'. Indicative is used throughout because nothing is presented as unreal or hypothetical; after verbs meaning 'hear', 'learn', 'discover', etc., the indicative is almost always found, the truth value of what is 'heard' being taken for granted; the unwillingness of the speaker to pay compensation and his propensity to have people killed are in no doubt.

(11)   **Norðmenn** ok **Danir** herj**uðu** mjǫk í vestrvíking ok k**ómu** optliga við eyjarnar, er **þeir** f**óru** vestr eða vestan, ok n**ámu** þar nesnám

'Norwegians and Danes harried much in west-viking and came often to islands-the when they went west or from-west, and took there headland-plunder'

'Norwegians and Danes made many raiding expeditions to the West and often called by the Orkneys when they were going west or (returning) east and plundered the headlands'

Herjuðu is 3rd pl. past indic. of weak *herja* (type 2). *Kómu*, *fóru* and *námu* are likewise 3rd pl. past indic., of strong *koma* (historically type 4, but highly irregular, see 3.6.9.3), *fara* (type 6) and *nema* (type 4). On the use of the indicative, see (1) and (2).

(12)   Fyrir ofdrambs sakar haf**ði hann** vill**zk** ok snú**izk** ífrá guði
       'For arrogance sake had he bewildered-*sk* and turned-*sk* from God'
       'Because of arrogance he had gone astray and turned from God'

Hafði is 3rd sg. past indic. of weak *hafa* (type 3, but irregular, see 3.6.7); together with the -*sk* supines *villzk* and *snúizk* (< *villt* + *sk*, from weak type 3 *villa*, *snúit* + *sk*, from irregular *snúa* (3.6.7), both with *ts* written 'z') it forms past perfect constructions (see (3)). Both the -*sk* forms are in origin probably reflexives ('led himself astray', 'turned himself'). On the use of the indicative, see (1) and (2).

(13)   Mun**tu** ok eigi vilj**a** vit**a** þat á þik, at **þú** ligg**ir** hér sem kǫttr í hreysi, þar er **ek** berj**umk** til frelsis hvárumtveggjum
       'Will-you also not want know that onto you, that you lie here like cat in cranny, there where I fight-*sk* for freedom for-both'
       'You will also not want to be accused of lying here like a cat in a cranny while I fight for the freedom of both of us'

Muntu (either *munt* + *þú* with assimilation *tþ* > *tt* and simplification *tt* > *t* after another consonant or *mun* + *þú* with loss of -*t* ending before *þú* and partial assimilation *nþ* > *nt*, see 3.2.1) is 2nd sg. present indic. of preterite present *munu*; together with infinitives *vilja* (weak type 1, but irregular, see 3.6.7, 3.6.9.1 point (11)) and *vita* (preterite present) it forms a double modal construction (i.e. two modal verbs 'will [future]' and 'want to' are involved). *Liggir* is 2nd sg. present subj. of strong *liggja* (type 5, but irregular, see 3.6.9.3). *Berjumk* is 1st sg. present of weak *berja* (type 1) with the -*umk* suffix (which replaces *-sk* in the 1st sg.). The *-sk* form of *berja* is in origin reciprocal ('beat each other'), but it comes to have the more general meaning 'fight' — in which 'each other' may or may not be understood. Of the three finite verbs in this example one is indic., one subj. and one indeterminate on the basis of form: *mun*(*t*) records what the speaker presents as fact, whereas *liggir* refers to a hypothetical event; *berjumk* is almost certainly indic. since the speaker is in no doubt about the fighting in which he will be involved.

(14) **Hverr vei**t, nema **ek** ver**ða** víða frægr
 'Who knows, but-that I become widely famous'
 'Who knows whether I may not become famous far and wide'

Veit is 3rd sg. present indic. of preterite present *vita*. *Verða* is 1st sg. present subj. of strong *verða* (type 3, but irregular, see 3.6.7). The first sentence contains a direct present-tense question introduced by an interrogative pronoun (*hverr*) and, like all sentences of this type, has a verb in the indicative. The second sentence is introduced by the conjunction *nema* which automatically triggers a subjunctive verb-form since it presupposes a hypothetical situation.

(15) Beið**ir** þá **Einarr**, at **Rǫgnvaldr** sk**yli** ráð**ask** til ferðar með þeim
 'Requests then Einarr that Rǫgnvaldr shall set-out-*sk* on journey with them'
 'Einarr then requests that Rǫgnvaldr should set out on the journey with them'

Beiðir is 3rd sg. present indic. of weak *beiða* (type 3). *Skyli* is 3rd sg. present subj. of preterite present *skulu*; together with inf. *ráðask*, *-sk* form of strong *ráða* 'advise', 'rule' (minor type), it forms a modal construction (see 3.6.3). *Ráðask* has various meanings, mostly different from those of *ráða*; the semantic development can often be hard to trace. *Beiðir* is indic. because it denotes what the writer regards as fact; *skyli*, in contrast, refers to what Einarr wants to happen, but which may or may not take place.

(16) Þá hr**uð**usk **skip** þeira Sigurðar ok Magnúss
 'Then cleared-*sk* ships their Sigurðr's and Magnús's'
 'Then Sigurðr's and Magnús's ships were cleared of men'

Hruðusk is 3rd pl. past indic. of *hrjóða* (strong type 2) with the *-sk* suffix. The sense of *-sk* here is clearly passive: some agency cleared the ships (i.e. killed those on board) but the goal of the action, 'ships', has been made subject and the agent is left unexpressed. On the use of the indicative, see (1) and (2).

(17)   Varð **engi uppreist** ímóti konungi gǫr
       'No rebellion was made against the king'

Varð is 3rd sg. past indic. of strong *verða* (type 3, but irregular, see 3.6.7); together with *gǫr*, pp. of *gøra/gera* (weak type 3, but irregular, see 3.6.7), it forms a passive construction (see (9)). *Verða*, as well as *vera*, may be used as the equivalent of English 'be' in passive verb phrases (see further 3.9.7.2). On the use of the indicative, see (1) and (2).

(18)   Þó at **þú** verð**ir** reiðr, þá **mældu** fátt
       'Though that you become angry, then speak-you little'
       'Though you become angry, yet say little'

Verðir is 2nd sg. present subj. of strong *verða* (type 3, see 3.6.7). The conjunction *þó at* or *þótt* (3.8.2.2), which introduces the first sentence, automatically triggers a subjunctive verb-form since it mostly presupposes a hypothetical situation. *Mældu* (*mæl* + *þú*, with partial assimilation *lþ* > *ld*, see 3.2.1) is the imperative of *mæla* (weak type 3) with the subject pronoun attached; it expresses an instruction.

(19)   Eigi **vil ek**, at **þit** hitt**izk** optarr
       'Not want I that you [dual] meet-*sk* more-often'
       'I do not want you two to meet again'

Vil is 1st sg. present indic. of weak *vilja* (type 1, but irregular, see 3.6.7, 3.6.9.1 point (11)). As a modal auxiliary, it is regularly followed by an inf., but here that is replaced by the dependent sentence *at þit hittizk*. *Hittizk* is 2nd pl. present of *hitta* (weak type 3) with the -*sk* suffix (*ðs* being written 'z'). The sense of -*sk* here is reciprocal: 'meet each other'. The mood of the verb cannot be deduced from the form, but it is almost certainly subj., determined by the sense of the preceding independent sentence: that which is wanted or wished for is hypothetical.

(20)   Ætl**aða ek** þá, at **ek** m**ynda** hvergi þess kom**a**, at **ek** m**ynda** þess gjald**a**, at **ek** vær**a** of friðsamr við óvini mína, en nú geld **ek** þess, er **ek** hef**i** þér grið gef**it**
       'Thought I then, that I would nowhere of-that come that I would for-that pay, that I was too peaceful towards enemies my, but now pay I for-that, that I have to-you quarter given'
       'I never thought then I would get into a situation where I would pay for being too easy on my enemies, but now I am paying for having given you quarter'

Ætlaða is 1st sg. past indic. of weak *ætla* (type 2). *Mynda* is 1st sg. past subj. of preterite present *munu*; together with infinitives *koma* (strong type 4 historically, but highly irregular, see 3.6.9.3) and *gjalda* (strong type 3, see 3.6.5.2) it forms modal constructions (3.6.3). *Væra* is 1st sg. past subj. of irregular *vera* (3.6.7). *Geld* is 1st sg. present indic. of strong *gjalda* (see above). *Hefi* is 1st sg. present indic. of weak *hafa* (type 3, but irregular, see 3.6.7); together with supine *gefit*, from *gefa* (strong type 5), it forms a perfect construction (see (3)). The three subjunctives, *mynda* (twice) and *væra*, all depend on *ætlaða* in the independent sentence: this is what the speaker thought would happen, but events have proved him wrong. With *geld*, we are back to statements the speaker presents as factual.

(21) **Hann** vei**tti** allri hirð sinni bæði mat ok mungát, svá at **menn** **þyrfti** eigi í skytning at gang**a**
      'He gave all his retainers both food and ale, so that men would not need to go to an inn'

Veitti is 3rd sg. past indic. of weak *veita* (type 3). *Þyrfti* is 3rd pl. past subj. of preterite present *þurfa*; together with inf. *ganga* (strong minor type) it forms a modal construction (see 3.6.3). Indic. *veitti* is used in what the writer presents as a statement of fact. The subjunctive *þyrfti* suggests a purpose rather than a result sentence: *svá at* 'so that' can mean either 'in order that' or 'with the result that' (see 3.8.2.2); the former is putative, normally requiring the subj., the latter factual, normally requiring the indic.

(22) Ef **hann v**æ**ri** heill at sumri, sa**gði hann**, at **þeir** sk**yldi** finn**ask**
      'If he were hale at summer, said he, that they should find-*sk*'
      'If he were alive when summer came, he said, they should meet'

Væri is 3rd sg. past subj. of irregular *vera* (3.6.7). *Sagði* is 3rd sg. past indic. of weak *segja* (type 3, but with vowel change in the past tense, see 3.6.9.2 point (5)). *Skyldi* is 3rd pl. past of preterite present *skulu*; together with inf. *finnask*, *-sk* form of strong *finna* 'find' (type 3, but irregular, see 3.6.9.2 point (2), 3.6.9.3), it forms a modal construction (see 3.6.3). The *-sk* form has reciprocal sense: 'find each other', and thus 'meet'. Indicative *sagði* presents what the writer regards as fact, namely that 'he' said the accompanying sentences. *Væri* conforms to the usage whereby past tense verbs in conditional sentences are almost always subjunctive (even when, as here, the condition is 'open', i.e. may or may not be fulfilled, and the past tense form is simply the reported speech equivalent of direct: 'if I am alive when summer comes'). The mood of *skyldi* cannot be deduced from the form, but it is certainly subj., referring to hypothetical circumstances dependent on the indirect-speech condition of *ef hann væri heill at sumri*.

(23) **Mun samþykki okkart** mest, at **vit** inn**imsk** lítt til um þann
 þriðjung landa
 'Will concord our [dual] greatest, that we allude-*sk* little to
 about that third of-lands'
 'Our concord will be greatest if we make little mention of
 that third of the country'

Mun is 3rd sg. present indic. of preterite present *munu*; *vera* 'be', with which it forms a modal construction, is omitted but understood (see 3.9.5.2). *Innimsk* is 1st pl. present subj. of weak *inna* (type 3) with the *-sk* suffix (*innim* + *sk*). The *-sk* form is in origin reciprocal: 'speak to each other'. Indicative *mun* expresses what the speaker regards as certain, subjunctive *innimsk* the hypothetical situation he envisages.

(24) Kall**aði hann** sér gef**it** haf**a** ver**it** þat ríki
 'Called he to-self given have been that realm'
 'He said that that realm had been given to him'

Kallaði is 3rd sg. past indic. of weak *kalla* (type 2). *Gefit* is the pp. of strong *gefa* (type 5), acc. n. sg., agreeing with *þat ríki*; together with *verit*, supine of irregular *vera* (3.6.7), it forms a passive construction (see (9)). *Verit* for its part joins with inf. *hafa* (weak type 3, but irregular, see 3.6.7) to form a perfect. We thus have a non-finite perfect passive construction. The lack of a finite verb arises because the complement of *kallaði* is what is known as an 'accusative and infinitive' clause — one that takes the object of the matrix verb as its subject. This is all somewhat complex, so a detailed analysis is now offered: *kallaði* (finite verb), *hann* (subject), *þat ríki* (direct object of *kallaði* and subject of *gefit*), *gefit hafa verit* (non-finite perfect passive construction), *sér* (indirect object of the infinitive clause, but coreferential with the subject of the independent sentence); a semi-literal translation is: 'he said that realm to have been given to himself'. (Some would argue that *sér* is subject of the infinitive clause and *þat ríki* object. These theoretical considerations need not concern the learner, but see 3.9.3. On acc. + inf. clauses, see further 3.9.4.)

(25) **Þér** skul**uð** nú frá mér þess mest njót**a**, er **þér** g**á**f**uð** mér líf
 ok leit**uðuð** mér slíkrar sœmðar sem **þér** m**áttuð**
 'You [pl.] shall now from me that most enjoy, that you [pl.]
 gave me life and sought for-me such honour as you [pl.] could'
 'What chiefly benefits you now as far as I am concerned is
 that you gave me my life and tried to show me as much honour as you could'

Skuluð is 2nd pl. present indic. of preterite present *skulu*; together with inf. *njóta* (strong type 2) it forms a modal construction (see 3.6.3). *Gáfuð* is 2nd pl. past indic. of strong *gefa* (type 5). *Leituðuð* is 2nd pl. past indic. of weak *leita* (type 2). *Máttuð* is 2nd pl. past indic. of preterite present *mega*; although not accompanied by an overt infinitive, it functions as a modal (the sense is 'as you could show me'). The indic. is used throughout because everything said is perceived by the speaker as factual.

3.6.8 Examples of verb usage — Exercise

1. In what different ways may the passive voice be expressed in Old Norse?
2. What are the principal factors that govern the choice between indicative and subjunctive?
3. What are the principal functions of the -*sk* form as revealed in the above examples?
4. What is meant by a 'covert subject'? Give an example.
5. In which of the above examples do modal constructions (modal auxiliary + inf.) occur? List all that you find.
6. In which of the above examples do passive constructions occur? List all that you find.
7. In which of the above examples do perfect and past perfect constructions occur? List all that you find.
8. Explain the following forms (i.e. state what inflexion or inflexions they have and the reasons for the inflexion(s)): *sefask* in example (5), *hafi fallit* (6), *váru drepnir* (9), *læt drepa* (10), *hafði snúizk* (12), *hruðusk* (16), *verðir* (18), *mældu* (18), *væri* (22), *máttuð* (25).

3.6.9 Important variations in verb inflexion

Difficulties in recognising verb-forms for what they are arise more from the irregularity of the principal parts than from the endings. Certainly, verb endings show the same degree of overlap and ambiguity as those of nouns and adjectives (3.1.6, 3.3.7), but they carry less meaning. Since in Old Norse the subject is virtually always expressed (unlike, say, in Latin or Italian), the endings are largely redundant for the purposes of denoting person and number. Thus in *hann drap tvá menn* 'he killed two men', we know that *drap* is 3rd sg. because that is the person and number of *hann*, the subject.

Other parts of the verbal system are equally transparent. Those who have studied the preceding sections will not fail to recognise *hann hafði drepit tvá menn* 'he had killed two men' as a past perfect construction and *tveir menn váru drepnir* 'two men were killed' as passive. The *-sk* suffix is also hard to confuse with any other ending (though occasional uncertainty may arise when it appears in its *-st*, *-zt* manifestations).

Less easy to spot is the difference between indicative and subjunctive mood. To get this right consistently the student will have to be familiar with the relevant endings, but quite often it is enough to recognise the form of the root (contrast *hann drap* 'he killed [indic.]' with *þótt hann dræpi* 'though he killed [subj.]'). How far it is essential to know whether a verb-form is indicative or subjunctive will depend on the context. As the examples in 3.6.8 show, the choice between the moods is sometimes automatic, sometimes dependent on meaning, though the differences of meaning can often be subtle and difficult to render in English.

In the light of these considerations, the deviations from the established patterns of verbal inflexion to be concentrated on here are chiefly those affecting principal parts. The presentation will be divided into three major sections. First, deviations that follow phonological rules the student can apply; second, unpredictable deviations that affect a group of verbs; third, idiosyncratic deviations.

3.6.9.1 Phonological variation

(1) In general, *v* is lost before rounded vowels. Strong type 3 *þverra* 'decrease', *verpa* 'throw', for example, have 3rd pl. past indic. *þurru*, *urpu* (past subj. root *þyrr-*, *yrp-*) and pp.s *þorrinn*, *orpinn* (cf. also *verða*, 3.6.7). Strong type 4 *vefa* 'weave' has pp. *ofinn*. Strong type 6 *vaða* 'wade', *vaxa* 'grow' have 3rd sg. and pl. past indic. *óð — óðu*, *óx — óxu* (past subj. root *æð-*, irregular *eyx-* or *yx-*).

(2) Strong verbs with vowel + *g* as the basic root have, or may have, a long monophthong and no *g* in the past sg. indic. Type 1 *stíga* 'step', for example, has 3rd sg. past indic. *sté* or *steig*, type 2 *fljúga* 'fly' has *fló* or *flaug*, type 5 *vega* 'kill' *vá*, type 6 *draga* 'drag' *dró*.

(3) Strong verb roots that end in *-d*, *-nd* and *-ng* undergo change to *-t*, *-tt* and *-kk* respectively in the imperative and the past sg. indic.

Type 3 *binda* 'bind' (on root vowel *i*, see 3.6.9.2 point (2)), *gjalda* 'pay', for example, have imp. *bitt*, *gjalt*, 3rd sg. past indic. *batt*, *galt*; minor types *ganga* 'walk', *halda* 'hold' have imp. *gakk*, *halt*, 3rd sg. past indic. *gekk*, *helt* (sometimes regular imp. forms are encountered — in the above cases: *bind*, *gjald*, *gang*, *hald*).

(4) Pp.s of type 6 and minor type strong verbs normally undergo front mutation of the root vowel when the root ends in -*g* or -*k*, e.g. *dreginn* from *draga*, *genginn* from *ganga*, *tekinn* from *taka* 'take'.

(5) Present roots of type 6 strong verbs undergo front mutation of the root vowel when *j* occurs before endings consisting of or beginning with *a* or *u*, e.g. *hefja* 'lift', *sverja* 'swear', 3rd sg. past indic. *hóf*, *sór* (see (1) above). Note also that the same conditions give root vowel *i* instead of *e* in type 5 strong verbs, e.g. *biðja* 'ask', *sitja* 'sit'.

(6) Pp.s of type 3 and 4 strong verbs have root vowel *u* rather than *o* when the immediately following consonant is *m* or *n*, e.g. *bundinn* from *binda* 'bind', *sprunginn* from *springa* 'spring' 'burst', *unninn* (see (1) above) from *vinna* 'work' (on root vowel *i*, see 3.6.9.2 point (2)), *numinn* from *nema* 'take'.

(7) Weak verbs undergo a number of consonantal assimilations and simplifications when the past tense and participial suffixes -*ð*, -*d*, -*t* are added. Such phonological adjustments are not restricted to verbs, but are found elsewhere in the language (see 3.1.7.4 point (1), 3.3.8.4 point (2), 3.3.8.5 point (2)). Verbs whose root ends in consonant + *ð*, *d* or *t* do not add a further *ð*, *d* or *t* to mark the past-tense or participial/ supine suffix, e.g. *virða — virði — virðr* 'value', *senda — sendi — sendr* 'send', *svipta — svipti — sviptr* 'deprive'. This applies equally when the root ends in *tt*, e.g. *rétta — rétti — réttr* 'straighten' 'stretch out'. Verbs whose root vowel is immediately followed by *ð* show assimilation *ðd > dd* in the past tense and past participle, e.g. *eyða — eyddi — eyddr* 'destroy', *gleðja — gladdi — gladdr* 'gladden'. The -*t* ending of the nom./acc. n. sg. of the pp. regularly amalgamates with the participial suffix (by processes of simplification or assimilation and simplification; see further 3.3.8.4 point (2) and 3.3.8.5 point (2)), e.g. *flutt* (< *flutt* + *t*) from *flytja* 'convey', *kastat* (< *kastað* + *t*) from *kasta* 'throw', *sent* (< *send* + *t*) from *senda*, *leyst* (< *leyst* + *t*) from *leysa* 'loosen', 'resolve', *hitt* (< *hitt* + *t*) from *hitta* 'meet'.

(8) As with nouns and adjectives (3.1.7.5 point (2), 3.3.8.5 point (4)), the vowels of endings tend to be dropped when they immediately

follow a long vowel of the same or similar quality. Thus weak type 3 *trúa* 'believe', for example, has a 1st pl. present indic. form *trúm* (< **trúum*)', *deyja* 'die' 3rd pl. past indic. *dó* (< **dóu*), *fá* 'get' 1st pl. present indic. *fám* (< **fáum*), *sjá* 'see' pp. *sénn* (< **séinn*) (these last three verbs are highly irregular and their principal parts are listed in 3.6.9.3).

(9) As with adjectives, *t* is lengthened when immediately following long, stressed vowels. Thus the 2nd sg. past indic. of strong type 1 *stíga* 'step' (see (2) above) is *stétt*, of *búa* 'prepare', 'dwell' (3.6.9.3) *bjótt*.

(10) Strong verbs whose root ends in *-ð* or *-t* suffer changes to these consonants in the 2nd sg. past indic. The *ð* assimilates to the *-t* ending (cf. (7) above), e.g. *reitt*, from strong type 1 *ríða* 'ride'. Where the root ends in *-t*, the usual ending is *-zt*, e.g. *bazt*, from strong type 3 *binda* 'bind' (3rd sg. past indic. *batt*, see (3) above; on root vowel *i* see 3.6.9.2 point (2)), *lézt*, from strong minor type *láta* 'let'. This latter change affects preterite present *vita* 'know' too (2nd sg. present indic. *veizt*). Some verbs with root final *-ð* may have the *-zt* ending as an alternative to *-tt*, e.g. *bazt* or *batt* from strong type 5 *biðja* (on root vowel *i*, see 3.6.9.1 point (5)). Some with root final *-t* may as an alternative add *t* in the normal way, e.g. *létt* from *láta* (see above), or have the same form as the 1st and 3rd sg. past indic., e.g. *helt* from strong minor type *halda* 'hold' (see (3) above). Strong verbs with root final *-st* have zero ending in the 2nd sg. past indic., e.g. *laust* from strong type 2 *ljósta* 'strike'.

(11) As in the case of nouns and adjectives (3.1.7.4 point (1), 3.3.8.4 point (1)), an *-r* ending may sometimes be assimilated to an immediately preceding *l*, *n* or *s*, e.g. 3rd sg. present indic. *vill* (< **vilr*), from irregular weak type 1 (3.6.7) *vilja* 'want', *skínn* (< **skínr*) from strong type 1 *skína* 'shine', *les*(*s*) (< **lesr*) from strong type 5 *lesa* 'gather', 'read'.

(12) The 2nd sg. past indic. *-t* ending of strong verbs is often dropped when the 2nd person pronoun immediately follows, e.g. *gekkt þú* or *gekk þú* 'you went', *tókt þú* or *tók þú* 'you took'.

(13) The 1st pl. *-m* ending is often dropped when the 1st person dual or pl. pronoun immediately follows, e.g. *tǫkum vit* or *tǫku vit* 'we two take', *tókum vér* or *tóku vér* 'we took'.

(14) The 2nd pl. *-ð* ending is often dropped when the 2nd person dual or pl. pronoun in the form *þit*, *þér* immediately follows, e.g. *takið þit* or *taki þit* 'you two take', *tókuð þér* or *tóku þér* 'you took'.

(15) The 3rd sg. present indic. -r ending of the verb þyk(k)ja 'seem' is often dropped when the dat. of the 1st or 2nd person sg. pronoun immediately follows, e.g. þyk(k)ir mér or þyk(k)i mér 'it seems to me'.

3.6.9.2 Morphological variation

(1) A few strong verbs of type 2 have present tense root vowel ú rather than jó or jú, e.g. lúta 'bend down', súpa 'sip'.

(2) Several strong verbs of type 3 have present tense root vowel i rather than e or ja, and a few have y or ø, e.g. binda 'bind', finna 'find', syngva/syngja (see (6) below) 'sing', søkkva 'sink'. The verbs with present tense i and y have root vowel u in the pp. (see 3.6.9.1 point (6)); those with present y and ø have root vowel ǫ in the past sg. indic., e.g. sǫng 'sang', sǫkk 'sank'.

(3) Some weak verbs of type 1 and type 3 have pp.s like those of type 2, e.g. hugaðr (or hugðr) from hyggja 'think' 'intend', viljat from vilja 'want', þorat from þora 'dare'. Many type 1 verbs have alternative pp. forms with connecting vowel -i-, e.g. barðr or bariðr 'beaten'. Because the nom./acc. n. sg. of the i-forms is identical with the nom./acc. n. sg. of the pp. of strong verbs (barit ~ farit), we also get analogical 'strong' pp.s of type 1 weak verbs, e.g. barinn nom. m. sg.

(4) A few weak verbs of type 3 have an -i ending in the imperative as well as zero, e.g. vak or vaki from vaka 'keep awake'. The imp. of þegja 'stay silent' is always þegi.

(5) The type 3 weak verbs segja 'say' and þegja (3rd sg. pres. indic. segir, þegir) have root vowel a in the past indic., e in the past subj., like type 1 verbs (3rd sg. sagði, þagði, segði, þegði respectively).

(6) As with nouns and adjectives (3.1.7.5 point (4), 3.3.8.5 point (5)), j may be found in some verbs before endings consisting of or beginning in a or u; in others v may be found before endings consisting of or beginning in a or i. With most verbs such insertions are found only in connection with the present root, but type 2 weak verbs have them throughout the paradigm. Examples are: svíkja 'betray' (strong type 1) — 1st pl. present indic. svíkjum — 3rd pl. past indic. sviku, syngva 'sing' (strong type 3, on root vowel y, see 3.6.9.2 point (2)) — 3rd pl. present subj. syngvi — 3rd pl. past subj. syngi, berja 'strike' (weak type 1) — 1st sg. past indic. barða, eggja 'incite' (weak type 2) — 3rd pl. past indic. eggjuðu

— supine *eggjat*, *bǫlva* 'curse' (weak type 2) — 3rd pl. past indic. *bǫlvuðu* — supine *bǫlvat*. Note that strong verbs with *v* insertion and *y* in the present tense root may alternatively have *j* insertion (e.g. *syngja*).

3.6.9.3 Idiosyncratic variation

A number of common verbs are irregular in varying degrees. While it would be possible to offer historical explanations for their irregularity and, where this has not already been done, assign them to one or other of the weak and strong types, it is easier for the learner simply to list their principal parts. For strong verbs inf., 3rd sg. and pl. past indic. and supine are given, for weak verbs inf., 3rd sg. past indic. and supine. Forms that cannot easily be deduced from these are described in the notes that follow, as are other peculiarities.

Strong verbs

blóta	*blét*	*blétu*	*blótit*	'sacrifice'
bregða	*brá*	*brugðu*	*brugðit*	'move'
búa	*bjó*	*bjoggu*	*búit*	'prepare', 'dwell'
deyja	*dó*	*dó*	*dáit*	'die'
draga	*dró*	*drógu*	*dregit*	'drag'
drekka	*drakk*	*drukku*	*drukkit*	'drink'
eta	*át*	*átu*	*etit*	'eat'
fá	*fekk*	*fengu*	*fengit*	'get'
fela	*fal*	*fálu*	*folgit*	'hide'
finna	*fann*	*fundu*	*fundit*	'find'
flá	*fló*	*flógu*	*flegit*	'flay'
fregna	*frá*	*frágu*	*fregit*	'ask', 'learn'
frjósa	*frøri*	*frøru*	*frørit*	'freeze'
ganga	*gekk*	*gengu*	*gengit*	'walk'
hanga	*hekk*	*hengu*	*hangit*	'hang'
heita	*hét*	*hétu*	*heitit*	'be called', 'promise'
hlæja	*hló*	*hlógu*	*hlegit*	'laugh'
hǫggva	*hjó*	*hjoggu*	*hǫggvit*	'strike', 'kill'
kjósa	*køri*	*køru*	*kørit*	'choose'
koma	*kom*	*kómu*	*komit*	'come'

liggja	lá	lágu	legit	'lie'
sjá	sá	sá	sét	'see'
slá	sló	slógu	slegit	'hit'
sofa	svaf	sváfu	sofit	'sleep'
standa	stóð	stóðu	staðit	'stand'
sveipa	sveip	svipu	sveipit	'wrap'
svima	svam	svámu	sumit	'swim'
troða	trað	tráðu	troðit	'tread'
tyggva	tǫgg	tuggu	tuggit	'chew'
þiggja	þá	þágu	þegit	'accept'
þvá	þó	þógu	þvegit	'wash'

Weak verbs

heyja	háði	há(i)t	'perform', 'conduct'
kaupa	keypti	keypt	'buy'
leggja	lagði	lagt	'lay' 'put'
ljá	léði	lét	'lend' 'grant'
selja	seldi	selt	'hand over', 'sell'
setja	setti	sett	'set' 'place'
sækja	sótti	sótt	'seek', 'attack'
yrkja	orti	ort	'work', 'make poetry'
þreyja	þráði	þrát	'long for'
þykkja	þótti	þótt	'seem'

Búa has past subj. root *bjǫgg-*, *bjøgg-* or *bygg-*.

Frjósa and *kjósa* have weak endings in the past sg. indic. Both alternatively have strong type 2 forms (*fraus — frusu — frosit*, *kaus — kusu — kosit*).

Hanga has a connecting vowel *i* in the present sg. indic. (e.g. *vápnit hangir* 'the weapon hangs'), as does *heita* in the sense 'be called'. *Hanga* lacks front mutation in the relevant forms.

Koma, *sofa*, and *troða* have certain alternative forms. Present sg. indic. root: *kem-* or *køm-*, *sef-* or *søf-*, *treð-* or *trøð-*; past pl. indic. root *kvám-*, *sóf-* (past subj. root is either *kæm-* or *kvæm-*, *svæf-* or *sæf-*).

Svima has an alternative inf. *symja*, and an alternative strong type 3 paradigm (with root final *mm*): *svimma — svamm — summu — summit*.

For the present tense of *sjá*, which has highly irregular inflexions, see p. 175.

3.6.9.1/3.6.9.2/3.6.9.3 Phonological variation/Morphological variation/Idiosyncratic variation — Exercise

1. Explain the following forms: 3rd pl. past indic. *urðu*, from *verða*; 1st sg. past indic. *hné*, from *hníga*; imp. *statt*, from *standa*; pp. *ekit*, from *aka*.
2. Why can *sverja* (past indic. root *sór-*) be said to belong to the same strong verb type as *fara* (past indic. root *fór-*)?
3. Which pp.s of type 3 and 4 strong verbs have root vowel *u* rather than *o*?
4. What is the past tense root of weak verbs *benda*, *hitta*, *myrða* and *skipta*, and why?
5. What is the past tense root of weak verbs *fæða* and *ryðja*, and why?
6. Give the 1st pl. present indic. of *búa*.
7. Give the 2nd sg. past indic. of strong verbs *láta* and *slá*, and the 2nd sg. present indic. of preterite present *vita*.
8. Give the 3rd sg. present indic. of *fregna*, *skilja*, *vaxa*.
9. Enumerate the different present tense roots of type 2 and type 3 strong verbs.
10. What variations does the imperative form exhibit?
11. In what way are the paradigms of *frjósa* and *kjósa* unusual?
12. Give the principal parts of *koma* and *sofa*, including all alternative forms.

3.6.10 Examples of verb inflexion

Complete paradigms of selected verbs are now given. As with adjectives, Old Norse grammars tend to be somewhat parsimonious in their exemplification of verbs. To be sure, most forms likely to be encountered can be identified using the guidance provided in the preceding sections, but this can often be a long and arduous process for the novice. The present grammar therefore gives more paradigms than strictly necessary, but not so many, one hopes, that the student is overwhelmed and unable to see the wood for the trees. To illustrate the main patterns, two strong verbs are displayed, one with root-final *t* (*skjóta*) and one with root *a* (*fara*), and three weak, one of each type (*berja*, *þakka*, *brenna*). In addition, a preterite present verb, *mega*, is presented, and *vera* and *sjá*, since not only are these two irregular and extremely common, but certain of their forms are easily confused. Finally, the paradigms of one strong (*fara*) and one weak verb (*berja*) are repeated with the *-sk* suffix added. Finite forms precede non-finite. The past participle is given in the nom./acc. n. sg. form. Rather than the abstract '1st sg.' etc., pronouns are used to indicate person and number; *hann* 'he' is used for the 3rd sg., *vér* for the 1st pl., *þér* for the 2nd pl., *þeir* for the 3rd pl. The imperative is always 2nd sg. (cf. 3.6.3).

Strong verb (type 2): *skjóta* 'shoot'

Present indicative		Present subjunctive	
ek	skýt	ek	skjóta
þú	skýtr	þú	skjótir
hann	skýtr	hann	skjóti
vér	skjótum	vér	skjótim
þér	skjótið	þér	skjótið
þeir	skjóta	þeir	skjóti

Past indicative		Past subjunctive	
ek	skaut	ek	skyta
þú	skauzt	þú	skytir
hann	skaut	hann	skyti
vér	skutum	vér	skytim
þér	skutuð	þér	skytið
þeir	skutu	þeir	skyti

Imperative	skjót
Infinitive	skjóta
Present participle	skjótandi
Past participle	skotit

Strong verb (type 6): *fara* 'go'

Present indicative
ek	fer
þú	ferr
hann	ferr
vér	fǫrum
þér	farið
þeir	fara

Present subjunctive
ek	fara
þú	farir
hann	fari
vér	farim
þér	farið
þeir	fari

Past indicative
ek	fór
þú	fórt
hann	fór
vér	fórum
þér	fóruð
þeir	fóru

Past subjunctive
ek	fœra
þú	fœrir
hann	fœri
vér	fœrim
þér	fœrið
þeir	fœri

Imperative	far
Infinitive	fara
Present participle	farandi
Past participle	farit

Weak verb (type 1): *berja* 'beat'

Present indicative
ek	ber
þú	berr
hann	berr
vér	berjum
þér	berið
þeir	berja

Present subjunctive
ek	berja
þú	berir
hann	beri
vér	berim
þér	berið
þeir	beri

Past indicative
ek	barða
þú	barðir
hann	barði
vér	bǫrðum
þér	bǫrðuð
þeir	bǫrðu

Past subjunctive
ek	berða
þú	berðir
hann	berði
vér	berðim
þér	berðið
þeir	berði

Imperative	ber
Infinitive	berja
Present participle	berjandi
Past participle	bart/barit

Weak verb (type 2): *þakka* 'thank'

Present indicative
ek þakka
þú þakkar
hann þakkar
vér þǫkkum
þér þakkið
þeir þakka

Present subjunctive
ek þakka
þú þakkir
hann þakki
vér þakkim
þér þakkið
þeir þakki

Past indicative
ek þakkaða
þú þakkaðir
hann þakkaði
vér þǫkkuðum
þér þǫkkuðuð
þeir þǫkkuðu

Past subjunctive
ek þakkaða
þú þakkaðir
hann þakkaði
vér þakkaðim
þér þakkaðið
þeir þakkaði

Imperative þakka
Infinitive þakka
Present participle þakkandi
Past participle þakkat

Weak verb (type 3): *brenna* 'burn' (transitive)

Present indicative
ek brenni
þú brennir
hann brennir
vér brennum
þér brennið
þeir brenna

Present subjunctive
ek brenna
þú brennir
hann brenni
vér brennim
þér brennið
þeir brenni

Past indicative
ek brennda
þú brenndir
hann brenndi
vér brenndum
þér brennduð
þeir brenndu

Past subjunctive
ek brennda
þú brenndir
hann brenndi
vér brenndim
þér brenndið
þeir brenndi

Imperative brenn
Infinitive brenna
Present participle brennandi
Past participle brennt

Irregular verb: *vera* 'be'

Present indicative
ek em
þú ert
hann er
vér erum
þér eruð
þeir eru

Present subjunctive
ek sjá/sé
þú sér
hann sé
vér sém
þér séð
þeir sé

Past indicative
ek var
þú vart
hann var
vér várum
þér váruð
þeir váru

Past subjunctive
ek væra
þú værir
hann væri
vér værim
þér værið
þeir væri

Imperative ver
Infinitive vera
Present participle verandi
Past participle verit

Irregular verb: *sjá* 'see'

Present indicative
ek sé
þú sér
hann sér
vér sjám/sjóm
þér séð
þeir sjá

Present subjunctive
ek sjá
þú sér
hann sé
vér sém
þér séð
þeir sé

Past indicative
ek sá
þú sátt
hann sá
vér sám
þér sáð
þeir sá

Past subjunctive
ek sæa
þú sæir
hann sæi
vér sæim
þér sæið
þeir sæi

Imperative sé
Infinitive sjá
Present participle sjándi
Past participle sét

Preterite present verb: *mega* 'be able to' 'be allowed to' 'can'

Present indicative		**Present subjunctive**	
ek	má	ek	mega
þú	mátt	þú	megir
hann	má	hann	megi
vér	megum	vér	megim
þér	meguð	þér	megið
þeir	megu	þeir	megi

Past indicative		**Past subjunctive**	
ek	mátta	ek	mætta
þú	máttir	þú	mættir
hann	mátti	hann	mætti
vér	máttum	vér	mættim
þér	máttuð	þér	mættið
þeir	máttu	þeir	mætti

Imperative *lacking*
Infinitive mega
Present participle megandi
Past participle mátt/megat

Strong verb (type 6): *farask* 'perish'

Present indicative		**Present subjunctive**	
ek	fǫrumk	ek	fǫrumk
þú	fersk	þú	farisk
hann	fersk	hann	farisk
vér	fǫrumsk	vér	farimsk
þér	farizk	þér	farizk
þeir	farask	þeir	farisk

Past indicative		**Past subjunctive**	
ek	fórumk	ek	fœrumk
þú	fórzk	þú	fœrisk
hann	fórsk	hann	fœrisk
vér	fórumsk	vér	fœrimsk
þér	fóruzk	þér	fœrizk
þeir	fórusk	þeir	fœrisk

Infinitive farask
Past participle farizk

> **Weak verb (type 1):** *berjask* 'fight'
>
> | **Present indicative** | | **Present subjunctive** | |
> |---|---|---|---|
> | ek | berjumk | ek | berjumk |
> | þú | bersk | þú | berisk |
> | hann | bersk | hann | berisk |
> | vér | berjumsk | vér | berimsk |
> | þér | berizk | þér | berizk |
> | þeir | berjask | þeir | berisk |
>
> | **Past indicative** | | **Past subjunctive** | |
> |---|---|---|---|
> | ek | bǫrðumk | ek | berðumk |
> | þú | barðisk | þú | berðisk |
> | hann | barðisk | hann | berðisk |
> | vér | bǫrðumsk | vér | berðimsk |
> | þér | bǫrðuzk | þér | berðizk |
> | þeir | bǫrðusk | þeir | berðisk |
>
> | **Infinitive** | berjask |
> |---|---|
> | **Past participle** | barzk/barizk |

Imperatives and present participles with the *-sk* suffix are uncommon and in many verbs unattested. To the extent they occur, they will be found to consist of the basic form + *sk*, e.g. *dvelsk* 'stay!', *dveljandisk* 'staying', from *dvelja* (weak type 1).

3.6.10 Examples of verb inflexion — Exercise

Identify the verb-forms printed in bold in the following sentences. If the form is non-finite, state whether it is an infinitive, present or past participle, and, if either of the latter, give the case, gender and number. If the form is finite, give its person (1st, 2nd or 3rd), number (sg. or pl.), tense (pres. or past), mood (indic., subj. or imp.) and voice (act. or pass.). In all cases, say what type of verb is involved (strong type X, weak type X, preterite present, etc.), and list its principal parts. Finally, comment, as appropriate, on the syntactic function and semantic role of the verb-forms, paying due attention to any with the *-sk* suffix.

(1) **Fóru** vinir á milli ok **leituðu** um sættir
  'Went friends be(-)tween and sought for settlement'
  'Friends intervened and tried to get a settlement'

(2) Hann **hljóp** fyrir borð ok **svam** til lands ok **bjó** svá um í hvílu sinni, at þar **sýndisk**, sem maðr **lægi**
'He jumped over side and swam to land and arranged thus around in bed REFL. POSS., that there showed-*sk* as man lay'
'He jumped overboard and swam to shore and arranged his bed in such a way that it looked as though a man lay there'

(3) 'Eigi **veit** ek þat', **segir** Skarpheðinn
'"Not know I that", says Skarpheðinn'
'"I don't know about that", says Skarpheðinn'

(4) **Heyrt hefi** ek, at þér **hafið kvisat** í milli yðvar, at ek **væra** ekki lítill maðr vexti
'Heard have I that you have whispered a(-)mong you that I was not little man in-stature'
'I have heard you whispering among yourselves that I was not a little man in stature'

(5) Þetta **þótti** ǫllum ráðligt, ok **var** þetta heit **fest**
'This seemed to-all advisable, and was this vow made'
'This seemed a good idea to everyone, and this vow was made'

(6) Eigi **vil** ek, at þit **séð** missáttir
'Not want I that you-two are discordant'
'I don't want you two to be on bad terms'

(7) Þeir **vǫrðusk** vel um hríð
'They defended themselves well for a while'

(8) Þeir **sjá**, hvar tveir menn **gengu** frá skálanum
'They see where two men went from hall-the'
'They see two men going from the hall'

(9) Hann **hafði** tvau skip ok jafnmarga menn, sem **mælt var**
'He had two ships and equally-many men as stipulated was'
'He had two ships and as many men as was stipulated'

(10) En því næst **laust** þú mik með hamrinum þrjú hǫgg
'But to-that next hit you me with hammer-the three blows'
'But then you hit me three blows with the hammer'

(11) **Væntir** hann þess, at þú **mynir** honum grið **gefa**, ef kastalinn **verðr unninn**
'Hopes he that, that you will to-him quarter give if castle-the is won'
'He hopes that you will spare his life if the castle is taken'

(12) **Ver** kátr bóndi, ok **grát** eigi
'Be cheerful, farmer, and cry not'
'Cheer up, master, and don't cry'

(13) Átján **váru drepnir**, en tólf **þágu** grið
'Eighteen were slain, and twelve received pardon'

(14) Ósœmt **er**, at líkamr **fœðisk** ok **klæðisk** ítarliga, en hinn iðri maðr **sé** óprúðr ok **missi** sinnar fœzlu
'Unseemly is that body feeds-*sk* and clothes-*sk* finely, but the inner man is unadorned and lacks REFL. POSS. food'
'It is unseemly that the body is finely fed and clothed, but the inner man is unadorned and goes without his food'

(15) En ek **á** nú norðr leið til fjalla þessa, er nú **munu** þér **sjá mega**
'But I have now northwards path to mountains these which now will you see be-able'
'But my path now lies northwards to these mountains which you will now be able to see'

(16) Ek **vil**, at vit **takim** menn til gørðar með okkr
'I want that we-two take men for arbitration between us-two'
'I want us to choose men to arbitrate between us'

(17) Eigi **er** þat kynligt, at þér **undrizk** þetta
'Not is that strange that you wonder-at-*sk* this'
'It is not strange that you are amazed at this'

(18) Hann **hafði loganda** brand í hendi
'He had a flaming brand in his hand'

(19) **Heyr** þú dróttinn bœn þá, er þræll þinn **biðr** þik í dag, at augu þín **sé** upp **lokin** ok eyru þín **heyrandi** yfir hús þetta dag ok nótt

'Hear you, Lord, prayer that which servant your asks you to(-)day, that eyes your be up opened and ears your hearing over building this day and night'
'Hear, O Lord, the prayer which your servant asks of you to-day, that your eyes be opened and your ears listening over this building day and night'

(20) Fyrir hví **reizt**u þessu hrossi, er þér **var bannat**?
'For why rode-you this horse which to-you was forbidden?'
'Why did you ride this horse which was forbidden to you?'

(21) Maðrinn **heilsar** þeim ok **spyrr**, hverir þeir **væri**
'The man greets them and asks who they were'

(22) Vel **má** ek **gøra** þat til skaps fǫður míns at **brenna** inni með honum, því at ek **hræðumk** ekki dauða minn
'Well can I do that for pleasure of-father my to burn inside with him, therefore that I fear-*sk* not death my'
'I can happily please my father by burning alive in the house with him, because I do not fear death'

(23) **Lézk** þar Adam byskup, ok **var** líkit lítt **brunnit**, er **fannsk**
'Lost-*sk* there Adam bishop, and was body-the little burnt when found-*sk*'
'Bishop Adam died there, and his body was scarcely burnt when it was found'

(24) **Sér** Þórr þá, at þat **hafði** hann **haft** of nóttina fyrir skála
'Sees Þórr then that that had he had during night-the for house'
'Then Þórr sees that that was what he had been using during the night as a house'

(25) Hann **skyldi halda** sætt ok frið við þá menn alla, er í þessi ráðagørð **hǫfðu vafizt**
'He should keep truce and peace with those men all who in this plot had entangled-*sk*'
'He was to keep the peace agreement with all the men who had become embroiled in this plot'

3.7 Prepositions

Prepositions are non-inflecting words that appear in conjunction with noun phrases and together with them form sentence elements known as preposition phrases. English examples, with the preposition given in bold, are: **with** John, **in** town, **for** two weeks, **about** them.

Usually a preposition will immediately precede its noun phrase, although in Old Norse other words may occasionally intervene (e.g. — with the preposition phrase given in bold — *nú ræðr þú, hversu þú skalt **við** una **þitt ørendi*** 'now decide you how you shall with be-content your mission [i.e. now it is up to you what satisfaction you derive from your mission]'). Where the noun phrase comes first, as can also happen in Old Norse, the term '**pre**position' is often replaced by the more precise '**post**position' (e.g. *mælti nú engi maðr því í móti* 'no man now spoke against it', with *því* 'it' preceding *í móti* 'against').

Although prepositions do not themselves inflect, in many languages they determine the case of the noun phrase they are used in conjunction with, and are thus said to 'govern' it (cf. *about them* above, not *about they).

Typically prepositions convey concepts like time, place, possession, instrumentality. This means that many preposition phrases are adverbials (cf. 3.5.4). In the English sentence *John did it during the interval*, for example, *during the interval* answers the question 'when?' and is reducible to the adverb *then*. Similarly, *outside the shop* in *we met outside the shop* answers the question 'where?' and can be reduced to the adverb *there*. Some prepositions, however, simply act as connectors between verb and noun phrase: contrast English *he visited them* with American *he visited with them*.

Old Norse has about thirty common prepositions, several of which occasionally function as postpositions. They trigger accusative, genitive and dative case in the noun phrases they govern, but never nominative. Some always trigger the same case, some trigger two, and one even three; among the second group, difference of case usually implies a difference of meaning.

In the following, the chief Old Norse prepositions are presented, ordered according to the case or cases they trigger. A selective range of their principal meanings is given, together with examples of usage. It should be noted, however, that prepositional usage is often very idiomatic, and one-to-one equivalence between the prepositions of Old Norse and English is not to be expected. ON *at*, for example, shares with English *at* a common form, origin and spatial sense, but appropriate English equivalents — as well as 'at' — can be 'against', 'to', 'along', 'around', 'near', 'by', 'in' and 'on', to name but some.

Observe that prepositions with initial *á*, *í*, *um* may also be found written as single words, e.g. *ámeðal*, *ímóti*, *umfram*.

3.7.1 Prepositions triggering the accusative

(í) **gegnum** 'through'

> Hallbjǫrn lagði í gegnum skjǫldinn
> 'Hallbjǫrn thrust through shield-the'
> 'Hallbjǫrn thrust his spear through the shield'

of   (a) [motion] 'over' 'across'

> Hann fór suðr of fjall
> 'He went south across the mountain'

   (b) 'during' 'in'

> Of aptan, er myrkt var, þá . . .
> 'In evening when dark was, then . . .'
> 'In the evening when it was dark, then . . .'

Occasionally *of* is construed with the dative case, either in sense (b) or with the locational meaning 'over' 'above' (e.g. *konungr sat of borði* 'the king sat over [i.e. at] table'). The latter usage is one *of* shares with the prepositions *um* and *yfir* (see below). In most functions *of* and *um* are interchangeable, and *of* was more or less ousted by *um*, and to a lesser extent *yfir*, in the course of the thirteenth century.

um   (a) [motion] 'around' 'over' 'across'

> Slógu þeir þá hring um þá
> 'Threw they then ring around them'
> 'Then they encircled them'

(b) 'during' 'in'

> Þeir váru þar um nóttina
> 'They were there during the night'

(c) 'about' 'concerning'

> Þeir tǫluðu þá um málit
> 'They spoke then about the matter'

Like *of*, *um* may occasionally be construed with the dative, either in sense (b) or, rarely, with the locational meaning 'over' 'above'.

um fram 'beyond' 'above' 'more than'

> Þat er þakt með ísum, umfram ǫll ǫnnur hǫf
> 'It is covered with ice, more than all other seas'

umhverfis 'around'

> Gengr hann umhverfis skemmuna
> 'He walks around the hut'

Apart from the above, there is a series of complex prepositions that trigger the accusative, made up of *fyrir* and a following adverb with the *-an* suffix (cf. 3.5.1). These indicate position relative to another (fixed) position, e.g. *fyrir vestan hafit* 'west of the sea', *fyrir neðan kné* 'below the knee' (further examples under 3.5.1). Sometimes the order *fyrir* + *-an* adverb may be reversed, but it should be noted that while, e.g., *fyrir ofan* always means 'above', *ofan fyrir* has two meanings: 'above' and 'down past' 'down along'; in the latter sense it is not a complex preposition but a sequence of adverb + preposition (see 3.7.4, *fyrir*).

3.7.2 Prepositions triggering the genitive

innan 'within'

> Innan kastalans var eitt munklífi
> 'Within the castle was a monastery'

Occasionally *innan* may be construed with the accusative or dative.

(á/í) meðal 'among' 'between'

> Hann settisk niðr á meðal þeirra
> 'He sat (himself) down between them'

(á/í) milli/millum 'among' 'between'

> Ríki guðs er yðar í milli
> 'The kingdom of God is among you'

Each of the three above prepositions can denote time as well as location (e.g. *innan lítils tíma* 'within a short time', *milli jóla ok fǫstu* 'between Christmas and Lent').

til   (a) 'to' 'towards'

> Hann fór vestr um haf til Þorfinns jarls
> 'He went west over the sea to Earl Þorfinnr'

(b) 'regarding' 'concerning'

> Þeim varð gott til manna
> 'To-them became good regarding men'
> 'They managed to gather together a good many men'

(c) 'to' 'until'

> Helt hertoginn ǫllu sínu ríki til dauðadags
> 'Kept duke-the all REFL. POSS. dominion till death-day'
> 'The duke kept all his lands until the day he died'

Somewhere between a preposition phrase and a preposition stands *fyrir . . . sakar/sakir/sǫkum*, *fyrir sakar/sakir/sǫkum* 'because of' 'regarding', which triggers the genitive (e.g. *fyrir sára sakir* 'because of wounds', *fyrir vits sakir* 'as regards intelligence', *fyrir sakar þess* 'for that reason').

3.7.3 Prepositions triggering the dative

af   (a) 'off' 'from'

>Rǫgnvaldr jarl kom af hafi við Hjaltland
>'Rǫgnvaldr earl came off sea at Shetland'
>'Earl Rǫgnvaldr landed in Shetland'

While *af* in this sense can simply denote [source] — where someone/something comes from — it often correlates with prepositions meaning 'on', first and foremost *á*: that which is 'on' something can come 'off' it (cf. the above example where Rǫgnvaldr has been on the sea sailing to Shetland).

(b) [time] '(gone) from'

>Þrjár vikur váru af sumri
>'Three weeks were from summer'
>'Three weeks of summer were gone'

(c) [partitive, cf. 3.2.6, sentence 20] 'of'

>Þorfinnr hafði mikinn hluta af Skotlandi
>'Þorfinnr had a big part of Scotland'

(d) [in passive constructions] 'by'

>Ek em sendr hingat af Starkaði
>'I am sent hither by Starkaðr'

(e) [cause] 'of' 'from' 'because of'

>Inn nørðri hlutr liggr óbyggðr af frosti ok kulða
>'The northern part lies uninhabited because of frost and cold'

at (a) 'at' 'to' 'towards'

>Hleypr Kolr þá at honum
>'Kolr then runs at him'

(b) 'at' 'in'

>Eigi má ek hér vera at hýbýlum mínum
>'Not can I here be at home my'
>'I cannot stay here at my home'

The above uses of *at* can be temporal as well as locational (e.g. *leið at kveldi* 'it passed on to evening', *at jólum gaf jarl honum gullhring* 'at Christmas the earl gave him a gold ring'). In addition *at* can signify future time (e.g. *at vári* 'next spring' 'when spring comes').

(c) 'from'

>Ari nam marga frœði at Þuríði
>'Ari gained much knowledge from Þuríðr'

(d) 'according to'

>Óláfi var gefit konungs nafn at upplenzkum lǫgum
>'To-Óláfr was given king's name according-to Upplandic laws'
>'Óláfr was declared king in accordance with the laws of Uppland'

At + acc. in the sense 'after' (particularly 'after someone's death') may also be encountered (e.g. *sonr á arf at taka at fǫður sinn* 'a son is to take inheritance after his father'). Historically this appears to be a different preposition from *at* + dat., probably an assimilated form of *apt*, related to *eptir* (see below).

frá (a) 'from'

>Þau róa frá skipinu
>'They row from the ship'

(b) 'concerning' 'about'

> Er mér svá frá sagt konungi
> 'Is to-me thus about said king'
> 'I am told so about the king'

As distinct from *af*, *frá* does not correlate with particular locational prepositions, but denotes source or origin of any kind. It can have temporal as well as locational function (e.g. *frá þessum degi* 'from this day').

gagnvart/gegnvart 'opposite'

> Skipaði Hrútr honum gagnvart sér
> 'Hrútr placed him opposite himself'

(í) **gegn** (a) 'against'

> Mestr hluti manna mælti honum í gegn
> 'Most part of-men spoke him against'
> 'Most of the men spoke against him'

(b) 'towards'

> Hann ríðr út í gegn þeim
> 'He rides out towards them'

hjá (a) 'at someone's (house)'

> Var hann á gistingu hjá Þóri
> 'Was he on night-stay at Þórir's'
> 'He was staying the night at Þórir's'

(b) 'close to' 'next to' 'by'

> Konungr bað hann sitja hjá sér
> 'The king bade him sit by him'

(c) 'past'

> Gengr kona hjá Þormóði
> 'A woman walks past Þormóðr'

(d) 'compared with'

> Þórr er lágr ok lítill hjá stórmenni því, er hér er með oss
> 'Þórr is short and small compared with the big men who are here with us'

In sense (a) and, to a certain extent, (b), ON *hjá* corresponds to French *chez*.

(**á/í**) **mót(i)** (a) 'against'

> Mælti þá ok engi maðr í mót honum
> 'Spoke then also no man a(-)gainst him'
> 'And indeed no man then spoke against him'

(b) 'towards'

> Gengu tveir menn í móti þeim
> 'Two men walked towards them'

nær 'near'

> Austmaðrinn kvezk vilja fyrir hafa land ok þó nær sér
> 'Easterner-the says-*sk* want for-it have land and yet near self'
> 'The Norwegian says he wants to have land in exhange for it, but near him'

Nær can have temporal as well as locational sense (e.g. *nær aptni* 'near evening'). Since *nær* is in origin an adverb, it has comparative and superlative forms (cf. 3.5.2), and occasionally these are also used with prepositional function (e.g. *nær(r) honum* 'nearer him', *næst hinum fremstum* 'closest to the foremost (people)').

ór/úr 'out of' 'from'

> Hann hafði í brot komizk ór brennunni
> 'He had a(-)way come-*sk* out-of burning-the'
> 'He had escaped from the burning'

Ór often correlates with prepositions meaning 'inside' 'within'; in the above example the escape was made from within a burning building.

undan 'away from'

> Ek get þess, at þú vilir eigi renna undan þeim
> 'I guess that, that you want not run away-from them'
> 'I do not imagine you want to run away from them'

Where one entity is moving and another following or due to follow in orderly fashion, *undan* corresponds to English 'ahead of' 'before' (e.g. *fara undan þeim* 'go ahead of them').

Also used with the dative is a series of constructions — with a wide range of meanings — consisting of preposition + various forms of the noun *hǫnd*. Like *fyrir . . . sakar* etc. (cf. 3.7.2), preposition + *hǫnd* constructions stand somewhere between a preposition phrase and a preposition. Among the most common are: *á hǫnd/hendr* 'against', *til handa* 'for' 'on behalf of' (e.g. *fara á hendr Rǫgnvaldi jarli* 'go against [i.e. attack] Earl Rǫgnvaldr', *biðja konu til handa honum* 'ask woman for him [i.e. ask for a woman in marriage on his behalf]').

3.7.4 Prepositions triggering the accusative and dative

Prepositions in this category are construed with the accusative or dative largely according to sense. The principal distinction is between motion (usually towards some goal) and location (rest), the former triggering the accusative, the latter the dative. Only *eptir*, *með* and *við* are unaffected by this dichotomy. *Eptir*, together with *fyrir*, tends to trigger the accusative when denoting time. *Með* may historically have been followed only or chiefly by the dative and *við* by the accusative, but in classical Old Norse the two prepositions have become somewhat mixed up and the one can rather often be found with the sense and/or case of the other. In connection with the motion : location dichotomy it is worth noting first that the movement or rest involved is often denoted or suggested by a word other than the preposition (usually a verb or adverb, cf., e.g., *á* + acc. (a) and *á* + dat. (a) below), and second that an English speaker's conception of movement and rest may not always tally with that of speakers of other languages (cf., e.g., *þeir sá boða mikinn inn á fjǫrðinn* 'they saw a great breaker [i.e. breaking wave] in the inlet [literally: (looking) into the inlet]').

á + acc. (a) 'onto' 'on' 'to'

> Hann gekk á land
> 'He went on land'
> 'He went ashore'

(b) 'during' 'at' 'in'

> Standa þar yfir vǫtn á vetrinn, en á várin . . .
> 'Stand there over waters in winter-the, but in springs-the . . .'
> 'It is covered with water in the winter, but in the spring . . .'

When used in a temporal sense *á* tends to trigger the accusative where the noun is accompanied by the definite article (contrast dat. (b) below). *Á* + acc. may indicate a point in time as well as a recurring period (e.g. *á laugardaginn næsta* 'on the next Saturday').

á + dat. (a) 'on' 'in'

> Reri hann yfir á Nes einn á báti
> 'Rowed he over to Nes one in boat'
> 'He rowed over to Caithness in a boat on his own'

Note the contrast between the accusative *yfir á Nes*, where the adverb *yfir* indicates motion towards a place, and the dative *á báti*, which implies location. The verb *reri* combines with both senses.

(b) 'during' 'at' 'in'

> Hann gaf Hrómundi gelding hvert haust, en lamb á várum
> 'He gave to-Hrómundr wether each autumn, but lamb in springs'
> 'He gave Hrómundr a wether each autumn, but a lamb in the spring'

Á + dat. may indicate a point in time as well as a recurring period (e.g. *á því sumri* 'in that summer').

(c) [inalienable possession] 'X's Y'

> Lagði hann í fótinn á honum
> 'Thrust he into leg-the on him'
> 'He thrust (his weapon) into his leg'

Á in this sense is typically used of body parts, but can also be found in other contexts (e.g. *allar dyrr á húsunum* 'all the doorways of the buildings').

eptir + acc. [time] 'after'

> Eptir orrostuna fór hann norðr til Þrándheims
> 'After the battle he went north to Þrándheimr'

Eptir + acc. can also be used in the sense of 'after someone's death' (e.g. *þá tók hann arf eptir fǫður sinn* 'then he took inheritance after his father').

eptir + dat. [motion] 'after' 'following'

> Hann reið eptir þeim
> 'He rode after them'

The sense 'following' can extend to 'along' (e.g. *gekk hann aptr eptir skipinu* 'he walked back along the ship'), and to 'according to' (e.g. *gekk allt eptir því, sem Hallr hafði sagt* 'everything went according to what [literally: that which] Hallr had said').

fyrir + acc. (a) [motion] 'before' 'in front of'

> Hann kom skildinum fyrir sik
> 'He came shield-the before self'
> 'He put the shield in front of him'

(b) [directional] 'over' 'past'

> Þeir drógu hann ofan fyrir brekkuna
> 'They dragged him down over the slope'

(c) [time] 'before'

> En litlu fyrir jól fór hann í Papey ina litlu
> 'But shortly before Christmas he went to Papa Stronsay'

(d) 'in return for' 'in place of'

> Þú skalt gjalda fyrir hana þrjár merkr silfrs
> 'You shall pay three marks of silver for her (a slave)'

fyrir + dat. (a) [location] 'before' 'in front of'

> Varð fundr þeira fyrir Rauðabjǫrgum
> 'Took-place meeting their before Rauðabjǫrg'
> 'They met off Roberry'

Locational *fyrir* has a number of extended meanings. Particularly common are: (1) 'in charge of', developed from the sense 'in front of' via the idea of 'leading' (e.g. *vera fyrir liði* 'be in charge of a body of men'), and (2) 'in the presence of', widely used with verbs of speaking (e.g. *mæla fyrir honum* 'say to [literally: before] him', *kæra fyrir þeim* 'complain to them').

(b) 'ago'

> Ek skilðumk við Óláf konung fyrir fjórum nóttum
> 'I parted from King Óláfr four nights ago'

í + acc. (a) 'into' 'in' 'to'

> Eigi miklu síðarr sendir hann menn í Suðreyjar
> 'Not much later he sends men to the Hebrides'

Í in the above sense may be used with abstract as well as concrete nouns (e.g. *kominn í allmikla kærleika við* 'come into very great friendship with [i.e. become very great friends with]').

(b) 'during' 'in' 'at'

> Í þenna tíma kom út Geirríðr
> 'At this time came out Geirríðr'
> 'At this time Geirríðr came to Iceland'

Í in this temporal sense is commonly used with the words *dagr* 'day' and *nótt* 'night' as well as the names of parts of the day and the seasons to indicate 'time now' or 'time closest to the present' (e.g. *í nótt* 'tonight', *í kveld* 'this evening', *í sumar* 'this summer').

í + dat. 'in'

> Dvalðisk Rǫgnvaldr skamma stund í Nóregi
> 'Rǫgnvaldr stayed a short while in Norway'

Í in this sense may be used with abstract as well as concrete nouns (e.g. *í miklum kærleikum við* 'in great friendship with').

með + acc. 'with'

> Hann fór til Íslands með konu sína ok bǫrn
> 'He went to Iceland with his wife and children'

Með here implies that 'he' took his wife and children to Iceland rather than simply going together with them (see *með* + dat. (a) below). Because it carries the notion of 'control' over whatever entity one is 'with', *með* + acc. is commonly found with nouns denoting inanimate objects (e.g. *kom Bárðr eptir þeim með horn fullt* 'Bárðr came after them with a full horn', i.e. carrying a horn full of drink).

með + dat. (a) 'together with'

>Dóttir hans fór með honum
>'His daughter went with him'

(b) [instrumental] 'with'

>Þeir urðu at verja sik með sverðum
>'They had to defend themselves with swords'

(c) [manner] 'with' 'in' 'by'

>Þriðju nótt varð gnýr með sama hætti
>'Third night happened clamour with same manner'
>'The third night there was a clamour in the same way'

(d) 'among'

>Þat er siðr með kaupmǫnnum, at . . .
>'It is a custom among merchants to . . .'

Case usage after *með* is more fluid than the above examples suggest. In particular it is not uncommon to find *með* + dat. in what appears to be the 'control' sense (cf. *með* + acc. above). As indicated in the preamble to this sub-section, *með* can sometimes take the place of *við*; thus we may attest, for example, *berjask með* + acc. for earlier *berjask við* + acc. 'fight with' 'fight against', where the noun phrase following the preposition denotes the goal of the action.

undir + acc. [motion] 'under'

>Lagði Þorfinnr jarl þá undir sik allar Eyjar
>'Laid Þorfinnr earl then under self all Islands'
>'Then Earl Þorfinnr placed all the Northern Isles under his rule'

undir + dat. [location] 'under'

>Þá brast í sundr jǫrðin undir hesti hans
>'Then burst a(-)sunder earth-the under horse his'
>'Then the earth burst open under his horse'

In either of the above senses *undir* may be used metaphorically (e.g. *gefa undir kirkjuna* 'give to the church', i.e. with the result that what is given comes under the church's control, *undir þeim biskupi eru ellifu hundruð kirkna* 'under that bishop are eleven hundred churches').

við + acc. (a) 'near' 'by'

> Þeir sátu lengi við bakelda
> 'They sat long by baking-flames'
> 'They sat by the fire warming themselves for a long time'

This use of *við* may be temporal as well as locational (e.g. *við sólarsetr* 'at sunset', *við þetta* 'at this (point)').

(b) [directional] 'to' 'towards' 'vis-à-vis'

> Engu skiptir mik, hversu þú hefir við aðra menn gort
> 'By-nothing concerns me how you have to other men done'
> 'It does not concern me at all how you have acted towards other men'

The noun following *við* in sense (b) denotes the entity at which an action is directed. The usage is commonly found *inter alia* with verbs of saying (e.g. *tala við konung* 'speak to the king'). Because of the directional sense, the noun following *við* can sometimes have the force of a direct object (the 'goal of the action', cf. 3.1.5, sentence 5). That is particularly the case with phrasal verbs (those consisting of two or more words), although many of these denote mental processes rather than actions (e.g. *fara til fundar við* 'go to meeting with', where the sense is more or less equivalent to the English transitive phrase *go to meet*, *verða varr við* 'become aware of', equivalent to *notice*, *vera hræddr við* 'be afraid of', equivalent to *fear*).

við + dat. 'against'

> Hann kastaði sér niðr við vellinum
> 'He threw himself down against the ground'

Sometimes *við* + dat. may have the related sense 'towards' (e.g. *horfa við* 'look towards'). As noted above, *við* and *með* have become confused, and we may thus find *við* + dat. in all the senses of *með* + dat. Potential ambiguities can usually be resolved by examining the sentence in which the preposition phrase stands or the wider context (e.g. *slá honum niðr við steininum* must mean 'throw him down against the rock' rather than 'strike him down with the rock' because of the dative *honum* — cf. (3.1.5, sentence 20) that verbs of throwing take the dative of the entity thrown).

yfir + acc. [motion] 'over' 'above'

>Þá tók Skaði eitrorm ok festi upp yfir hann
>'Then took Skaði poisonous-snake and fixed up above him'
>'Then Skaði took a poisonous snake and tied it up above him'

yfir + dat. [location]

>Hvers manns alvæpni hekk yfir rúmi hans
>'Each man's weapons hung above his seat'

In either of the above senses *yfir* may be used metaphorically (e.g. *hafa vǫxt yfir aðra menn* 'have growth beyond [i.e. be taller than] other men', *konungr yfir Englandi* 'king over England').

3.7.5 Prepositions triggering the accusative and genitive

The only preposition regularly to trigger both accusative and genitive is *útan*. It has two senses, and either case may have either sense.

útan + acc./gen. (a) 'outside'

>Hann nemr stað í garðinum útan hurð klaustrsins
>'He takes stand in yard-the outside door of-convent'
>'He stops in the yard outside the door of the convent'

>Þeir fóru heldr útan heraðs til kaupa
>'They went rather outside district to tradings'
>'They preferred to go outside the district to trade'

(b) 'without'

> Eigi er enn við honum tekit útan þitt ráð
> 'Not is yet with him taken without your consent'
> 'He has not yet been received without your consent'

> ... ef þeir eru útan sætta
> '... if they are without a settlement'

3.7.6 Preposition triggering the accusative, genitive and dative

The only preposition to trigger all three cases is *án*. The meaning is the same, irrespective of case.

án + acc./gen./dat. 'without'

> Kristnin mátti eigi vera lengi án stjórnarmanninn
> 'The Church could not be long without its leader'

> Þess máttu Gautar illa án vera
> 'That could Gautar ill without be'
> 'The people of Gautland could not afford to be without it'

> Giptisk hon Valgarði án ráði allra frænda sinna
> 'Married-*sk* she to-Valgarðr without consent of-all kinsmen REFL. POSS.'
> 'She married Valgarðr without the consent of any of her kinsmen'

3.7.7 Residual remarks

Two further matters concerning Old Norse prepositions should be noted.

First, they often combine with adverbs, particularly those that indicate direction. Thus a journey to Caithness from Orkney may be described as *yfir á Nes*, one in the opposite direction as *út í Eyjar*, and one into the hinterland of Scotland as *upp í Skotland*. Sometimes such combinations develop idiomatic senses considerably removed from the meanings of the two elements of which they are made up, e.g. *framan at* 'to the front side of [literally: from the front to]' (cf. also 3.7.1 on the many combinations of *fyrir* + *-an* adverb). When confronted by an adverb + preposition (or preposition + adverb) sequence that does not appear to make immediate sense, the student is advised to look up the adverb first since often it will mainly be this that gives the sequence its meaning.

Second, prepositions in Old Norse are often converted into adverbs by the omission of the noun phrase they govern. Sometimes the noun phrase can be clearly understood from the context (e.g. *hann kom svá á óvart, at eigi varð fyrr vart við en* . . . 'he came so on unawares that not became before aware of than . . . [i.e. he arrived so unexpectedly that no one became aware of (him) before . . .]'. In other cases the reference is less specific (e.g. *niðamyrkr var á* 'pitch-darkness was on [i.e. it was pitch-dark]'. Students should be particularly on their guard against prepositions used adverbially that yet appear to be prepositions because they are immediately followed by a noun phrase (e.g. *hann finnr, at þar var stungit í sverði Sigmundar* 'he notices that there was thrust into with-sword of-Sigmundr [i.e. that Sigmundr's sword was thrust into it]', where *sverði* is an instrumental dative (cf. 3.1.5, sentence 20) and *í* belongs with the adverb *þar*, giving the adverb phrase *þar í* 'therein', or, more idiomatically, 'into it'). As can be seen from the translation, *þar* is here the equivalent of a pronoun, and *þar í* therefore effectively a preposition phrase. This type of construction is very common in Old Norse; mostly it involves *þar*, but *hér* 'here' also occurs (cf. *nú verðr þar frá at hverfa* 'now becomes there from to turn [i.e. now we must turn from that]'; . . . *svá bjǫrt, at þar af lýsti* '. . . so bright [n. pl.] that there from shone [i.e. so bright that they shone]'; *ǫll sannindi hér um* 'all truth here about [i.e. all the truth about this]'). (See further 3.9.8.3.)

3.7 Prepositions — Exercise

1. Define and exemplify 'preposition', taking your examples from Old Norse.
2. Do Old Norse prepositions always immediately precede the noun phrase they govern?
3. List the prepositions that trigger the accusative, the genitive or the dative only.
4. How far can case usage after Old Norse prepositions be related to meaning?
5. What differences, if any, are there between the meanings of *af*, *frá* and *ór*?
6. In what senses and with what cases may *fyrir* be used?
7. In what senses and with what cases may *með* be used?
8. What is the difference in meaning between *ofan* and *fyrir ofan*?
9. Which Old Norse prepositions may have temporal sense?
10. Identify the basic meaning of each of the following prepositions (printed in bold); state, where appropriate, the case of the noun phrase governed and the reason for the choice of case (where a preposition is found to be used adverbially, discuss its relationship with other words in the sentence):
    (a) Var Kálfr þá **í** miklum kærleikum **við** Þorfinn jarl
    'Kálfr was then on very friendly terms with Earl Þorfinnr'
    (b) **Eptir** þat sendi Þorfinnr menn út **í** Eyjar
    'After that Þorfinnr sent men out to the Orkneys'
    (c) Hann kærir **fyrir** þeim, at þeir ætla at fara **með** her **á hendr** honum
    'He complains to them that they intend to advance against him with an army'
    (d) Hann sigldi þegar **á** haf **um** nóttina ok svá austr **til** Nóregs
    'He sailed straight to sea during the night and then east to Norway'
    (e) Konungr sat **yfir** mat
    'The king sat over food'
    (f) Var kominn **á** byrr
    'A fair wind had sprung up'
    (g) Hann er jarðaðr **at** Kristskirkju
    'He is buried at Christ's Church'
    (h) Mǫrg lǫnd hafði hann lagt **undir** sik **með** hernaði
    'Many countries he had placed under his rule by warfare'
    (i) Goðin skǫpuðu þar **ór** mann
    'The gods created a man out of it'

3.8 Conjunctions

Conjunctions differ from most other words in that they do not form part of a sentence, but stand outside it. Their function, as the term conjunction suggests, is to join constituents together, and the constituents may be anything from sentences to single sentence elements (though even the latter can mostly be analysed as reduced sentences).

A distinction is made between coordinating and subordinating conjunctions. The former join together constituents of the same level, the latter constituents of different levels. Commonly, coordinating conjunctions connect independent sentences (also known as matrix sentences or main clauses), i.e. sentences that can stand on their own as a complete utterance. The two most frequently occurring coordinating conjunctions in English are *and* and *but*. In:

Peter sat down **and** poured himself a drink

and connects the sentences *Peter sat down* and *[Peter] poured himself a drink* (in the second sentence *Peter* is omitted because unless specified, the subject of *poured* will be understood to be the same as the subject of *sat down*). Both these sentences are independent in the sense that they require nothing further to complete them. The conjunction *but*, while introducing an element of contrast not present in *and*, functions in a similar way. In:

Anne opened the door **but** did not go in

the sentences joined together are again both independent: (1) *Anne opened the door*; (2) *[Anne/she] did not go in*.

Subordinating conjunctions typically function as connectors between independent and dependent sentences, introducing the latter (also known as embedded sentences or subordinate clauses). Dependent sentences are those that cannot stand on their own as complete utterances. Examples of subordinating conjunctions in English are *because*, *when*, *if*. In:

I like the summer **because** it is light

because joins the dependent *because it is light* to the independent

I like the summer. The former, unlike the other sentences so far adduced, is not a complete utterance. To say *because it is light*, which details a reason, requires that we specify the action, event or state to which the reason applies. Equally, the dependent *when he arrives*, introduced by *when*, needs to be completed by an independent sentence which details an action, event or state that stands in a time relation to 'his' arrival, e.g.:

>We will eat **when** he arrives

The conjunction *if* introduces the notion of condition: one action, event or state is conditional upon another. The action/event/state that will/would take place/ensue if the condition is/were met is expressed as an independent, the condition as a dependent sentence, e.g.:

>Joan will write the letter **if** you help her

Subordinating conjunctions are often grouped according to their meaning, and the groups given designations such as 'causal' (e.g. *because*, *since*), 'temporal' (e.g. *when*, *while*), 'conditional' (e.g. *if*, *unless*), 'final' (e.g. *in order that*), 'consecutive' (*so that* [i.e. 'with the result that']). As will be seen from these examples, some conjunctions consist of more than one word.

Not all words that introduce dependent sentences have traditionally been reckoned conjunctions. English *who(m)*, *which* and *whose* are often termed 'relatives' or even 'relative pronouns', the latter designation based on the observation that such words can have the same function as noun phrases (appearing as subjects and objects of sentences, for example), cf.:

>Bill helped the girl **who** was drunk (subject)

>This is a prize **which** you can win (object)

Whatever other functions they may have, however, it is undeniable that *who*, *which* in examples like the above (and in similar fashion *whom*, *whose*) join together sentences, and to that extent can be classed as conjunctions in the same way as *because*, *when*, etc.

For *who(m), which* we may often substitute *that* in English (... *that was drunk*, ... *that you can win*). A different function of *that* — likewise conjunctional, though, again, not always recognised as such — is to introduce what are often called *that*-clauses. These have a number of functions, but are often the complements of verbs such as *say, know, think, suppose, hope*, or, in a different type of construction, of *be*, e.g.:

He said **that** it was interesting

The upshot was **that** they all left

In such cases *that* is, of course, not interchangeable with *who(m), which*.

We are dealing here with three fundamentally different types of dependent sentence: (1) those reducible to an adverb (e.g. ... *when he arrives = then*); (2) those reducible to an adjective (e.g. ... *which you can win = winnable*); (3) those reducible to a noun phrase (e.g. ... *that it was interesting = it, the (following) thing*, etc.). All dependent sentences are reducible in this way, which accounts for their dependent status. They represent expanded versions of adverbial, adjectival or nominal elements in independent sentences. Different though the three main types of dependent sentence may be, it is unhelpful to divide the words that introduce them into three separate categories since their common function as dependent sentence introducers is thereby obscured. In keeping with this view, all Old Norse words that join sentences together will in the following be treated as conjunctions.

3.8.1 Coordinating conjunctions

The principal coordinating conjunctions in Old Norse are *ok* 'and' and *en* 'but' 'and moreover' 'and'. Others are *eða* 'or' 'but', *né* 'nor'. Note further the expanded constructions *bæði ... ok* 'both ... and', *annattveggja ... eða* 'either ... or' and *hvárki ... né* 'neither ... nor'. As can be seen from the translations offered, the meanings of Old Norse coordinating conjunctions are sometimes less clear-cut than those of their modern English equivalents, and the student may need to examine carefully the contexts in which they appear in order to determine the precise meaning.

The following examples illustrate typical usage.

Conjunctions

> Eptir þat fór Þorfinnr jarl til Orkneyja **ok** sat þar um vetrinn
> 'After that went Þorfinnr earl to Orkneys and sat there during winter-the'
> 'After that Earl Þorfinnr went to the Orkneys and stayed there over the winter'

> Þessu játa þeir brœðr, **en** Óláfr ferr heim
> 'To-this agree those brothers, but Óláfr goes home'
> 'The brothers agree to this, but Óláfr goes home'

> Lét ek ok þar fé nǫkkut, **en** ek var leikinn sjálfr háðuliga
> 'Lost I also there property some, but I was treated myself shamefully'
> 'I also lost some property there, and moreover I was myself treated shamefully'

Here *ok* appears not as a conjunction, but as an adverb with the sense 'also'. For further uses of *ok*, see 3.8.2.4 and 3.9.9.

> Hvárt sem hann bað fyrir óvinum **eða** hann ávitaði þá . . .
> 'Whether that he prayed for enemies or he rebuked them . . .'
> 'Whether he prayed for his enemies or rebuked them . . .'

Note that the sentences joined by *eða* in this example are both dependent.

> Ver vel kominn! **Eða** hvat mey er þat, er þér fylgir
> 'Be well come! Or what maid is that who you follows?'
> 'Welcome! But what maid is that who is with you?'

This use of *eða* to bridge two different themes is very common, especially where the sentence it introduces is a question.

> Nú mun faðir minn dauðr vera, ok hefir hvárki heyrt til hans styn **né** hósta
> 'Now will father my dead be, and has neither heard to him groan nor cough'
> 'Now my father must be dead, and neither a groan nor a cough has been heard from him'

Although *né* joins together the two nouns *styn* and *hósta*, the second of these can be seen as a reduced sentence: *hefir hvárki heyrt til hans styn né* [*hefir heyrt til hans*] *hósta*.

3.8.2 Subordinating conjunctions

As is the case with many languages, Old Norse boasts far more subordinating than coordinating conjunctions. The field is so broad, not least because of the tendency for adverbs to metamorphose into subordinating conjunctions, that no attempt can be made here to provide a complete list. For the student the most important thing is in any case not the meaning of each individual conjunction. That can be looked up in a dictionary. It is rather to grasp those features of the system that constantly recur, in particular any which may not be immediately transparent to the learner.

3.8.2.1 The particle **er**

Old Norse *er* is an all-purpose subordinating conjunction. Having lost any meaning of its own, it is used to introduce a wide variety of dependent sentences, either alone or together with one or more other words. In order to interpret *er* correctly, the student will usually need to understand clearly the context in which it appears. Consider the following sentences (where the semantic emptiness of *er* is signalled by the literal rendering COMP (= complementiser), indicating a general complementising — sentence introducing — function):

(a) Ok **þá er** þessi orðsending kom aptr til jarls, bjó hann ferð sína
'And then COMP this message came back to earl, prepared he journey REFL. POSS.'
'And when this message got back to the earl, he made ready to leave'

(b) En **er** hann kom á Péttlandsfjǫrð, **þá** hafði hann þrjá tigi stórskipa
'But COMP he came into Pentland-Firth, then had he three tens of-large-ships'
'And when he got into the Pentland Firth, he had thirty large ships'

(c) En **um morguninn, er** menn váru vaknaðir, var kominn á byrr
'And in morning-the, COMP men were woken-up, was come on favourable-wind'
'And in the morning, when men were awake, a favourable wind had sprung up'

(d) Ok **er** þeir váru búnir, sigldu þeir í haf
'And COMP they were prepared, sailed they to sea'
'And when they were ready, they sailed out to sea'

(e) Þorfinnr jarl var **þá** fimm vetra gamall, **er** Melkólmr Skotakonungr gaf honum jarlsnafn
'Þorfinnr earl was then five of-winters old COMP Melkólmr king-of-Scots gave him earl's-name'
'Earl Þorfinnr was five years old when Melkólmr, king of the Scots, gave him the title of earl'

In (a) *er* is immediately preceded by *þá*, an adverb of time meaning 'then'. The latter (in conjunction with the tense of the verbs) supplies past-time sense, while *er* introduces the dependent sentence; together they form a temporal subordinating conjunction with the meaning 'when [past time]'. (b) has *er* as a sentence introducer without preceding *þá*. The sense of the dependent sentence it introduces can, however, be deduced from the occurrence of the adverb *þá* at the beginning of the following independent sentence: the earl commanded thirty ships 'then', i.e. at the point when he entered the Pentland Firth. In (c) the time adverbial *um morguninn* performs much the same function as *þá* in (a), even though *um morguninn* is more obviously than *þá* part of the independent sentence that, as it were, 'frames' its dependent partner (*en um morguninn* [. . .] *var kominn á byrr*). Past-time sense is given by the tense of the verbs (*váru, var*). (d) lacks any adverbial that could indicate the sense of *er*. Here we must be guided by context, and the context is a sequence of events occurring at a particular time in the past. Immediately following (d) is the sentence: *þat var á ǫndverðum vetri* 'that was at the beginning of winter'. This makes a temporal interpretation of *er þeir váru búnir* the obvious one. (e) is similar to (b) in that the *er* introducing the dependent sentence is rendered unambiguous by the occurrence of *þá* 'then' in the accompanying independent sentence. The difference lies in the order of the two sentences and in the placing of *þá*: in (b) it is the first element in the independent sentence, in (e) it follows the verb.

The particle *er* appears in many temporal contexts. It commonly combines with the adverbs *meðan* 'meanwhile', *síðan* 'since', *þegar* 'at once' (yielding the conjunctions *meðan er* 'while', *síðan er* 'since', *þegar er* 'as soon as'), with the adverb phrase *þar til* 'thereto' 'up to that point' (conjunction: *þar til er* 'until'), and with preposition phrase adverbials (see 3.5.4) such as *eptir þat* 'after that' (conjunction: *eptir þat er* 'after'), *frá því* 'from that' (conjunction: *frá því er* 'since'), *í því* 'in that' (conjunction: *í því er* 'at the moment when'), *til þess* 'to that' (conjunction: *til þess er* 'until'). In most of these cases (and also with *þá*) *er* can be omitted, and there is then formal identity between conjunction and temporal adverbial (3.5.4) — as with English *since* (cf. *since* (conj.) *he came* . . . , *it has since* (adv.) *been lost*). The following can serve as a general example illustrating the use of temporal conjunctions with and without *er*.

> Vér sœkjum þangat miskunn guðs, **þegar er** vér komum í heim, ok þangat **meðan** vér erum í heimi, ok þangat **þá er** vér fǫrum ór heimi
> 'We seek thither mercy of-God at-once COMP we come into world, and thither while we are in world, and thither then COMP we go from world'
> 'We seek God's mercy there (in church) as soon as we enter the world, and (we seek it) there while we are in the world, and (we seek it) there when we leave the world'

Observe that the temporal contexts in which *er* operates are not restricted to past-time reference.

Location is another type of context in which *er* is commonly to be found, usually in combination with a locational adverbial. We find *þar er* 'where' (adverb *þar* 'there'), *þangat er* (sometimes *þangat til er*) 'to where' (adverb *þangat* 'thither', adverb *til* 'to' (cf. 3.7.7)), *þaðan er* 'from where' (adverb *þaðan* 'thence'), and the further series *hvar(gi) er* 'wherever' (adverb *hvar* 'where'), *hvert(ki) er* 'to wherever' (adverb *hvert* 'whither'), *hvaðan er* 'from wherever' (adverb *hvaðan* 'whence').

Typical examples are:

> Helt hann **þangat, er** hann spurði til Þorfinns
> 'Proceeded he thither COMP he heard of Þorfinnr'
> 'He proceeded to where he heard Þorfinnr was'

> Guð heyrir bœnir várar, **hvar er** vér biðjum fyrir oss af ǫllu hjarta
> 'God hears prayers our where COMP we pray for ourselves of all heart'
> 'God hears our prayers wherever we pray from our whole heart'

Er can introduce several other types of adverbial sentence. Some of these are easy enough to interpret since the words with which *er* combines are common and impart their characteristic meanings — e.g. *hversu, hvé* 'how', *hverr* 'who', which give the conditional-concessives *hversu er, hvégi er* 'however' (as in *hversu/hvégi lengi er . . .* 'however long . . .'), *hverr er* 'whoever'. The circumstantial *at því er* 'insofar as' is not immediately deducible from its component parts, but its sense is clear and unambiguous. Circumstantial or causal *þar er*, on the other hand, can only be distinguished from the formally identical locational conjunction (see above) by the context. In, for example:

> Tǫlðu þeir þat óráð at leggja til bardaga við Þorgeir, **þar er** hann hafði lið meira
> 'Said they that bad-counsel to go to battle with Þorgeirr, there COMP he had force bigger'
> 'They said it was a bad idea to go to battle with Þorgeirr since he had the bigger force'

there can be no question of a locational interpretation since no locations are mentioned. On the other hand, in:

> Muntu ok eigi vilja vita þat á þik, at þú liggir hér sem kǫttr í hreysi, **þar er** ek berjumk til frelsis hvárumtveggjum

cited as 3.6.8, sentence 13, it can be hard to determine the precise meaning of *þar er*. There is the implied contrast of *þar* with *hér* 'here', suggesting a locational interpretation, but the greater contrast seems to be circumstantial: hiding away as opposed to participating in desperate action. The translation offered in 3.6.8 is 'while'; 'given that' 'seeing that' are possible renderings too.

Another very common use of *er* is to introduce relative (adjectival) sentences. This arises because Old Norse has no relative pronoun proper (though in Latinate style interrogative *hverr* 'who?' is sometimes used as a relative in the same way as *who(m)*, *which*, *whose* in English). Since *er* is semantically empty, it is usual for the antecedent noun phrase modified by the relative sentence to be accompanied by the appropriate form of the demonstrative *sá* or *sjá/þessi* (3.2.2). E.g.:

> Erlendr átti **þá konu**, **er** Þóra hét
> 'Erlendr had that woman COMP Þóra was-called'
> 'Erlendr was married to the woman who was called Þóra'

where *konu* is the antecedent noun phrase, *þá* the accompanying demonstrative and *er Þóra hét* the relative sentence. Note however that *þá* is in the same (independent) sentence as *konu* and agrees with it in case, gender and number (acc. f. sg.). It is thus of no help in indicating the function of whatever correlates with (i.e. refers to the same entity as) *konu* in the relative sentence. Whether we take this to be *er* or a relative pronoun that is absent but understood, it has subject function ('the woman/she was called Þóra'), and nominative would therefore be the appropriate case. This is not, however, shown, the only marker, *er*, being uninflected, and the student thus has to deduce the function of the correlate from the context.

Further examples will make the problem clearer, and indicate strategies for solving it. In:

> Hann beiddisk **þess þriðjungs**, **er** átt hafði Einarr jarl
> 'He demanded that third COMP owned had Einarr earl'

the antecedent and its accompanying pronoun are in the genitive (governed by *beiddisk*), but what of the correlate? The student may ponder two possibilities: 'which had owned Earl Einarr' ('which' = subject) or 'which Earl Einarr had owned' ('which' = object). The latter will be preferred as by far the more likely statement, and any residual doubt can be resolved by the form *Einarr*. *Einarr* is nom. (acc. *Einar*). Since *eiga* '[to] own' is construed with nom. subject and acc. direct object, the subject of the relative sentence must be *Einarr*, leaving the correlate of *þess þriðjungs* as the object (accusative, though unmarked as such). The idiomatic translation is thus:

> 'He demanded the third which Earl Einarr had owned'

In:

> Váru **þeir menn** þá út dregnir, **er** grið váru gefin
> 'Were those men then out dragged [from the burning building] COMP truces were given'

the antecedent and its accompanying pronoun are in the nominative (the subject of *váru . . . dregnir*). The main verb of the relative sentence is to be found in the pp. form *gefin*, from *gefa* '[to] give'. Verbs of giving are normally construed with nominative subject, accusative direct object and dative indirect object in Old Norse, but in passive constructions, which is what we have here, nominative subject (what was given) and dative indirect object (to whom it was given) normally suffice (see 3.6.8, sentence 24). The only noun phrase in the relative sentence is *grið*, and this will be found to be n. pl. The auxiliary verb-form *váru* is pl. and its subject could thus be either the correlate of *þeir menn* or *grið*; however, pp. *gefin* is either nom. f. sg. or nom./acc. n. pl. (3.3.9, paradigm 7) and cannot therefore agree with a m. pl. subject. The correlate must be indirect object ('to whom truces were given'), and an idiomatic rendering would be:

> 'The men who were given quarter were then pulled out'

Note finally that antecedent and relative sentence are discontinuous (i.e. *þá út dregnir* intervenes), a common enough phenomenon in Old Norse. In:

> Rǫgnvaldr segir, at **þann hlut** Eyja, **er** þeir kalla til, hefði hann tekit í lén af Magnúsi konungi
> 'Rǫgnvaldr says that that part of-Islands COMP they call to, had he taken in fief from Magnús king'

the antecedent and its accompanying pronoun are in the accusative (the object of *hefði tekit*). The verb phrase of the relative sentence consists of verb (*kalla*) + preposition (*til*). Since the verb is 3rd pl., its subject cannot be the correlate of *þann hlut* and must therefore be nom. pl. *þeir*. This means the correlate of *þann hlut* is governed by *til*. An idiomatic rendering is then:

> 'Rǫgnvaldr says that he had taken in fief from King Magnús the part of the Orkneys to which they are laying claim'

(Observe that in Old Norse constructions of this type the preposition regularly comes at the end of the sentence; word-order equivalent to English *to which*, *from whom*, etc., is seldom found, and never where the particle *er* is used.)

This last example indicates that the correlate can have functions (in addition to reference to the antecedent) other than those of subject, direct and indirect object. The instrumental dative and the various relationships expressed by the genitive — to mention the most common — can also be 'built in' to the correlate. Consider the following two examples:

> **Sá þvengr**, **er** muðrinn Loka var saman rifaðr, heitir Vartari
> 'That thong COMP mouth-the of-Loki was together sewn is-called Vartari'
> 'The thong with which Loki's mouth was sewn up is called Vartari'

(*er* (or an understood correlate, cf. above) = instrumental dat. 'with which')

> **Sjá maðr**, **er** vér segjum nú frá jartegnum, átti marga lærisveina
> 'This man, COMP we say now from miracles, had many disciples'
> 'This man, of whose miracles we are now telling, had many disciples'

(*er* (or understood correlate) = subjective gen. 'whose')

Although pronoun + noun or noun + pronoun is the most common antecedent of a relative sentence, a noun or pronoun may also occur on its own. E.g.:

> Ǫzurr átti **son**, **er** Leifr hét
> 'Ǫzurr had a son who was called Leifr'

> Svínbeygt hefi ek nú **þann**, **er** ríkastr er með Svíum
> 'Made-root-like-a-pig have I now that-one [m.] COMP most-powerful is among Swedes'
> 'I have thoroughly humbled him who is most powerful among the Swedes'

Occasionally — mostly in early writings — a personal or demonstrative pronoun or possessive adjective may be included in the relative sentence to make the function of the correlate clearer. E.g.:

> Ekkja heitir **sú**, **er** búandi **hennar** varð sóttdauðr
> 'Widow is-called that-one [f.] COMP husband her was dead-from-illness'
> 'She whose husband died from illness is called a widow'

Sometimes the particle *er* is replaced by *sem*. This is particularly common with relative, conditional-concessive (*hverr er/sem* 'whoever' etc.) or locational '-ever' sentences (*hvar er/sem* 'wherever' etc.). E.g.:

> Gengu út **þeir**, **sem** gløggsýnastir váru at sjá
> 'Went out those COMP most-clear-sighted were to look'
> 'Those who were most clear-sighted went out to look'

> Hann var kenndr at illu **hvar sem** hann fór
> 'He was known for bad where COMP he went'
> 'He had a bad reputation wherever he went'

More problematically, *er* is interchangeable with *at*, another extremely common Old Norse particle which participates in a wide range of constructions (3.8.2.2).

For example:

> En **þeir** allir, **at** þau tíðindi heyrðu, lofuðu sannan guð
> 'But those all, COMP those tidings heard, praised true god'
> 'And all who heard that news praised the true God'

English-speaking learners may be helped by the quirk that *that* can introduce both *that-* (noun) and relative (adjective) sentences (cf. 3.8), making 'and all that heard that news . . . ' a possible English rendering of the above. This superficial similarity will not help in all cases where *at* is substituted for *er*, however, nor where *er* is used for expected *at*, so it is important to understand the sentence structure. In, for example:

> **Þegar at** haustaði, tóku at vaxa reimleikar
> 'At-once COMP became-autumn, began to grow hauntings'
> 'As soon as autumn arrived the hauntings began to increase'

þegar combines with *at* rather than *er* to form a temporal subordinating conjunction. Here it is quite impossible to think of *at* as the equivalent of English 'that'. For the beginner the best advice is to try substituting *er* for *at* and vice versa when either is met in a context where it does not make obvious sense.

3.8.2.2 The particle at

Used on its own, *at* introduces noun sentences and adverbial sentences of purpose. The former are far commoner. Typical examples of *at* noun sentences are provided by:

> Þeir segja, **at** hann væri þar á hǫfðanum hjá þeim
> 'They say that he was there on the headland with them'

> En ek vil, Sveinn, **at** þú farir í Orkneyjar
> 'But I want, Sveinn, that you go to Orkneys'
> 'But I want you, Sveinn, to go to the Orkneys'

An adverbial sentence of purpose introduced by *at* is contained in:

> Mun ek veita þér slíkt lið, sem þú vill, **at** þetta fari fram
> 'Will I give you such aid as you want that this goes forward'
> 'I will give you as much aid as you want so that this may be accomplished'

Noun sentences are sometimes anticipated by a demonstrative pronoun standing in the associated independent sentence, e.g.:

> Ræð ek **þat**, **at** vér vindim segl várt
> 'Advise I that that we hoist sail our'
> 'I advise that we hoist our sail'

> Er **sú** bœn Kveldúlfs, **at** þú takir við Þórólfi
> 'Is that [f.] request of-Kveldúlfr that you take with Þórólfr'
> 'It is Kveldúlfr's request that you receive Þórólfr'

where *at vér vindim segl várt*, the object of *ræð*, is represented by *þat* in the independent sentence, and *at þú takir við Þórólfi*, the subject of *er*, by *sú* (agreeing with *bœn*, f.).

At regularly combines with other words to form subordinating conjunctions; these introduce various kinds of adverbial sentence. More often than plain *at* the purpose conjunction is *til þess at* 'in order that' 'so that' (*til þess at* can alternatively, but less commonly, have the temporal sense 'until'). Sentences of reason or cause may be introduced by *því at*, *af því at*, *fyrir því at*, *með því at* 'because' 'since'; of concession by *þó at* or *þót*(*t*) (the latter a compound of the former) 'although' 'even though'; of result by *svá at* 'so that' 'with the result that'; and of comparison by *svá . . . at* 'so . . . that'. Examples are:

> Skulu [3.6.9.1 point (13)] vér frændr þínir veita þér styrk, **til þess at** þú komir aldrigi síðan í slíkt ǫngþveiti
> 'Shall we kinsmen your give you support to that that you come never subsequently into such straits'
> 'We your kinsmen will give you support so that you never again get into such straits'

Hrauð hann skipin skjótt, **því at** þar var borðamunr mikill
'Cleared he ships-the quickly therefore that there was difference-in-height great'
'He cleared the ships (of men) quickly because there was a great difference in height (between his ships and the others)'

Kallar hann þat meirr verit hafa **fyrir því** játtat, **at** þeir váru þá komnir í greipr Óláfi konungi
'Calls he that more been have for that agreed that they were then come into clutches [belonging] to-Óláfr king'
'He says it was agreed more readily because they had then fallen into the clutches of King Óláfr'

Þó at hann deyi í mǫrgum syndum, þá lifir hann í trú sinni
'Though that he dies in many sins, then lives he in faith REFL. POSS.'
'Even though he may die full of sin, he lives in his faith'

Lǫgðu þeir á flótta, **svá at** fá ein skip váru eptir með jarls skipi
'Set-off they to flight, so that few only ships were behind with earl's ship'
'They took to flight, so that only a few ships were left with the earl's ship'

Ekki eru þeir enn **svá** nær oss, **at** eigi væri betr, at ek hefða sofit
'Not are they yet so near us that not were better that I had slept'
'They are not yet so near us that it would not have been better if I had slept'

Note that conjunctions that consist of more than one word can be discontinuous (*fyrir því . . . at*; comparative *svá . . . at* is always so).

Sometimes whole sentences may intervene between the different elements, e.g.:

> **Af því** eigum vér, góðir vinir, at leggja mikla rœkt á kirkjur várar, **at** vér sœkjum þangat miskunn guðs
> 'From that ought we, good friends, to place great care on churches our that we seek thither grace of-God'
> 'We ought, dear friends, to take great care of our churches because we seek there the grace of God'

This in no way exhausts the list of subordinating conjunctions incorporating *at*, but students will find that once the basics are understood the sense of most can be deduced from the context. In addition to result and comparison, for example, *svá at* can introduce sentences of purpose, e.g.:

> Af því er oss nauðsyn, góðir brœðr . . . at vér hreinsim brjóstkirkjur várar, **svá at** ekki finni guð í mysteri sínu . . . þat er hann styggvisk við
> 'From that is to-us necessity, good brothers . . . that we cleanse breast-churches our, so that not finds God in temple REFL. POSS. . . . that COMP he offends-*sk* with'
> 'Therefore it is necessary for us, dear brethren . . . to purify the churches of our hearts, so that God does not find in his temple . . . anything by which he is offended'

Note that *af því* here is the adverbial 'therefore', and does not belong with the following *at*, which introduces the noun sentence subject of *er oss nauðsyn* ('that we purify the churches of our hearts is to us a necessity'). Observe also a further example of a correlate in a relative sentence governed by a preposition: *er hann styggvisk við* (3.8.2.2.1).

3.8.2.3 Interrogative pronouns and adverbs

The interrogative pronouns *hverr* 'who' 'which' 'what', *hvat* 'what' and *hvárr* 'which of two', and interrogative adverbs such as *hvar* 'where', *hvaðan* 'whence', *hvert* 'whither' 'where', *hvárt* 'whether', *hvé, hversu, hvernig* 'how', *nær, hvenær* 'when', *hví* 'why', introduce noun sentences. Typically such sentences occur after verbs of 'asking' or 'knowing', denoting the thing asked or known, but they may be found in many other contexts. Since these interrogatives are among the most common words in Old Norse and their meaning is usually clear, the dependent sentences they introduce are unlikely to cause the learner many difficulties. It is worth noting, however, that the pronouns always appear in a case, gender and number appropriate to their function in the dependent sentence. A selection of examples follows to illustrate the range of Old Norse 'indirect questions' — as dependent sentences introduced by interrogatives are often called.

> Hann lét frétta eptir, **hverr** fyrir eldinum réði
> 'He let ask after who of fire-the had-command'
> 'He had people ask who was responsible for the fire'

Hverr is the subject of the verb *réði* and thus nominative (cf. 3.1.5, sentence 1). The noun sentence *hverr fyrir eldinum réði* is governed by the preposition *eptir* (3.7.4) in the independent sentence: if *hverr fyrir eldinum réði* were reduced to a noun or pronoun, its case would be dative (e.g. *hann lét frétta eptir því* 'he had people ask about that').

> Ek vil vita, **hverju** þú vill bœta mér bróður minn
> 'I want know with-what you will compensate to-me brother my'
> 'I want to know what compensation you will give me for my brother's death'

Hverju is an instrumental dative denoting the means of compensation — with or by what someone or something is compensated (cf. 3.1.5, sentence 20). The noun sentence introduced by *hverju* is the object of the verb *vita* in the independent sentence: it describes what the speaker wants to know (cf. 3.1.5, sentence 5, 3.2.6, sentence 6).

> Leitaði hann þá eptir, **hvern** styrk þeir vilja veita honum
> 'Sought he then after what support they will give him'
> 'He then enquired what support they are willing to give him'

Styrk, with which *hvern* agrees, is accusative — the object of *veita* (what 'they' (may) give). As in the first example, the noun sentence is governed by the preposition *eptir*.

> Þat vil ek vita, **hvat** þú vill veita oss
> 'That want I know what you will give us'
> 'I want to know what you are willing to give us'

Hvat, like *hvern styrk* in the preceding example, is the object of *veita*. Observe that the noun sentence is anticipated by (and reduced to) *þat* in the independent sentence: 'I want to know that — namely, what you will give us'. Such anticipation by a demonstrative pronoun is not uncommon. *Þat* is acc., because it and the noun sentence it stands for are the object of *vita*.

> Eigi þykki mér skipta, í **hvárum** flokki ek em
> 'Not seems to-me matter in which-of-the-two party I am'
> 'It does not seem to me to matter in which of the two parties I am'

Hvárum agrees with *flokki*, which is dat., governed by the preposition *í* (3.7.4). The noun sentence introduced by *í hvárum flokki* is the subject of the independent sentence — in which of the two parties the speaker finds himself is what does not seem to him to matter.

> Veit ek eigi, **hvaðan** þjófsaugu eru komin í ættar várar
> 'Know I not whence thief's-eyes are come into families our'
> 'I do not know from where thief's eyes have come into our kin'

> Engi veit, **nær** sú stund kømr
> 'No one knows when that time will come'

> Nú vil ek vita, **hvárt** þú vill þessa ferð fara með mér
> 'Now want I know whether you will this journey go with me'
> 'Now I want to know whether you will make this journey with me'

Hvaðan, *nær* and *hvárt* are interrogative adverbs and thus not inflected. The noun sentences they introduce are the objects of *veit*/*vita* — what the speaker does not know, what no one knows, and what the speaker wants to know.

> Engu skiptir mik, **hversu** þú hefir við aðra menn gǫrt
> 'By-nothing concerns me how you have to other men done'
> 'It does not concern me at all how you have treated other men'

Hversu is an interrogative adverb. The noun sentence it introduces is the subject of *skiptir* — what does not concern the speaker.

> Hann spurði, **hví at** eigi skyldi drepa flugumenn
> 'He asked why that not should kill assassins'
> 'He asked why assassins should not be killed'

Hví is an interrogative adverb. The noun sentence it introduces is the object of *spurði* — what is asked. Observe that not only *hví* but also the particle *at* is used to introduce the dependent sentence. Such 'doubling' is not uncommon and can also involve *er*, e.g.:

> En nú haf þú njósn af, **nær er** þeir koma til bœjarins
> 'But now have you watch of when COMP they come to town-the'
> 'But now keep watch and see when they come to town'

The addition of *at* or *er* makes no difference to the meaning. It strengthens the impression of these particles as general complementisers, and suggests that interrogatives were sometimes felt to be unequal to the task of introducing dependent sentences on their own.

3.8.2.4 Other adverbial sentence introducers

We have already seen that the particles *er* and *at* can introduce adverbial sentences (3.8.2.1, 3.8.2.2). There are in addition several conjunctions with more specific meaning that perform this task. Commonest among these are the conditionals *ef* 'if', *nema*, *útan* 'unless', the temporals *áðr* 'before', *unz* 'until', the temporal and circumstantial *síðan* 'since' 'seeing that' (see 3.8.2.1), and the comparatives *en* 'than', *sem* 'as' 'as though'. The following examples illustrate typical usage.

> (a) En **ef** vart verðr við vára ferð, þá látum vér enn hafit gæta vár
> 'But if aware becomes of our movement, then let we again sea-the guard us'
> 'But if people notice our movements then we will once again let the open sea hide us'

(a) provides a good illustration of the way in which dependent sentences are reducible to a single word. The adverb *þá* 'then' 'in that case', which heads the independent sentence, encapsulates and repeats the adverbial sense of the preceding conditional *en ef vart verðr við vára ferð*. Observe further that the conditional sentence has no subject (cf. 3.9.3).

(b) Nú þykki mér Rǫgnvaldr eigi vel launa mér, **ef** ek skal nú eigi ná bróðurarfi mínum, **nema** ek berjumk til
'Now seems to-me Rǫgnvaldr not well repay me if I shall now not get brother's-inheritance my unless I fight-*sk* for'
'Now it seems to me Rǫgnvaldr is not repaying me well if I am not now to get my brother's inheritance unless I fight for it'

(c) Nú sé ek, at ek mun deyja, **útan** þú hjálpir mér
'Now I see that I shall die unless you help me'

Conditional sentences introduced by *nema* or *útan* are most often dependent on a negative, as in (b).

(d) Þeir kómu þar árdegis, **áðr** menn váru uppstaðnir
'They came there early-of-day before men were risen'
'They came there early in the day before men had got up'

(e) Ferr hann í Geirþjófsfjǫrð ok er þar **unz** haustar
'Goes he into Geirþjófsfjǫrð and is there until becomes-autumn'
'He goes to Geirþjófsfjǫrð and stays there until autumn arrives'

As in (a), the dependent sentence of (e) is subjectless.

(f) Einarr hafði verit með Óláfi Svía konungi **síðan** Sveinn jarl andaðisk
'Einarr had been with Óláfr of-Swedes king since Sveinn earl died-*sk*'
'Einarr had been with Óláfr, the Swedish king, since Earl Sveinn died'

(g) Villtu, at ek gæta vitans, **síðan** ek geri ekki annat?
'Want-you that I look-after beacon-the, since I do nothing other?'
'Do you want me to look after the beacon seeing that I am not doing anything else?'

Observe that *síðan* may have circumstantial as well as temporal meaning, testifying to the close relationship between a temporal sequence and the closed condition or premise (*síðan ek geri ekki annat*) that ties a circumstantial sentence to an independent fellow expressing the conclusion (*villtu . . . ?*). (In English *since* and *as* function as temporal, circumstantial and also as causal conjunctions.)

(h) Þeir létu ok eigi fleiri menn sjá á skipinu **en** jarli hǫfðu fylgt
 'They let also not more men see on ship-the than earl had followed'
 'Nor did they let more men be seen on the ship than had accompanied the earl'

(i) Hann létti eigi fyrr **en** hann kom á fund Magnúss konungs
 'He stopped not earlier than he came to finding of-Magnús king'
 'He did not stop before he found King Magnús'

Just as English *than*, ON *en* requires a comparative adjective (here *fleiri*) or adverb (*fyrr*) in the independent sentence. It is possible to analyse *fyrr en* as a complex temporal conjunction (cf. the idiomatic English rendering 'before'), although, like most other compound conjunctions in Old Norse, it may be discontinuous (i.e. the parts may be separated) as in: *eigi varð **fyrr** vart við **en** þeir hǫfðu tekit allar dyrr á húsunum* 'not became earlier aware of than they had taken all doorways on buildings-the [i.e. people did not become aware of anything before they had seized all the exits from the buildings]'.

(j) Konungr bauð honum með sér at vera, svá lengi **sem** honum líkaði
 'King invited him with self to be as long as him pleased'
 'The king invited him to stay with him as long as he pleased'

(k) Muntu gǫrr sekr, slíkir menn **sem** hér eigu eptirmæli
 'Will-you made outlawed, such men as here have prosecution'
 'You will be condemned to outlawry, seeing what kind of men have to follow up the case'

(l) Magnús konungr bað hann fara **sem** honum líkaði
 'Magnús king bade him go as him pleased'
 'King Magnús said he could go as he pleased'

(m) Sveinn lét, **sem** hann heyrði eigi
'Sveinn acted as-though he heard not'
'Sveinn pretended he did not hear'

Comparative *sem* is often dependent on a preceding *svá* (j) or *slíkr* (k) — with *slíkr* in the appropriate case, gender and number — though it may appear without either (l), and commonly does when the sense is 'as though' (m). The precise syntactic function of *svá* and *slíkr* — with or without accompanying adverb or noun phrase — can be difficult to analyse (true also of comparative *svá . . . at* constructions, 3.8.2.2). In (j) and (k) above *svá lengi* and *slíkir menn* stand outside the independent sentence but before the *sem* which introduces the dependent, comparative sentence. Since, however, similar constructions — equally difficult to analyse — are found in English, understanding is unlikely to prove a problem for the learner. (On the lack of an Old Norse equivalent of 'be' in (k)'s *muntu gǫrr sekr*, see 3.9.5.2.) Note that comparative *sem* is sometimes replaced by *ok*. This normally only occurs where the comparative is dependent on an antecedent meaning 'same' or 'similar'. E.g.:

> Þat segja sumir menn, at hann yrði aldri sami maðr ok áðr
> 'That say some men that he became never same man and before'
> 'Some men say that he was never the same man as (he was) before'

3.8 Conjunctions — Exercise

1. What is the principal function of conjunctions? In what way do they differ from most other words?
2. What is implied by the term 'coordinating conjunction'? What are the main coordinating conjunctions in Old Norse?
3. How can the meaning of *er* be deduced?
4. Outline the main sentence types introduced by *er*.
5. What types of sentence are introduced by *at* on its own?
6. With what words does *at* combine to form complex subordinating conjunctions? Give the Old Norse forms and their meaning(s).
7. List the interrogative pronouns that introduce dependent sentences in Old Norse and give their meaning(s).
8. Apart from *er* and *at*, which simplex (single-word) conjunctions introduce adverbial sentences in Old Norse? Give the words and their meaning(s).
9. Find three examples of discontinuous conjunctions (either from sentences in this section or elsewhere) and quote them.

10. Analyse the conjunctions (printed in bold) in the following sentences. State whether they are coordinating or subordinating and, if subordinating, the type of sentence they introduce (noun, adjectival, adverbial; conditional, temporal, causal, etc.).

   (a) Þá spurði hann, **at** Haraldr var farinn yfir til Kataness
   'Then he learnt that Haraldr had gone across to Caithness'
   (b) Er þér eigi forvitni á, **hversu** mér líkar sagan?
   'Aren't you curious to know how I like the story?'
   (c) Fór þá Erlendr austr í Nóreg, **en** Anakol var eptir í Orkneyjum
   'Then Erlendr went east to Norway, but Anakol remained in the Orkneys'
   (d) Íþrótt er þat, **ef** þú efnir
   'That is a feat if you can perform it'
   (e) Hann var þá barn at aldri, **er** hann tók ríkit
   'He was only a child when he came to the throne'
   (f) **Þó at** þú verðir reiðr, þá mældu fátt
   'Though you become angry, yet say little'
   (g) Konungr kallaðisk þá vilja fá honum skip **ok** lið, svá **sem** hann þurfti
   'The king said he would give him ships and men then as (many as) he needed'
   (h) Tóku þeir þá byrðinginn **ok** allt þat, **er** á var
   'They then seized the cargo-boat and everything that was on it'
   (i) Þeir váru í Orkahaugi, **meðan** él dró á
   'They were in Orkahaugr, while a storm passed over'
   (j) Gaf hann meir en fjórðung biskupsdóms síns, **til þess at** heldr væri tveir biskupsstólar á Íslandi **en** einn
   'He gave more than a quarter of his bishopric so that there should be two episcopal seats in Iceland rather than one'
   (k) Sveinn skyldi fyrir sjá, **hvert** ráð **er** skyldi taka
   'Sveinn was to decide what plan should be adopted'
   (l) Konungr varð svá reiðr Agli, **at** hann vill eigi fara at finna hann
   'The king became so angry with Egill that he will not go to see him'
   (m) Hann sendi þá orð ǫðrum hǫfðingjum þeim, **er** honum var liðs at ván
   'He then sent word to the other leaders from whom he expected help'
   (n) **Því** var hann kallaðr blóðøx, **at** maðrinn var ofstopamaðr
   'He was called "bloodaxe" because he was an overbearing man'

3.9 Residual points of syntax

The aim of this section is to introduce the learner to various aspects of Old Norse syntax that may cause difficulty (some will have been briefly alluded to in earlier parts of this *Grammar*). Only the essentials are dealt with. For more thorough accounts, see Faarlund 2004, Haugen 2001, Heusler 1932, Iversen 1973, Nygaard 1905.

3.9.1 Sentence word-order

Word-order in Old Norse is freer than in modern English. That does not mean, however, that words may appear in any sequence. One clear rule is that the finite verb must be the first or second element in a sentence, in dependent sentences most often the second. Awareness of this pattern can help to determine whether a sentence is to be analysed as independent and beginning with an adverb or dependent and introduced by a conjunction. For example:

(a)   Síðan gekk hann til messu

and:

(b)   Síðan hann gekk til messu . . .

are to be interpreted differently. (a) is an independent sentence in which the adverb *síðan* 'then' occupies first position, the finite verb *gekk* 'went' second, and the subject *hann* 'he' third. (b) is a dependent sentence introduced by the subordinating conjunction *síðan* 'since', in which the subject *hann* occupies first position and the finite verb *gekk* second. The full meaning of (a) is thus 'then he went to mass' and of (b) 'since he went to mass . . .' Being dependent, (b) requires the addition of an independent sentence to complete the utterance (cf. 3.8).

In English a finite verb in first position normally signals either a question (*can you come?*) or a command (*come here!*). In Old Norse declarative sentences too may have verb-first order. Thus:

Hefir þú mikit lið

may either be the question 'have you a big force?' or the declarative 'you have a big force'. Normally the context will make clear how such a sentence is to be understood. Ambiguity can also be avoided by the use of the question introducer *hvárt* (in origin nom./acc. n. sg. of the interrogative pronoun *hvárr* 'which of two', cf. 3.2.5). Thus, while

> Lifir hann enn
> 'Lives he still'

may either be the question 'is he still alive?' or the statement 'he is still alive',

> Hvárt lifir hann enn?

can only be the question.

As noted in 3.1.5 and elsewhere, the unmarked order of noun phrases in Old Norse (order not deliberately altered for emphasis) is subject — object. Often the subject will precede the finite verb giving subject — verb — object:

> Þeir fundu konung
> 'They met the king'

However, where some other word is in first position (a) or the verb is first (b), the order will be verb — subject — object (cf. above):

(a)   Þar fundu þeir konung

(b)   Fundu þeir konung

The position of the direct and indirect object in relation to one another is not fixed, morphological case (mostly) indicating the function (see 3.1.5, sentences 5, 16–19). A tendency for the indirect to precede the direct object is however noticeable.

The subject complement (3.1.5, sentence 1) also follows the subject in unmarked word-order, and the object complement (3.3.6, sentence 7) the object, as in:

> Var hann inn mesti hǫfðingi
> 'Was he the greatest ruler'
> 'He was a very great ruler'

> Þeir gerðu hann þegar líflátinn
> 'They made him at-once life-lost'
> 'They killed him at once'

Many sentences will of course contain more than subject, finite verb, object(s) and/or complement. However, the learner is unlikely to be much confused by the order in which such additional elements appear, even though this can vary considerably. Three features are worth noting. First, non-finite verb-forms may follow as well as precede objects and complements. E.g.:

> Hann hafði heit strengt
> 'He had oath sworn'
> 'He had sworn an oath'

> Eigi var hann jafnaðarmaðr kallaðr
> 'Not was he fair-man called'
> 'He was not called a fair man'

Second, although a finite verb may immediately follow a subordinating conjunction, it is common to insert a sentence element between them. This element may be of almost any type. E.g. (with intervening pronoun *vér*, supine *byggt* and adverb *þar* in bold):

> Af þeira ætt er sú kynslóð komin, er **vér** kǫllum Ása ættir, er **byggt** hafa Ásgarð ok þau ríki, er **þar** liggja til
> 'From their union is that family-line come COMP [3.8.2.1] we call of-Æsir kinsfolk, COMP inhabited have Ásgarðr and those realms COMP there lie to'
> 'From them has come the family line we call the Æsir kinsfolk, who have inhabited Ásgarðr and the realms which belong to it'

Third, provided the subject is the only noun phrase in the sentence, it may be postponed to the end. E.g.:

> Tók þá brátt at brenna bœrinn
> 'Took then soon to burn farmhouse-the'
> 'Then the farmhouse soon began to burn'

Not uncommonly, an object or complement is fronted (moved into first position), either because it is an established discourse topic or to give it emphasis. These are cases of marked word-order (see 3.1.5, sentence 1). A fronted object will usually be detectable from the fact that it has a case other than the nominative and one different from that of any other noun phrase in the sentence, but a complement will have the same case as one of the other noun phrases (cf. above and 3.1.5, sentence 1, 3.3.6, sentence 7), often the nominative. Thus, in:

> Ásu dóttur sína gipti hann Guðrøði konungi
> 'Ása, daughter REFL. POSS., married he to-Guðrøðr king'
> He gave his daughter, Ása, in marriage to King Guðrøðr'

the accusative case of *Ásu dóttur sína* should warn the student against trying to interpret it as subject, notwithstanding it is the first noun phrase in the sentence. The student will either know, or can ascertain from a dictionary, that *gipta* is construed with a nominative subject, accusative direct object and dative indirect object. Since *Guðrøði konungi* is clearly dat., and *Ásu dóttur sína* clearly acc., *hann* must be nom. (rather than acc., cf. 3.2.1) and is thus the only candidate for subject. On the other hand, in:

> Vitr maðr ertu
> 'Wise man are-you'
> 'You are a wise man'

both *vitr maðr* and *þú* (*ertu* = *ert þú*, cf. 3.2.1) are nominative. There is nevertheless no doubt that *þú* is subject and *vitr maðr* subject complement. In sentences of the *X is Y* type *X* is the topic and *Y* the comment. Thus, *you are a wise man* is acceptable English since *you* can be interpreted as an established discourse topic about which something is being said, whereas *<i>a wise man is you</i> is impossible because of the difficulty of interpreting *a wise man* as topic and *you* as something said about it. Not all examples are as clear-cut as this. Consider:

>Dóttir Njarðar var Freyja
>'Daughter of-Njǫrðr was Freyja'
>'Freyja was Njǫrðr's daughter'

Here we may legitimately wonder what is subject and what subject complement. The reason for identifying *Freyja* as subject is that *dóttir Njarðar* is more likely as a description of a named individual than a named individual is as a description of *dóttir Njarðar* (cf. English *?John's daughter was Sally*).

It is not only objects and complements that are fronted in Old Norse. Adverbials (cf. *þar fundu þeir konung*, *eigi var hann jafnaðarmaðr kallaðr* above) and non-finite verbs (*þakka viljum vér yðr* 'we want to thank you') may also be topicalised or emphasised in this way.

Observe that in all these cases of fronting the finite verb remains the second sentence element (though not necessarily the second word). This is even the case where a dependent precedes an independent sentence — the former being reducible to a single element (cf. 3.8), e.g.:

>Er jarl heyrði þetta, varð hann reiðr mjǫk
>'COMP earl heard this, became he angry much'
>'When the earl heard this, he became very angry'

Dependent *er jarl heyrði þetta* can be reduced to *þá* 'then', and where *þá* heads an independent sentence the finite verb, here *varð*, must be the next element.

3.9.1 Sentence word-order — Exercise

1. What sentence positions may the finite verb occupy in Old Norse? Give three examples.
2. In what order do the different noun phrases appear in an unmarked Old Norse sentence? Give three examples.
3. What is meant by fronting? Give three examples.
4. Analyse the word-order of the following sentences:

   (a) Fé þat allt gaf hann liðsmǫnnum sínum
   'He gave all that wealth to his followers'
   (b) Fornjótr hefir konungr heitit
   'There was a king called Fornjótr'
   (c) Hugðu þeir, er fyrir váru, at Rǫgnvaldr jarl myndi þar fara
   'Those who were present thought that Earl Rǫgnvaldr would be on the move there'

3.9.2 Word-order in noun phrases

Noun phrase word-order, like word-order in general, is freer in Old Norse than English. Words modifying a noun may, with certain restrictions, appear either before or after it. Thus we find both *gamall maðr* (adj. + noun) and *maðr gamall* (noun + adj.) 'old man', *þann guð* (pron. + noun) and *guð þann* (noun + pronoun) 'that god'. Phrases containing a pronoun, definite article and adjective may have three different orders (cf. 3.3.5): *sá (h)inn blindi maðr* (pron. + def. art. + adj. + noun), *maðr sá (h)inn blindi* (noun + pron. + def. art. + adj.), and *sá maðr (h)inn blindi* (pron. + noun + def. art. + adj.) 'the blind man'.

Possessive adjectives tend to come after the noun they modify unless they are stressed: *lið várt* 'our army', *móðir mín* 'my mother', *tungu hennar* 'her language', but *þat er ekki mitt skap* 'that is not my inclination' — with stress on 'my'. This applies also to genitive modifiers: *þræll konungs* 'the king's slave', *haugr Hálfdanar* 'Hálfdan's mound', but *margra manna vitorð* 'many men's knowledge [i.e. known to many men]' with stress on 'many'. Regularly placed after the noun are epithets and appositional modifiers: *Eiríkr rauði* 'Eiríkr the red', *Þorfinnr jarl* 'Earl Þorfinnr'.

Comparative and superlative adjectives normally precede the nouns they modify: (h)in stærri skipin 'the larger ships', (h)inir spǫkustu menn 'the wisest men'. This is also true of adverbs modifying adjectives, though a few, such as the common mjǫk, vel, betr, bezt, tend to follow their head word: ákafliga reiðr 'furiously angry', but gott mjǫk 'very good', hærðr vel 'well haired [i.e. with fine hair]'.

A further feature of noun phrases in Old Norse of which students should be aware is their proneness to discontinuity. Elements which belong together may be found at some distance from each other, separated by other elements. Consider the following examples (with the separated elements in bold):

> Er **menn** váru út dregnir **flestir**, gekk maðr út í dyrrnar
> 'COMP men were out dragged most, went man out into doorway'
> 'When most men had been dragged out, a man went out into the doorway'

> **Maðr** gekk í lyptingina í rauðum kyrtli **mikill ok vaskligr**
> 'Man went onto poop-deck-the in red tunic large and manly'
> 'A large and valiant-looking man in a red tunic came up onto the poop-deck'

> Þorfinnr hafði **mikit** skip **ok vel búit**
> 'Þorfinnr had a large and well-equipped ship'

> **Þórr** fór fram á leið **ok þeir félagar**
> 'Þórr went forward on way and those companions'
> 'Þórr and his companions went on their way'

Such discontinuity should not on the whole cause students too much difficulty provided they pay proper attention to case, gender and number. The inflexions of nouns, pronouns and adjectives will normally suffice to make clear what belongs with what.

3.9.2 Word-order in noun phrases — Exercise

1. Where is the place of the adjective (including the possessive) in relation to the noun in Old Norse noun phrases? Give four examples, two indefinite, two definite, of Old Norse noun phrases containing adjectives.
2. Where is the place of genitive modifiers in relation to the noun in Old Norse?
3. Where is the place of adverbs in Old Norse in relation to the adjectives they modify?
4. What is meant by discontinuity? Give two examples of its occurrence in Old Norse noun phrases.

3.9.3 Impersonal constructions

Certain verbs in Old Norse are construed without a subject. Many of these have to do with the weather, with the coming of the seasons or of parts of the day or night. Common to all of them is that they denote an event which has no obvious instigator; it is the event itself that the sentence 'is about' (cf. 3.1.5, sentence 1). Examples are (with the subjectless verb in bold):

Frost var veðrs, en áðr hafði **snjófat** nǫkkut
'Frost was of-weather, but earlier had snowed somewhat'
'The weather was frosty, but earlier it had snowed a bit'

Þegar at **haustaði**, tóku at vaxa reimleikar
'At-once COMP became-autumn, began to grow hauntings'
'As soon as autumn arrived the hauntings began to increase'

En at morni þegar **dagaði**, stendr Þórr upp ok þeir félagar
'But in morning as-soon-as dawned gets Þórr up and those companions'
'But in the morning as soon as dawn broke Þórr and his companions get up'

Because of their lack of a subject, constructions such as these are often known as 'impersonal' — a reference to the absence both of an instigator and of person agreement in the verb (cf 3.3.1, 3.6.1), 3rd person sg. being used as the default form. 'Impersonal' is not only applied to cases where the verb cannot have a subject, however, but also to those where a potential subject is left unexpressed. This often happens in Old Norse when the focus is on the object and the subject is of no interest in the context, e.g. (once again with the relevant verb(s) in bold):

(a) Hér **hefr** kristni sǫgu
    'Here begins of-Christianity saga'
    'Here begins the history of the Church (in Iceland)'

(b) Standi menn upp ok taki hann, ok **skal** hann **drepa**
    'Stand men up and seize him, and shall him kill'
    'Let men stand up and seize him; he is to be killed'

(c) **Sjá má** nú, at ekki nýtir þú hér af
    'See can now that nothing benefit you here from'
    'One can see now that you get no benefit at all from this'

It is not uncommon for learners to take *sǫgu* in (a) or the second *hann* in (b) as the subject. However, the form *sǫgu*, which differs from nom. *saga*, and the meaning of *hann*, which can hardly be agent, warn against such hasty conclusions. *Sǫgu* is acc., the object of *hefr*, and the sense is something like 'here one begins the history of the Church'. The Old Norse sentence has no word corresponding to 'one', however, and given that the subject and agent — the person or thing beginning the history — is unspecified, there are several ways of rendering the sense into English, e.g. 'here we begin . . . ', rather than 'here one begins' or the passive 'here is begun' (cf. 3.6.4 and further below). Similarly in (b) both occurrences of *hann* are acc., the objects of *taki* and *drepa*, but whereas *taki* (3rd pl. pres. subj.) has *menn* as its subject (understood because coreferential with the expressed subject of *standi*), *drepa* is subjectless; *menn* cannot be subject here since the finite verb, the auxiliary *skal*, is sg. In English we must once again introduce an unspecified 'one', 'we', 'you', etc. as subject and agent — the person or persons who are to do the killing — or we can make the rendering passive, whereby the Old Norse object *hann* will correspond to the English subject and the agent can be omitted: 'he shall be killed', 'he is to be killed' — by whom in particular is neither here nor there in the context. In (c) the impersonal construction is slightly easier to spot because there is no noun phrase at all in the independent sentence *sjá má nú*, the object of *sjá* being the dependent *at ekki nýtir þú hér af*. Otherwise (c) is not different in type from (a) or (b): the focus is on the object of *sjá* — the thing seen — not the subject — the person or persons who see. The seer or seers are unspecified and can thus be rendered 'one', 'people', etc. in English, or omitted altogether by substituting a passive for the Old Norse active phrase: 'that you get no benefit at all from this can now be seen'.

Insofar as the direct object in active verb phrases becomes the subject when the verb is made passive, active phrases lacking a direct object will, if turned directly into passives (i.e. without further change), tend to be without a subject. In English such passivisation does not occur: we may say *the bed was slept in*, but not **was slept in the bed*. In Old Norse, on the other hand, subjectless passives are a regular feature. Thus, active:

> Þá lǫgðu þeir at jarlsskipinu
> 'Then laid they at earl's-ship-the'
> 'Then they attacked the earl's ship'

> Gekk hann inn nǫkkut fyrir lýsing
> 'Went he in somewhat before dawn'
> 'He went in shortly before dawn'

correspond to passive:

> Þá var lagt at jarlsskipinu
> 'Then was laid at earl's-ship-the'
> 'Then the earl's ship was attacked'

> Var gengit inn nǫkkut fyrir lýsing
> 'Was gone in somewhat before dawn'
> 'Someone went in shortly before dawn'

Students should take careful note of these and the other types of 'impersonal' construction mentioned above. By one means or another they will have to supply a subject when translating them into English.

The designation 'impersonal' has further been applied to Old Norse verbs construed without a nominative, or where the nominative noun phrase is not the first in unmarked word-order (see 3.9.1, 3.1.5, sentence 1). This is a moot point. Where there is no nominative, there is no person agreement in the verb — the default 3rd sg. being used (see above); to that extent 'impersonal' might be deemed an appropriate term. On the other hand, it has been shown that oblique (non-nominative) noun phrases that appear first in unmarked word-order behave like subjects in virtually every respect except the triggering of person agreement. And such phrases may certainly denote 'persons'. While the question how constructions of this type are best described is not of primary concern to the learner, it is important for him/her to realise that where a noun phrase in a case other than the nominative is the first in a sentence, it is not automatically to be taken as a fronted object (see 3.9.1). Thus, in:

> Þá skal hana engan hlut skorta
> 'Then shall her no thing lack'
> 'Then she shall lack nothing'

> Ávalt er ek sé fagrar konur, þá minnir mik þessarrar konu
> 'Always COMP I see beautiful women, then reminds me of-this woman'
> 'Whenever I see beautiful women, then I remember this woman'

> Tók konungi at orna undir feldinum
> 'Began to-king to warm undir cloak-the'
> 'The king began to get warm under the cloak'

> Líkaði yðr vel Finnskattrinn, er Þórólfr sendi yðr?
> 'Liked to-you well Lapp-tribute-the COMP Þórólfr sent to-you?'
> 'Were you pleased with the Lapp-tribute that Þórólfr sent you?'

the accusatives *hana* and *mik* and the datives *konungi* and *yðr* are the first noun phrases in sentences whose word-order is not obviously marked. Even in *líkaði yðr vel Finnskattrinn*, where the second noun phrase is nominative, the difficulty of showing that dat. *yðr* has been fronted makes it hard to cast it in the role of object, and that in turn raises doubts about whether *Finnskattrinn* can be subject. In semantic terms, *hana*, *mik*, *konungi* and *yðr* represent 'experiencers' (the people experiencing the events denoted by the verbs), a sense regularly conveyed by the nominative in modern English and certain other European languages (cf. *I lack, I remember, I get warm, I am pleased*) — seemingly reflecting a common tendency to make the experiencer subject rather than the thing experienced. Certainly, natural English translations of Old Norse sentences like the above will tend to bring out the subjecthood of the first noun phrase.

Also regularly construed without nominatives are the passives of verbs whose direct object is in the genitive or dative, e.g.:

>Þess var leitat við jarl
>'Of-that was sought of earl'
>'That was asked of the earl'

>Mǫnnum var borgit flestum
>'To-men was saved most'
>'Most people were saved'

In the active, *leita* 'seek' 'ask' has a nominative subject and genitive object, *bjarga* 'save' a nominative subject and dative object. When passivised such verbs lose their nominative subject in the normal way (3.6.4), but the object does not become the new nominative subject. It remains in its original case. However, since in unmarked word-order (cf. 3.1.5, sentence 1) it precedes the verb phrase in the passive sentence, there is some justification for treating it as subject. It certainly becomes the theme of the sentence — 'what it is about' (cf. 3.1.5, sentence 1).

Only partially analogous are passives of verbs construed in the active with a nominative subject, a dative indirect object and a further argument in the genitive or dative. To active:

> Þeir ljá jarli lífs
> 'They grant [to-]earl [of-]life'
> 'They spare the earl's life'
>
> Þeir hétu honum bana
> 'They promised [to-]him [with-]death'
> 'They threatened him with death'

correspond passive:

> Engum er alls lét
> 'To-none is [of-]all granted'
> 'No one is granted everything'
>
> Honum var heitit bana
> 'To-him was promised [with-]death'
> 'He was threatened with death'

In the passive versions the nominative subject is lost as before, but it is the indirect object (*engum, honum*) which moves into subject position rather than gen. *alls* or dat. *bana*. Although genitive and dative arguments of this type have been termed 'direct objects' (e.g. 3.1.5, sentences 11, 12, 16, 18, 19 and above in this section), their failure here to move into subject position suggests they retain something of the original syntactic and semantic role that caused them to be expressed by the genitive or dative in the first place. Just as, for example, the dative with which *kasta* is construed can be viewed either as direct object or instrumental phrase — '[to] throw something' or '[to] throw with something' (cf. 3.1.5, sentence 20) — so *ljá* + dat. + gen. may be taken as '[to] grant someone something' or '[to] give to someone possession of something', and *heita* + dat. + dat. as '[to] promise someone something' or '[to] threaten someone with something'.

Nominativeless passive constructions are relatively easy to spot, and — where relevant — the student will normally be able to render the, or the first, genitive or dative noun phrase as the subject when translating, as above. More difficult is to recognise the accusative, genitive or dative that precedes other noun phrases in an active sentence not because it is fronted, but because the verb is thus construed. The student should try to be alert to verbs that do not have a nominative subject (relatively few) and make an effort to learn them as a special category. It is important this be done. Subject and object can otherwise easily be confused. (See further the 'postscript' pp. 262–3.)

3.9.3 Impersonal constructions — Exercise

1. What do you understand by the term 'impersonal'?
2. Give Old Norse examples (a) of a verb always construed without a subject, and (b) of a construction in which a potential subject is left unexpressed.
3. How would you translate examples (a) and (b) in your answers to the previous question into English?
4. In what circumstances do Old Norse passive constructions lack a subject?
5. The first noun phrase in an Old Norse sentence is often in the accusative, genitive or dative case. What are the different possibilities of interpretation in such examples?
6. How are the main verbs in the following sentences construed?

   (a) Líðr fram haustinu ok tekr at vetra
   'The autumn passes and winter comes on'
   (b) Þess er enn ekki hefnt
   'That is not yet avenged'
   (c) Ekki sá skipit fyrir laufinu
   'The ship could not be seen for the foliage'
   (d) Draum dreymði mik í fyrri nátt
   'I dreamt a dream the night before last'
   (e) Engum mun bóta synjat
   'No one will be refused compensation'

3.9.4 Accusative and infinitive

In English we may say: *I saw her open it, he asked the boys to sing*. What follows *saw* and *asked* is sometimes described as a non-finite clause object: we have a clause or sentence which is the equivalent of an object (cf. *I saw the letter, he asked a favour*), and it contains an infinitive (*open*, *sing*) but no finite verb. This analysis, however, leaves out of account the fact that in a sense *her* is both the object of *saw* and the subject of *open*, and *the boys* both the object of *asked* and subject of *sing* (cf. (*I saw that*) *she opened it*, (*he asked the boys that*) *they should sing*). The term mostly used to describe the Old Norse counterparts of such English constructions is 'accusative and infinitive'. While hardly achieving descriptive adequacy, this designation has the merit of emphasising accusative case, which marks direct object status, and suggesting a connection between the accusative and the following infinitive. Above all, it is a more precise term than non-finite clause object, which can cover a variety of constructions.

Old Norse accusatives and infinitives occur regularly after verbs of saying, thinking, and experiencing. E.g.:

> Magnús bað hann fara sem honum líkaði
> 'Magnus bade him go as to-him pleased'
> 'Magnús said he could go as he pleased'

> Vér ætlum hana litla hríð svá hafa verit kallaða
> 'We think her little while thus have been called'
> 'We think she has been called that only a short while'

> Opt hefi ek heyrt yðr þat mæla
> 'Often have I heard you that say'
> 'I have often heard you say that'

In cases where the accusative object/subject of the infinitive is identical with the subject of the finite verb, the former is not expressed as a separate word; instead it is denoted by the -*sk* suffix (3.6.5.3), which can be considered to have reflexive function. Thus in:

> Hon sagðisk vera dóttir Þorkels
> 'She said-*sk* be daughter of-Þorkell'
> 'She said she was Þorkell's daughter'

the -*sk* can be interpreted literally as 'herself'. Observe that the subject complement *dóttir* is nominative. This is the rule where the accusative of an acc. + inf. construction is to be found in the -*sk* suffix.

Where the accusative appears as a separate word denoting an entity different from the subject of the finite verb, a subject complement will agree with it by also appearing in the accusative — cf. acc. f. sg. *kallaða* in the second example above agreeing with *hana*, and:

> Hann sagði Sigmund vera óbættan
> 'He said Sigmundr be unatoned'
> 'He said Sigmundr was unatoned [i.e. his death was uncompensated]'

where acc. m. sg. *óbættan* agrees with *Sigmund*.

In the case of the verb *þyk(k)ja* 'seem' 'think' we normally find a 'nominative and infinitive' construction. There are two variants of this. Occasionally the subject of the infinitive is 'raised' (i.e. moved into the higher sentence) and becomes the subject of *þyk(k)ja* (a), but more commonly *þyk(k)ja* appears in the default 3rd sg. form, with dative experiencer — denoting the person to whom the matter of the infinitive sentence 'seems' — as its most likely subject (see 3.9.3) and a nominative as the subject of the infinitive (b).

(a)   Eiríki konungi . . . þóttu þeir mjǫk hafa spottat sik
       'To-Eiríkr king seemed they much have mocked self'
       'King Eiríkr thought they had mocked him greatly'

(b)   Þá þótti mér þeir sœkja at ǫllum megin
       'Then seemed to-me they come against on-all sides'
       'Then it seemed to me they attacked on all sides'

In (a) nom. *þeir* is the subject of *þóttu* as can be seen from the 3rd pl. verb-form. In (b), on the other hand, where *þótti* is 3rd sg., *þeir* can only be the subject of inf. *sœkja*. When the subject of the infinitive is 3rd sg., as it often is, the two constructions are difficult to distinguish. In:

> Þótti honum hon vel hafa gert
> 'Seemed to-him she well have done'
> 'He thought she had acted well'

hon can according to traditional analysis be the overt subject either of *þótti* or of *gert*. In some modern approaches dat. *honum*, the first noun phrase, would be deemed the subject of *þótti*, as also *mér* in (b) above.

Subject raising is the norm with *þyk(k)ja* where the subject of the following infinitive denotes the same person as the experiencer (the person to whom the matter of the infinitive sentence 'seems'). In, for example:

> Þú þykkisk of fá drepit hafa mína hirðmenn óbœtta
> 'You seem-*sk* too few killed have my retainers unatoned'
> 'You think you have killed too few of my retainers without paying compensation'

a putative **þykkir þér þú of fá drepit hafa* . . . is restructured in such a way that *þú*, the subject of *drepit*, becomes the subject of the finite sentence and the dative experiencer is converted into an -*sk* suffix. This is not unlike what happens with the *hon sagðisk vera* . . . type of construction above, though there there is no subject raising and the -*sk* suffix takes the place of an accusative rather than a dative. If we render -*sk* in the above example as 'to yourself', and translate fairly literally 'you seem to yourself to have killed too few . . . ' we get something of the flavour of the original.

Concerning *þyk(k)ja*, it should finally be noted that the 3rd singular present indicative is often *þyk(k)i* rather than *þyk(k)ir* (see 3.6.9.1 point (15)).

Sometimes in accusative and infinitive constructions a past infinitive is encountered (see 3.6.6). In prose this is only likely to involve the forms *mundu*, *skyldu*, *vildu*, and occurs chiefly when the finite verb is past tense. E.g.:

> Hann lézk heldr mundu at sinni gefa upp ríkit
> 'He said-*sk* rather would for time give up earldom-the'
> 'He said he would rather give up the earldom for the time being'

> Þórðr kvað beggja þeira ráð þetta vera skyldu
> 'Þórðr said of-both their decision this be should'
> 'Þórðr said this should be their joint decision'

It is difficult to get the literal sense of *mundu* and *skyldu* across since English 'would' and 'should' are finite forms. Semi-literal renderings may be helpful here, using the infinitive marker *to* to direct attention to the past infinitive.

> 'He said himself rather to would give up the earldom . . . '

> 'Þórðr said this their joint decision to should be'

3.9.4 Accusative and infinitive — Exercise

1. Why are Old Norse accusative and infinitive constructions so called?
2. What happens to the accusative in an accusative and infinitive construction when it denotes the same entity as the subject of the finite verb?
3. Describe the different kinds of nominative and infinitive construction in which the verb *þyk(k)ja* is found.
4. In what type of construction do past infinitives occur in Old Norse?

3.9.5 Omissions

Certain elements are regularly omitted from Old Norse sentences. Some can be readily understood from the context and will cause the learner no difficulty. A subject that is already established, for example, is usually omitted in Old Norse just as in English. Thus, in:

> Karl hljóp á annat skip ok bað þá taka til ára
> 'Karl jumped onto another ship and bade them take to oars'
> 'Karl jumped onto another ship and told them to start rowing'

the subject of *bað* is not expressed — any more than in the English renderings — because it refers to the same person as the subject of the previous sentence, *Karl*.

3.9.5.1 Objects

Slightly more problematic for the learner, because characteristic of Old Norse but not of English, is the omission of the object where already established. E.g.:

(a) Njáll tók fésjóðinn ok seldi Gunnari
     'Njáll took money-bag-the and gave to-Gunnarr'
     'Njáll took the bag of money and gave it to Gunnarr'

(b) Konungr greip til sverðs ok brá
     'King grasped at sword and drew'
     'The king grabbed hold of the sword and drew it'

Here 'it', referring in (a) to the bag of money, in (b) to the sword, is lacking in Old Norse. This is because there is identity of reference with a preceding noun, *fésjóðinn* in (a), *sverðs* in (b). Observe that object omission is not dependent on case equivalence. In (a) the missing noun phrase would have had accusative case, just as *fésjóðinn*, but in (b) it would have been dative, while *sverðs*, the noun establishing the reference in (b), is genitive, governed by the preposition *til* (3.7.2). Indirect objects, too, may be omitted, as in:

> Konungr lét skíra Hákon ok kenna rétta trú
> 'King let baptise Hákon and teach true faith'
> 'The king had Hákon baptised and taught the true faith'

Note that the idiomatic English rendering obscures the omission; insertion of 'him' between 'taught' and 'the' would give a different sense — that it was the king himself who taught Hákon the true faith.

3.9.5.2 vera

The verb *vera* is often omitted, especially the infinitive (a) in connection with auxiliary verbs and (b) in accusative and infinitive constructions. The student should pay particular attention to this phenomenon since it can often cause misunderstanding.

Consider the following examples:

> Þú munt þá ekki hér vel kominn
> 'You will then not here well come'
> 'You will not then be welcome here'

> Þat mæltu sumir, at leitat skyldi um sættir
> 'That said some, that sought should about settlement'
> 'Some said that an attempt should be made to reach a settlement'

> Þorfinnr kvað þat ósannligt, at . . .
> 'Þorfinnr said that unjust that . . .'
> 'Þorfinnr said it was unjust that . . .'

> Tǫlðu sumir várkunn, at hann vildi eigi miðla ríkit
> 'Said some cause that he wanted not divide earldom-the'
> 'Some said there was understandable cause for his unwillingness to divide the earldom'

In the first example the copula (*vera*, the verb 'be') is the missing link needed to connect subject *þú* and the subject complement *vel kominn* (cf. *þú ert vel kominn* 'you are welcome'). In the second *vera* is required to complete the passive construction *leitat skyldi vera* 'should be sought'. The third and fourth examples illustrate accusative and infinitive constructions from which the infinitive is omitted. In the third the copula is what is wanted to connect *þat* and its complement *ósannligt* (cf. *þat er ósannligt* — subject + copula + subject complement), so the construction is to be understood as *Þorfinnr kvað þat ósannligt vera, at* . . . The fourth example too requires *vera* to be understood since *várkunn* can only be the object of *tǫlðu* in an accusative and infinitive construction (i.e. *tǫlðu sumir várkunn vera at* . . . is perfectly acceptable, but **tǫlðu sumir várkunn* without the ellipsis of *vera* is not).

Because all four contexts so clearly demand *vera*, it is readily understood or supplied by the reader familiar with Old Norse. The beginner will have to proceed more slowly and analytically: faced by a sentence that seems to lack an infinitive, and in doubt about the meaning, s/he should always try supplying *vera*. In most cases this will provide the solution.

Finite forms of *vera* are also sometimes omitted. As with the above, the prerequisite seems to be that the verb should be recoverable from the context. Consider:

> Fimm menn hǫfðu bana af liði Helga, en sárir allir aðrir
> 'Five men had death from force of-Helgi, but wounded all others'
> 'Five of Helgi's men were killed, and all the others were wounded'

The finite verb of the first sentence is *hǫfðu*, but that will not fit the context of the second. What we have in *sárir allir aðrir* is a fronted subject complement (*sárir*) followed by the subject (*allir aðrir*), and the copula is needed to connect them. The second sentence is thus to be understood: *en sárir váru allir aðrir*.

3.9.5.3 Verbs of motion

The infinitives of verbs of motion are often omitted when modified by an adverb or preposition phrase indicating destination. E.g.:

> Sámr sagðisk vilja heim aptr
> 'Sámr said-*sk* want home again'
> 'Sámr said he wanted to go back home'

> Ætlaði hann yfir á Nes
> 'Intended he over to Nes'
> 'He intended to go across to Caithness'

Because of the clear directional sense indicated by adverb or preposition phrase, such constructions are unlikely to cause the learner great problems.

3.9.5 Omissions — Exercise

1. In what circumstances may the object be omitted in Old Norse? Give examples.
2. In what kinds of construction is *vera* commonly omitted? Give examples.
3. What is understood in the sentence: *nú býsk hann út til Íslands* 'now he gets ready to go to Iceland'?

3.9.6 Points of nominal syntax

Important aspects of nominal syntax not dealt with elsewhere are (1) certain idiomatic uses of personal pronouns and possessive adjectives; (2) what are often loosely termed 'the genitive and dative of respect'.

3.9.6.1 Idiomatic uses of personal pronouns and possessive adjectives

Sometimes in Old Norse personal names are accompanied appositionally by a 3rd person pronoun of the same gender and number. Instead of *þar sitr Selsbani* 'there sits Selsbani', we find *þar sitr hann Selsbani* 'there sits he [i.e. that fellow] Selsbani', instead of *hann var faðir Eiríks hins sigrsæla ok Óláfs* 'he was the father of Eiríkr the victorious and Óláfr', *hann var faðir þeira Eiríks hins sigrsæla ok Óláfs* 'he was the father of-them [i.e. of the pair] Eiríkr the victorious and Óláfr'. More commonly a 3rd plural or 1st or 2nd dual or plural pronoun is found together with a single name. E.g.:

> Báru þeir Rǫgnvaldr eld at bœnum
> 'Carried they Rǫgnvaldr fire to house-the'
> 'Rǫgnvaldr and the others set fire to the house'

> Vit Arnviðr munum fara
> 'We-two Arnviðr will go'
> 'Arnviðr and I will go'

Here, as will be seen from the idiomatic translations, the pronouns are only partly in apposition to the personal names since they also contain a reference to one or more other people known from the context. The dual pronouns denote one additional person, the 1st and 2nd plural more than one. Thus *vér Arnviðr* would mean 'Arnviðr and we (others)', *þit Arnviðr* 'Arnviðr and you [sg.]', *þér Arnviðr* 'Arnviðr and you (others)'. Since there is no dual 3rd person pronoun, *þeir Rǫgnvaldr* can mean 'Rǫgnvaldr and he' as well as 'Rǫgnvaldr and the others', depending on the context. Where men and women or a man and a woman are involved, the 3rd person neuter plural is used (cf. 3.2.1):

> Þau dróttning tala jafnan
> 'They queen talk constantly'
> 'The queen and he talk constantly'

From the context of this particular example we know that only the queen and a single male are involved; in another context *þau dróttning* could mean 'the queen and the others (including at least one male)'.

This usage is not confined to personal pronouns, but can also be found with possessive adjectives. E.g.:

> Hverja ætlan hefir þú á um deilu ykkra Óláfs digra?
> 'What view have you on about quarrel your-two Óláfr's stout?'
> 'What is your view of Óláfr the stout's and your quarrel?'

Here the dual 2nd person possessive *ykkra* carries the same 'inclusive' sense as the personal pronouns in the previous examples. There is however a significant syntactic difference between *ykkra Óláfs digra* and, say, *vit Arnviðr*. The pronoun *vit* stands in the same case as *Arnviðr* (nom.), whereas *ykkra* takes its case (and gender and number) from *deilu* (acc. f. sg.) while *Óláfs digra* is in the genitive. The difference is occasioned by the fact that *vit* and *Arnviðr* form a joint subject, a pairing of two noun phrases, whereas *ykkra* and *Óláfs*, though both modify *deilu*, represent different word classes: adjective and noun. The possessive signals its modifier role by case, gender and number agreement, but the noun cannot — instead it goes into the genitive (the 'possessive' case, see 3.1.5, sentence 13). The close relationship between possessive adjectives and genitives is shown by the 3rd person pronouns (non-reflexive), whose genitive forms, *hans*, *hennar*, *þess*, *þeira*, double up as possessives (3.3.8.5 point (6)).

It should be observed that the juxtaposition of possessive adjectives and genitive noun phrases is also common in more unambiguous cases of apposition. E.g.:

> Er þat vili várr búandanna
> 'Is that will our of-farmers-the'
> 'That is the will of us farmers'

Two further points of nominal syntax involving possessives and pronouns require discussion.

In partitive constructions (3.2.6, sentence 20, 3.4.2, sentence 9) where a pronoun is the head word denoting the part, and the modifier denoting the whole would be expected to be a personal pronoun, the latter is usually replaced by the corresponding possessive adjective, which agrees in case, gender and number with the head word. E.g.:

> Skal hverr yðvarr fara í friði fyrir mér
> 'Shall each your go in peace before me'
> 'Each of you shall go in peace as far as I am concerned'

> Þá skal sá okkarr kjósa bœn af ǫðrum, er sannara hefir
> 'Then shall that-one our-two choose favour of other COMP truer has'
> 'Then the one of us (two) who is right shall choose a favour of the other'

Instead of nom. m. sg. *hverr* 'each' + gen. *yðvar* 'of you' and nom. m. sg. *sá* 'that one' + gen. *okkar* 'of us two', we find nom. m. sg. *hverr yðvarr* 'each your' and nom. m. sg. *sá okkarr* 'that one our-two'. Students should take careful note of this construction since experience has shown it can cause much confusion.

Contemptuous reference is a further case in which a possessive adjective is used where on the basis of English one might expect a personal pronoun. This can occur in both direct and indirect speech. Thus we find not only *fóli þinn* 'fool your [i.e. you fool!]', but also:

> Hann bað þegja bikkjuna hans
> 'He bade be-silent bitch-the his'
> 'He told the dog to shut up'

where 'the dog' is used insultingly of a man.

3.9.6.2 The genitive and dative of respect

The genitive and dative can be used in Old Norse to specify the applicability of the verb phrase. The basic sense of such constructions is 'with respect to' 'in respect of' 'as regards', but idiomatic English will usually require a different translation. E.g. (with the genitive or dative phrases in bold):

> Þegi þú **þeira orða**
> 'Be-silent you of-those words'
> 'Keep quiet with those words'

Vesall ertu **þinnar skjaldborgar**
'Wretched are-you of-your shield-fortification'
'You and your wretched wall of shields!'

Er Haraldr konungr varð **þessa tíðinda** víss, þá dró hann her saman
'When Haraldr king became of-these tidings aware, then drew he army together'
'When King Haraldr got news of these events, he gathered together an army'

Ǫll váru bǫrn Svíakonungs vel **viti** borin
'All were children of-Swedes-king well with-wit endowed'
'All the children of the Swedish king were endowed with a good understanding'

Varð **þeim** mart talat
'Became to-them much talked'
'There was much talk between them'

Vín er **honum** bæði drykkr ok matr
'Wine is to him both drink and food'

Dative phrases of respect often have the force of possessives. This applies notably where they complement preposition phrases denoting body parts. E.g. (with dative and preposition phrase in bold):

Skarði fell **fyrir fœtr Þorkeli**
'Skarði fell before feet to-Þorkell'
'Skarði fell in front of Þorkell's feet'

Loki greip upp mikla stǫng ok rekr **á kroppinn erninum**
'Loki grasped up big pole and drives onto body-the to-eagle-the'
'Loki seized a big pole and drove it against the eagle's body'

Þá laust hann sverðit **ór hǫndum honum**
'Then struck he sword-the out-of hands to-him'
'Then he struck the sword out of his hands'

3.9.6 Points of nominal syntax — Exercise

Analyse the phrases printed in bold in the following sentences:

(a) **Þeir Þorfinnr** dvǫlðusk í eyjunni um nóttina
 'Þorfinnr and the others stayed on the island for the night'
(b) Með henni mun nú vera **beggja ykkur** hamingja
 'With her lies the good fortune of you both now'
(c) En ek hefi hér vitnismenn þá, er handsal **okkart jarls** sá
 'But I have witnesses here who saw the earl's and my agreement'
(d) **Hverjum yðrum** þótti þat ráðligast?
 'Which of you thought it most advisable?'
(e) Hrani sagði henni **hverra erinda** Haraldr fór á fund Sigríðar dróttningar
 'Hrani told her for what purpose Haraldr had gone to see Queen Sigríðr'
(f) Þá lét Loki fallask **í kné Skaða**
 'Then Loki let himself drop onto Skaði's knees'

3.9.7 Points of verbal syntax

A few remarks on verbal syntax need to be added to the basics set out at various points in section 3.6. These concern four areas: (1) the perfect and past perfect (3.6.2, 3.6.8, sentence 3); (2) the passive (3.6.4); (3) the 'dative absolute'; (4) present participles expressing potentiality or obligation.

3.9.7.1 The perfect and past perfect

The perfect and past perfect of intransitive verbs of movement and change are construed with *vera* as well as *hafa*. E.g.:

> Hann hafði komit út með Þorkatli
> 'He had come out with Þorkell'
> 'He had come to Iceland with Þorkell'

> Maðr er hér kominn úti fyrir durum
> 'Man is here come outside before doorway'
> 'A man has arrived here outside the door'

Svá mun Hallgerði sýnask, sem hann hafi eigi sjálfdauðr orðit
'So will to-Hallgerðr seem, as he has not self-dead become'
'It will seem to Hallgerðr as though he has not died a natural death'

Þá er myrkt var orðit, leituðu þeir sér til náttstaðar
'Then COMP dark was become, searched they for-self for night-place'
'When it had become dark, they looked for a place to spend the night'

The choice of auxiliary depends on the sense. Where the focus is on the action itself, *hafa* is used, where the state following the action is emphasised, we find *vera* (contrast English *he has gone there a lot recently* and *he is gone* (= *he is no longer present*)). Thus the first example above focuses on the travelling to Iceland rather than the being there, the third on the dying rather than the being dead. In the second and fourth examples, in contrast, the emphasis is on the man's being outside the door and the state of darkness in which the searching took place.

It will be observed that where *vera* is the auxiliary, the past participle inflects as an adjective, agreeing with the subject in case, gender and number (cf. 3.6.6). Thus *maðr* and *kominn* are both nom. m. sg. (*þá er myrkt var orðit* has no subject, so the nom. n. sg. (*orðit*) is used as the default form). With *hafa* as the auxiliary, on the other hand, the past participle tends to adopt the neuter nom./acc. sg. form, and is then often known as the supine (3.6.8, sentence 3). The reason for this difference lies in the auxiliaries themselves. Elements linked by *vera*, whatever its function, stand in the same case, the one element modifying the other, whereas non-auxiliary *hafa* is construed with a nominative subject and accusative object (cf., e.g., *hann hafði tvá knǫrru* 'he had two merchant ships'). In perfect constructions with *hafa* the past participle does not normally modify anything; it combines with the auxiliary to form a single verb phrase. Thus in *hann hafði keypt tvá knǫrru* 'he had bought two merchant ships' *hafði keypt* is the verb phrase of which *tvá knǫrru* is the object. In origin, however, the perfect seems to have been a subject — verb — object — object complement construction ('I have them bought'), which was gradually re-analysed as subject — verb phrase — object ('I have bought them').

One of the chief reasons for assuming this development is that in early Old Norse texts the past participle quite often agrees with an accusative object (never a genitive or dative, since *hafa* governed the accusative only). It seems, however, that at this relatively late stage in the history of the Old Norse perfect, participle-object agreement had ceased to carry the original 'I have them bought' meaning. Agreement and non-agreement give the appearance of being interchangeable — indeed, sometimes we find an inflected and an uninflected participle dependent on the same auxiliary, e.g. (with the participles in bold):

> En jarlsmenn hǫfðu **barða** marga eyjarskeggja, en **tekit** Kúga bónda ok **settan** í fjǫtra
> 'But earl's-men had beaten many islanders, but taken Kúgi farmer and placed in shackles'
> 'But the earl's men had beaten many islanders and taken the farmer, Kúgi, and put him in shackles'

There is agreement here between *barða* and *marga eyjarskeggja* (acc. m. pl.), and *settan* and *Kúga bónda* (acc. m. sg.), but not between *Kúga bónda* (acc. m. sg.) and *tekit* (nom./acc. n. sg.). The function of the participle is however the same in all three cases: each combines with *hǫfðu* to form a verb phrase of which *marga eyjarskeggja* or *Kúga bónda* are the objects. The student may thus consider inflected participles in perfect constructions as ordinary supines and treat them in exactly the same way they would their uninflected counterparts (as in modern French).

Several other verbs combine with past participles to form periphrastic constructions, but of these only *fá* and *geta* are at all common. Both have the basic sense 'get', and their use with past participles is paralleled in English (cf. *he got it done*). As in the *hafa* constructions, the participle may either agree with an accusative object or not; where the object is genitive or dative, or there is no object, the nom./acc. n. sg. form is always used. E.g. (with the periphrastic verb phrases in bold):

> Abraham **gat frelsta** frændr sína
> 'Abraham got saved kinsmen his'
> 'Abraham was able to save his kinsmen'

Ambáttirnar **fengu dregit** steininn
'Bondwomen-the got dragged stone-the'
'The bondwomen managed to drag the stone'

Sá **fekk** þó **borgit** sér nauðuliga
'He got though saved self narrowly'
'He just about managed to save himself, though'

In the first example *frelsta* agrees with *frændr sína* (acc. m. pl.), in the second and third examples the nom./acc. n. sg. form of the participle is used, once where the object is acc. m. sg. (*steininn*), once where it is dat. reflexive.

3.9.7.2 The passive

The Old Norse periphrastic passive formed with *vera* may be dynamic or static, just as its English counterpart with *be*. Dynamic passives denote an action or event, static passives the state after an action or event. Two typical examples illustrating the difference are:

Var sá hǫggvinn fyrr, er síðar gekk
'Was he cut-down earlier COMP later walked'
'He (of two) who walked behind was slain first'

Hann nefndi mennina þá, er vegnir váru
'He named men-the those COMP slain were'
'He named the men who were slain'

The passive *var sá hǫggvinn, er . . .* is the equivalent of the past tense active: *þeir hjoggu þann, er . . .* 'they slew the one who . . .', whereas *er vegnir váru* corresponds to the past perfect active *er þeir hǫfðu vegit* 'whom they had slain', and could itself be expressed as a past perfect: *er vegnir hǫfðu verit* 'who had been slain'. Of itself, *vera* + pp. is ambiguous; it is the context that determines whether the construction is to be understood as dynamic or static, just as in English (cf., e.g., ambiguous *the house was sold*, which may be expanded into the dynamic *the house was sold by the new agent* or the static *the house was already sold*). A further contrastive pair of Old Norse examples illustrating present tense usage is:

> Fjórir hleifar brauðs eru honum fœrðir hvern dag
> 'Four loaves of-bread are to-him brought each day'
> 'Four loaves of bread are brought to him each day'

> Frá þessu segir í flokki þeim, er ortr er um Þormóð
> 'From this says in poem that COMP composed is about Þormóðr'
> 'It tells of this in the poem that is composed about Þormóðr'

The passive *eru honum fœrðir* is dynamic, the equivalent of active *þeir fœra honum* 'they bring to him', while *ortr er* is static, corresponding to active *einnhverr hefir ort* 'someone has composed'.

Sometimes passives are formed with auxiliary *verða* rather than *vera*. Such passives are always dynamic, and usually have one or more additional senses — commonly the notion of futurity and/or possibility. E.g.:

> Hversu megu synir hans, þeir er getnir verða í útlegð, njóta þeira gjafa?
> 'How may sons his, those COMP born are in exile, enjoy those gifts?'
> 'How may his sons, those who will be born in exile, enjoy those gifts?'

> Varð engi uppreist í móti konungi gǫr í þat sinn í Þrándheimi
> 'Was no uprising a(-)gainst king made on that occasion in Þrándheimr'
> 'No rebellion was made against the king on that occasion in Þrándheimr'

In the first example the talk is of sons who *may* be born *in the future*. The interpretation of the second example is less certain: it need be no more than a dynamic passive, but it could carry the additional sense that an uprising against the king was not possible on that occasion (because of his superior force). More firmly endowed with the notion of (im)possibility is:

> Hallbjǫrn hleypr til búðar, en sveinarnir til skógar, er þar var nær, ok verða cigi fundnir
> 'Hallbjǫrn runs to booth, but boys-the to scrub, COMP there was near, and are not found'
> 'Hallbjǫrn runs to the booth, but the boys run into the scrub which was nearby and cannot be found'

Occasionally in *verða*-passives the agent may be expressed by the dative, e.g.:

> Honum varð litit upp til hlíðarinnar
> 'By-him was looked up to hillside-the'
> 'He looked up at the hillside'

Such constructions usually carry the implication that the action was a chance one, a sense of *verða* being '[to] happen' (cf. *slíkt verðr opt ungum mǫnnum* 'such things often happen to young men'). A more precise idiomatic rendering of the above would therefore be: 'He chanced to look up at the hillside'.

3.9.7.3 *The 'dative absolute'*

The Old Norse 'dative absolute' construction consists of a noun phrase in the dative accompanied by a present or past participle in agreement, the two conveying what would otherwise be expressed by a dependent temporal sentence. Commonly the construction takes the form of a prepositional phrase introduced by *at*, but in more formal style the preposition may be dispensed with. E.g. (with the dative absolute in bold):

> Ok **at liðnum þrimr nóttum** fór hann at finna vísendamann
> 'And with passed three nights went he to find soothsayer'
> 'And when three nights had passed he went to find the soothsayer'

Vér skulum hér koma svá margir þingmenn, sem nú eru til nefndir, **at uppverandi sólu**
'We shall here come as many assembly-members as now are to appointed, with up-being sun'
'We are to come here, as many assembly members as are now appointed for the purpose, when the sun is up'

Þessum þrettán útgengnum váru aðrir þrettán inn leiddir
'These thirteen out-gone were other thirteen in led'
'When these thirteen had gone out, another thirteen were led in'

Hǫfum vér þar um talat **herra Erlingi ok ǫðrum góðum mǫnnum hjáverǫndum**
'Have we there about spoken lord Erlingr and other good men present-being'
'We have spoken about it in the presence of Lord Erlingr and other good men'

The idiomatic English renderings make clear the equivalence between dative absolutes and dependent temporal sentences. An alternative to 'in the presence of Lord Erlingr and other good men' is 'when Lord Erlingr and other good men were present'. The construction with the past participle corresponds to a finite perfect or past perfect, that with the present to a finite present or past, depending on the context.

3.9.7.4 Present participles expressing potentiality or obligation

Present participles can appear in Old Norse as subject complements with the sense of what is suitable, possible or necessary, and with a passive interpretation. In this function, *geranda*, for example, means 'do-able' — 'fit to be done', 'able to be done' or 'necessary to be done', according to the context. A few examples will suffice to make the usage clear:

Hann fór suðr með landinu at leita, ef þar væri byggjanda
'He went south along land-the to search if there might-be settleable'
'He went south along the coast to see if it might be suitable for settlement there'

Jarl kvað þetta vera ópolanda
'Earl said this be intolerable'
'The earl said this was intolerable'

At kveldi er dagr lofandi
'At evening is day to-be-praised'
'The day should be praised when evening comes (and not before)'

The clarity of the context will determine the degree of precision with which the participle can be translated into English.

Outside this construction, the Old Norse present participle tends to correspond to the English *-ing* form of the verb and will give the learner little trouble: e.g. *hlæjandi* 'laughing', *skínandi* 'shining', *sofandi* 'sleeping'.

3.9.7 Points of verbal syntax — Exercise

1. When is *hafa* and when *vera* used to form perfect and past perfect constructions?
2. To what in Old Norse does the term 'supine' refer?
3. What is the difference between an inflected past participle and an inflected supine in Old Norse?
4. Give an example of a dynamic and a static passive in Old Norse and explain the difference.
5. What characterises *verða*-passives?
6. What is the Old Norse 'dative absolute'? Give examples of the construction.
7. Explain the meaning of the present participle in: *þat þótti þó ógeranda, at konungr vissi eigi þetta.*

3.9.8 Points of syntax affecting more than one type of phrase

Three matters require brief treatment: (1) adjectival and adverbial complements; (2) agreement between subject, verb and subject complement; (3) -*sk* verb forms and 'preposition adverbs'.

3.9.8.1 Adjectival and adverbial complements

Complements of *vera* '[to] be' and *verða* '[to] become' are sometimes adverbs in Old Norse. In the case of the pair *vel* 'well' and *illa* 'badly', English tends to use adjectives in corresponding phrases. E.g.:

> Þat er vel
> 'It is good' 'It is right'
>
> Konungr segir, at þat var illa at Arnljótr hafði eigi farit á hans fund
> 'King says that it was badly that Arnljótr had not gone on his meeting'
> 'The king says that it was bad that Arnljótr had not gone to see him'
>
> Þú skalt heita þræll, ok svá vera
> 'You shall be-called slave and so be'
> 'You shall be called a slave and be so'
>
> Varð Eyjólfr þá framarlega
> 'Became Eyjólfr then forward'
> 'Eyjólfr then came to be near the front'

In contradistinction to usage in the first two of the above sentences, adjectives may stand in apposition to subjects, objects or prepositional complements in Old Norse where English would employ an adverb or adverbial (cf. 3.5.4). This applies to comparatives and superlatives where a sequence or order is denoted, to quantifiers such as *einn* 'one', *allr* 'all', *hálfr* 'half', and to the locational terms *miðr* 'middle', *þverr* 'transverse'. E.g.:

Skuluð þit brœðr fyrstir fara
'Shall you-two brothers [as the] first go'
'You two brothers shall go first'

Þrym drap hann fyrstan
'Þrymr killed he [as the] first'
'He killed Þrymr first'

Hann var einn konungr yfir landi
'He was one king over country'
'He alone was king over the country'

Hví ertu í blóði einu allr?
'Why are-you in blood one all?'
'Why are you completely covered in blood?'

Kom sú á hann miðjan
'Came she onto him middle'
'It hit him in the middle (of his body)'

(Cf. also 3.1.5, sentence 20.)

3.9.8.2 Agreement between subject, verb and subject complement

Although the verb in Old Norse normally agrees in number with the (nominative) subject of the sentence (3.1.1, 3.2, 3.6.1), there are exceptions to the rule. Where the verb precedes one or more of a sequence of conjoined subjects, it will often appear in the same number as the subject which is closest. E.g. (with the relevant agreement in bold):

Var þá **Ulfr** ok allir stafnbúarnir komnir at lyptingunni
'Was then Ulfr and all forecastle-men-the come to poop-deck-the'
'Then Ulfr and all the forecastle men had got to the poop-deck'

> **Týndisk fé allt** ok meiri hlutr manna
> 'Lost-*sk* property all and greater part of-men'
> 'All the property was lost and most of the men'
>
> **Konungr var** allmjǫk drukkinn ok bæði þau
> 'King was all-much drunk and both they'
> 'The king was very drunk and she as well'

Observe that in the first sentence the past participle *komnir* agrees with the plural subject *allir stafnbúarnir* (or, equally possible, both subjects together) rather than the singular subject *Ulfr* and the singular verb. (On the use of *þau* in the last sentence, see 3.9.6.1.)

Even where it precedes a lone plural subject, a verb may appear in the singular if several words intervene. E.g. (with the singular verb in bold):

> Eptir þat **dreif** at þeim fóstbrœðrum vinir þeira ór Firðafylki
> 'After that drifted to those foster-brothers friends their from Firðafylki'
> 'After that their friends from Firðafylki thronged to (join) the foster-brothers'

In sentences of the type *X is Y*, the verb often agrees in number with *Y*, the subject complement, especially when the subject is *þat* 'that' 'it' or *þetta* 'this'. E.g. (with the relevant agreement in bold):

> **Váru** þat **lítil sár** ok **mǫrg**
> 'Were that small wounds and many'
> 'The wounds were small and many'
>
> Ekki **munu** þetta **friðarmenn** vera
> 'Not will this peace-men be'
> 'These will not be men of peace'
>
> Slíkt **eru konungsmenn**, sem þú ert
> 'Such are king's men as you are'
> 'You are the sort of person to be a king's man'

Notice further the propensity of past participles in such constructions to agree with the subject complement rather than the subject:

> Var þat **mikill fjǫlði orðinn**
> 'Was it great multitude become'
> 'It had become a great number'

Sometimes, however, agreement is with the subject:

> **Þat var** Þorkell nefja, Karlshǫfuð, ok Þorsteinn ok Einarr þambarskelfir
> 'That was Þorkell nefja, Karlshǫfuð, and Þorsteinn and Einarr þambarskelfir'

> **Þat** var síðan **kallat** Kvernbítr
> 'It was thereafter called Kvernbítr [m.]'

3.9.8.3 -sk *verb forms and 'preposition adverbs'*

As pointed out in 3.6.5.3, the *-sk* form may have reflexive and reciprocal function. Often this is combined with use of a preposition, which, in an abstract sense, governs the reflexive or reciprocal to which the *-sk* form gives expression. Since, however, there is no overt prepositional complement in such constructions, the preposition has the appearance of an adverb (cf. 3.7.7). E.g. (with the *-sk* form and preposition given in bold):

> Kormakr lita**sk um**
> 'Kormakr looks-*sk* around'
> 'Kormakr looks around him'

> Þeir lǫgðusk allir niðr fyrir kirkjunni ok báðu**sk fyrir**
> 'They laid-*sk* all down before church-the and prayed-*sk* for'
> 'They all laid themselves down before the church and prayed for themselves'

Ek hefi nú vel **um** búi**zk**
'I have now well around prepared-*sk*'
'I have now protected myself all around'

Áttu**sk** þeir **við** drykkju ok orðaskipti
'Had-*sk* they with drinking and conversation'
'They had drinks and conversation with each other'

Horfðu**sk** þeir Gizurr **at** hǫfðunum
'Faced-*sk* they Gizurr towards with-heads-the'
'Gizurr and he faced towards each other with their heads'

Where the preposition is immediately followed by a noun phrase (or noun phrases) as in the last two sentences, the student should be particularly careful not to jump to the conclusion that the two belong together. Neither *við drykkju ok orðaskipti* nor *at hǫfðunum* is a preposition phrase, *drykkju ok orðaskipti* being the accusative direct object of *áttu*, *hǫfðunum* a manner adverbial in the dative case.

3.9.8 Points of syntax affecting more than one type of phrase — Exercise

1. Old Norse sometimes employs adverbs as complements of *vera* '[to] be' and *verða* '[to] become'. Give examples and compare and contrast Old Norse usage with English in this respect.
2. In Old Norse an adjective standing in apposition to subject, object or prepositional complement often corresponds to an adverb or adverbial in English. Give examples and compare and contrast Old Norse usage with English in this respect.
3. In what circumstances may an Old Norse verb not agree in number with a nominative subject?
4. Give a grammatical analysis of the sentence *þau ræddusk opt við* 'they often talked together'.

3.9.9 Adverbial ok

Sometimes *ok* appears at the beginning of an independent sentence with a sense equivalent to *þá* 'then'. In such cases a dependent temporal or conditional sentence almost always precedes (indeed, the *ok* or *þá* represents a recapitulation, in the form of an adverb, of the dependent sentence, cf. 3.8, 3.9.1). E.g.:

> Ok í annat sinn er þeir raufa seyðinn, þá er stund var liðin, ok var ekki soðit
> 'And for second time COMP they open cooking-pit-the, then COMP short-while was passed, and was not cooked'
> 'And the second time they break open the cooking pit after a short while had passed, then it was not cooked'

> Ef maðr andask í úteyjum, ok eru þeir menn skyldir at fœra lík til kirkju, er . . .
> 'If man dies-*sk* in out-islands, and are those men bound to take body to church, COMP . . .'
> If a man dies on some outlying island, then those men are responsible for taking the body to a church, who . . .

The second example is from a law text, where this use of *ok* for *þá* is very common.

A postscript on 'impersonal' constructions

The student may legitimately wonder why some verbs in Old Norse are construed without a nominative, and thus, apparently (cf. 3.9.3), without a subject. It was explained in 3.9.3 that sometimes this is because the focus is on the object and the subject is of no interest in the context. In, e.g.,

> Hér hefr kristni sǫgu
> 'Here begins of-Christianity saga'
> 'Here begins the history of the Church (in Iceland)'

the writer draws attention solely to the work and its commencement. Who caused it to commence is of no relevance, and indeed the individual(s) concerned would probably be hard to identify. There is a similarity here with some passive constructions in English. In, e.g.,

> The church was built in the fourteenth century

the point of interest is the time at which the building work took place, not who carried it out, which, as in the ON example, may not be (generally) known.

What is missing in both the ON and the English sentence is of course the agent — which is nevertheless there in the background, understood although unspecified. But it has been argued by some that an agent has also been omitted from those types of ON 'impersonal' (i.e. non-nominative) construction in which an animate instigator cannot be conceived (e.g. *daga* 'dawn', *skorta* 'lack', *dreyma* 'dream'; cf. further 3.9.3, pp. 230, 233–4). The verbs concerned tend to denote natural events, the passing of time, (chance) occurrences, want, feelings, impressions, etc. What is suggested is that at the time such constructions arose there was a belief in a mythological agency or agencies which controlled the events by which people were affected. Thus in, e.g.,

> Gaf þeim vel byri
> 'Gave to-them well winds'
> 'They got favourable winds'

Rak þá víða um hafit
'Drove them widely across sea-the'
'They drifted far across the sea'

Ragnhildi dróttning dreymði drauma stóra
'Ragnhildr queen [acc.] dreamt dreams big [acc.]'
'Queen Ragnhildr dreamt great dreams'

a recognised but (for whatever reason) unspecified power may have been conceived as directing the wind, driving boats across the sea, causing people to dream, and so on (cf. the further examples pp. 230, 233).

It is not claimed that speakers of Old Norse thought in these terms; rather that they were using linguistic constructions inherited from an earlier age (many Indo-European and non-Indo-European languages exhibit similar types of phrase). The interconnection between nominative case and agent role suggested by this line of reasoning can also be viewed as having a historical basis. In 3.1.2 it was stressed that no morphological case is uniquely associated with a particular syntactic function in Old Norse, and that is equally true of semantic roles. It is conceivable, however, that to begin with each case did have a unique semantic role and syntactic function, and that in this pristine system nominative denoted the agent. Then, over the thousands of years that followed, much restructuring took place, including perhaps loss and amalgamation of several cases — leading to the Old Norse system in which morphological case, syntactic function and semantic role are far less obviously interconnected.

Regardless of the correctness or otherwise of these ideas, the student may find them helpful in getting to grips with 'impersonal' constructions — a type alien to modern English. The closest equivalents are constructions such as *it is raining*, where *it* simply fills what would otherwise be an empty subject slot, or *it seems to me*, where the experiencer does not become subject but is presented as the recipient of external stimuli. We may also note the archaic construction *methinks*, comparable to ON *þyk(k)ir mér*.

References to linguistic terms explained in the *Grammar*

References (by page number) are to the place or places where the term is most clearly explained and/or exemplified, usually the first occurrence. Items which form the subject matter of a (sub-)section or (sub-)sections of the *Grammar* are not normally included; these can be located using the list of contents (pp. vii–xi). Terms that are used only once or twice and are explained where they occur are also mostly omitted.

absolute superlative 93
accusative 22–7
accusative and infinitive 236–40
active 135–6
adverb of degree 128
adverb of intensification 129
adverb of manner 127
adverb of place 127
adverb of time 127
agent 31
agreement 38, 77–8, 131–2
analogical levelling 42
anaphoric pronoun 27
antecedent 208
attributive 77
auxiliary verb 133

back vowel 42

comparative 79
complementiser 204
consonant cluster 13
copula 242
correlate 208–11

dative 22–7
dative absolute 253–4
definite article 56
dependent sentence 200–02
determiner 78–9
diphthong 9–10
direct object 32–3
discontinuity 220, 229

dual 62

experiencer 70, 234

front(ing) [vowels] 41–2
fronting [sentence elements] 226–7

genitive 22–7
genitive of type 35

imperative 135
independent sentence 200
indicative 134–5
indirect object 32–3, 35
infinitive 140, 147–8
instrumental(ity) 24
intonation 4

labial 39
lexical item 147

marked 226–7
matrix sentence 200
modal auxiliary 152
monophthongisation 102
morphology 22
mutation 39, 41

nominative 22–7
noun phrase 31–2

object 32–3
object complement 89

objective genitive 34, 90
oblique 72

paradigm 28
partitive 74
passive 135–6, 251–3
past infinitive 147–8, 239–40
past participle 147
periphrastic 133
positive 79
possessive adjective 83
possessive genitive 34
postposition 181
preaspiration 18–19
predicate 131
predicative 77
preposition phrase 181
present participle 147
principal parts 148–9

raised subject 238–9
reciprocal 146

reflexive 62
reflexive possessive 83
relative (pronoun) 201
relative sentence 208
rounded, rounding 39

subject 31
subject complement 32, 224–7
subjective genitive 34, 91
subjunctive 134–5
subordinate clause 200–02
superlative 79
supine 156
syntax 22

that-clause 202

unmarked 31–2
unvoiced 12

voiced 12
vowel gradation 141–2

Select glossary of linguistic terms not explained in the *Grammar*

apposition The relationship between two or more sentence elements with the same syntactic function and identity or similarity of reference. E.g. *hann átti Ragnhildi, dóttur Hrólfs* 'he was married to Ragnhildr, the daughter of Hrólfr', where *Ragnhildi* and *dóttur Hrólfs* are in apposition.

assimilation The influence of one sound on another, so that they become more alike or identical. E.g. *lykill* 'key' < **lykilr*, with assimilation *lr* > *ll*.

beneficiary The entity to which something is given, said, etc. or for which something is done, made, etc. E.g. *þeir veittu honum lið* 'they gave him support', where *honum* is the beneficiary.

complement A syntactic element that 'completes' another element. E.g. *var hann inn mesti hǫfðingi* 'he was a very great ruler', where *hann* is the subject and *inn mesti hǫfðingi* the subject complement; *í þenna tíma* 'at this time', where *í* is a preposition and noun phrase *þenna tíma* the prepositional complement.

complex Consisting of two or more separate elements. E.g. the preposition *fyrir norðan* 'north of'.

compound Consisting of two or more elements which are combined. E.g. *fjárskipti* 'division of property' a compound noun made up of gen. *fjár*, from *fé* 'property' 'money', and *skipti* 'division'.

covert Not expressed, understood. In, e.g., *þeim var engi kostr í brott at fara* 'there was no possibility for them to go away', the subject of *fara* is not expressed, but is understood as identical with the *þeim* of *þeim var engi kostr*.

declarative A sentence type used for statements, contrasting with interrogative, imperative, etc. E.g. *Páll jarl fór til Orkneyja* 'Earl Páll went to the Orkneys' is a declarative sentence, whereas *hvárt fór Páll jarl til Orkneyja?* 'did Earl Páll go to the Orkneys?' is interrogative and *farðu til Orkneyja!* 'go to the Orkneys!' imperative.

goal The entity affected by the action expressed by a verb. In, e.g., *þeir brenndu hann inni* 'they burnt him in his house', *hann* 'him' is the goal of the action, the person burnt.

govern(ment) A syntactic linkage whereby one word requires a particular morphological form of another word. E.g. the ON verb *hefna* 'avenge' governs the genitive of the person or thing avenged (*hann hefndi bróður síns* 'he avenged his brother'); the preposition *frá* governs the dative (*frá skipinu* 'from the ship').

head word The central word in a phrase. E.g. in *maðr gamall* 'an old man', the noun *maðr* is the head word, on which the adjective *gamall* is dependent; we find *maðr gekk út* 'a man went out', but not **gamall gekk út* 'old went out'.

infinitive clause A clause (sentence) with one or more infinitives but no finite verb — one of several types of non-finite clause. E.g. in *dvel þú eigi at snúask til dróttins* 'do not wait to turn to the Lord', *at snúask til dróttins* is an infinitive clause whose covert (understood) subject is the *þú* of the finite *dvel þú eigi* (see **covert**).

infix An affix (a word element that can only be used when joined to another form) added within a word (see p. 65).

inflexion A change to any part of a word (root, affix, ending) signalling grammatical relations (case, gender, number, tense, mood, etc.), e.g. *hestr* 'horse' (nom. sg.), *hests* (gen. sg.); *horð* 'hard' (nom. f. sg., nom./acc. n. pl.), *harðir* (nom. m. pl.); *bít* 'bite' (1st sg. pres. indic.), *beit* (1st/3rd sg. past indic.).

intransitive A verb which cannot take a direct object, e.g. *liggja* 'lie' 'be situated'.

modifier (modify) A word that is dependent on another word or phrase and qualifies its meaning. In, e.g., *sá inn gamli maðr* 'the old man', the words *sá inn gamli* are all dependent on the head word *maðr*: they qualify the meaning of *maðr*, introducing the attribute of age and making the phrase definite. In *draumr Hálfdanar*, the genitive *Hálfdanar* is dependent on *draumr* and qualifies its meaning, indicating whose the dream was (see **head word**).

overt Expressed, observable in the structure (see **covert**).

past perfect A verb construction found in Germanic (and some other) languages consisting of the past tense of *have* (*hafa* etc.) and a supine, usually expressing a time prior to some past point of time. In, e.g., *er þeir hofðu upp borit fongin, fóru þeir á land* 'after they had carried up the baggage, they went ashore', the carrying precedes the going ashore, which is itself in the past.

perfect As **past perfect**, but consisting of the present tense of *have* (*hafa* etc.) and a supine, and commonly expressing time viewed in relation to the present. In, e.g., *vér hofum fengit mikinn skaða á monnum várum* 'we have suffered great losses to our men', the losses are presented as relevant to the situation in which the words are spoken.

phrase A sentence element consisting of one or more words, but usually reducible to a single word. E.g. *skrín ins helga Magnúss jarls* 'the shrine of St Magnús the earl' is a noun phrase, reducible to *þat* 'it'; *í þann* *tíma* 'at that time' is a preposition phrase functioning as an adverbial, reducible to *þá* 'then'.

root The basic form of a word, to which nothing has been added. E.g. *tak*-, root of the verb *taka* 'take', *heið*-, root of the feminine noun *heiðr* 'moor', 'heath', *lang*-, root of the adjective *langr* 'long'.

semantics The study of meaning in language; sometimes simply used as a synonym for meaning.

sentence The largest unit of grammar or syntax, i.e. the largest unit over which a grammatical or syntactic rule can operate. A sentence will always include one finite verb, and one only. Thus (finite verbs given in bold) **Go**! or *John* **kicked** *the ball into the net* are each sentences, whereas *Gosh!* or *Looking to the future* are not. The utterance *She* **smiled** *because she* **was** *given a toy, but she often* **scowls** contains three sentences: the independent (3.8) *she smiled* and [*but*] *she often scowls* and the dependent [*because*] *she was given a toy*. In traditional grammatical parlance what is here termed 'sentence' is known as a 'clause', 'sentence' being employed for broader and less clearly defined concepts such as 'a statement that can stand on its own'.

sentence element Used in the *Grammar* synonymously with **phrase**.

simplex Consisting of a single element — non-complex or non-compound. E.g. *á* 'on [etc.]' is a simplex preposition as opposed to the complex *fyrir norðan* 'north of'; *konungr* 'king' is a simplex noun as opposed to the compound *konungsmaðr* 'king's man'.

stress Prominence given to a particular syllable because of the degree of articulatory force used in producing it. In, e.g., *Skotlandi* 'Scotland' (dat. n. sg.) there is primary stress on the first syllable, secondary stress on -*land*-, and little or no stress on the dative -*i* ending.

substantive An alternative term for 'noun' — the part of speech denoting persons, places, concrete objects, concepts (e.g. *Hrólfr*, *Ísland* 'Iceland', *hús* 'house', *gleði* 'joy'). Formally substantives/nouns display certain types of inflexion, in Old Norse number: *konungr* 'king', *konungar* 'kings', case: *konungr* (nom.), *konungi* (dat.), and to a certain extent gender: *dropi* (m. with -*i* ending) 'drop', *gata* (f. with -*a* ending) 'path'. Substantives/nouns also perform specific syntactic functions, appearing, e.g., as subject or object of a sentence or the complement of a preposition in a preposition phrase (examples under 3.1.5).

substantivised Used as a substantive/noun. The term is applied to adjectives that stand in place of a substantive/noun, e.g. *gott* 'good [nom./acc. n. sg.]', *fáir* 'few [nom. m. pl.]', *hit ellra* 'the older [nom./acc. n. sg.]' (see 3.3, 3.3.6, sentences 19–22, 26).

suffix An affix (see **infix**) coming after the form to which it is joined. Examples of ON suffixes are the weak past tense markers *-ð*, *-d*, *-t* (cf. *kasta-ð-i* 'threw', with root *kasta-*, past tense suffix *-ð* and 3rd sg. ending *-i*), and the definite article *-inn* (cf. *hest-r-inn* 'the horse', with root *hest-*, nom. sg. ending *-r* and suffixed nom. m. sg. def. art. *-inn*).

transitive Verb which can take a direct object, e.g. *drepa* 'kill', *hefna* 'avenge'.

Bibliography

Cleasby, Richard and Gudbrand Vigfusson 1957. *An Icelandic–English Dictionary* (2nd ed.). Oxford: Clarendon Press.

Faarlund, Jan Terje 2004. *The Syntax of Old Norse*. Oxford: Oxford University Press.

Gordon, E. V. 1957. *An Introduction to Old Norse* (2nd ed.). Oxford: Clarendon Press.

Haugen, Einar 1972. *First Grammatical Treatise* (2nd ed.). London: Longman.

Haugen, Odd Einar 2001 (and later printings). *Grunnbok i norrønt språk* (4th ed.). Oslo: Ad Notam Gyldendal.

Heusler, Andreas 1932 (and later printings). *Altisländisches Elementarbuch* (3rd ed.). Heidelberg: Carl Winter.

Hreinn Benediktsson 1972. *The First Grammatical Treatise*. Reykjavík: University of Iceland.

Höskuldur Thráinsson 1994. 'Icelandic'. In: (E. König and J. van der Auwera eds) *The Germanic Languages*. London: Routledge, 142–89.

Iversen, Ragnvald 1973 (and later printings). *Norrøn grammatikk* (7th ed.). Oslo: Aschehoug.

Noreen, Adolf 1923. *Altisländische und altnorwegische Grammatik* (4th ed.). Halle: Niemeyer.

Nygaard, M. 1905. *Norrøn syntax*. Kristiania: Aschehoug.

Spurkland, Terje 1989. *Innføring i norrønt språk*. Oslo: Universitetsforlaget.

Stefán Einarsson 1945 (and later printings). *Icelandic*. Baltimore: John Hopkins.

Thomson, Colin D. 1987. *Icelandic Inflections*. Hamburg: Helmut Buske.

Zoëga, Geir T. 1910. *A Concise Dictionary of Old Icelandic*. Oxford: Clarendon Press.